"Tom Nelson has written a wonderful field guide for every pastor who shares in this sentiment. If you are a pastor who values not only building a flourishing congregation but also your own flourishing soul, I cannot recommend this book highly enough."

Scott Sauls, senior pastor of Christ Presbyterian Church in Nashville, Tennessee, and author of *Jesus Outside the Lines*

"This book makes clear the irreducible foundation ministerial vocation: intimacy with God that roots one for integrity and resilience. It coaches pastors in a vital, practical skill: discipling congregants in connecting their work and worship. While unpacking it all, Nelson writes with a pastor's heart, and it's easy to see why he has been a beloved mentor to many a young pastor."

Amy L. Sherman, author of *Kingdom Calling: Vocational Stewardship for the Common Good*

"I've been waiting for this book for a long time. Pastor, just read the first chapter alone and you'll realize how much you need to sit, read, and hang out with Tom Nelson."

John Yates II, rector of The Falls Church (1979–2019)

"You won't find simple solutions to the complexities of pastoral ministry here. What you will find is humility and wisdom that come from a lifetime of ministry, as well as some great ideas for your next message."

Chris Dolson, pastor emeritus, Blackhawk Church in Madison, Wisconsin

"Tom Nelson is the pastor I want to teach me how to flourish in ministry. He reminds us that nothing but intimacy with Jesus can help us recover the lost art of shepherd leadership."

Collin Hansen, vice president of content and editor in chief of The Gospel Coalition, coauthor of *Rediscover Church: Why the Body of Christ Is Essential*

"Traditionally there are three parts to the ordained ministry—preaching, pastoring, and leading. In our religious world today, preaching and leading are the most highly valued. But while it is not so visible and attention grabbing, skillful knowledge of and pastoring of the human soul is perhaps the most fundamental of the three. Talented preachers and leaders who are not mature and wise pastors may draw a crowd, but they will not help believers 'grow in grace' (2 Pet 3:18) and Christlikeness in both their private and public lives. Tom Nelson's fine book will help rehabilitate the importance of the work of shepherding in our churches."

Timothy Keller, Redeemer City to City

"Drawing from a deep well of scriptural insight and his own wealth of pastoral experience, Nelson reveals a pathway that leads to flourishing leadership, both personally and organizationally. Pastoral leaders of the present and future would be wise to heed his words."

Terry Timm, lead pastor of Christ Community Church of the South Hills, Pittsburgh

"Grounded and beautiful, *The Flourishing Pastor* brings necessary healing and hope not only to pastors but also to those of us in their care."

Curt Thompson, author of *The Soul of Shame* and *Anatomy of the Soul*

"I remember the first time I heard Tom speak, the words of a prophet in a winsome spirit, and now this book. The gospel is deeply imbedded in each page, a clarion call to pastors everywhere, asking what is at the heart of their call and exploring the painful reality of what happens to the kingdom when it is not embraced. Coming out of Covid-19 this may be the most important book for you to get your hands on."

Nancy Ortberg, CEO of Transforming the Bay with Christ

"With pastoral wisdom and fidelity to the Scriptures, Tom Nelson offers a tapestry of biblically informed encouragement to pastoral leaders of all experience levels. Tom skillfully interacts with current research to bring needed insight to pressing and perennial pastoral concerns."

Donald C. Guthrie, professor and director of the PhD educational studies program at Trinity Evangelical Divinity School

"Theologically rich and practically informed, *The Flourishing Pastor* will challenge the reader to adopt a deeper understanding of sabbath rest, physical health, and emotional health. I highly recommend this book for anyone seeking a deeper, fuller, and richer understanding of pastoral leadership in the midst of a fractured world."

Jimmy Dodd, founder and CEO of PastorServe, author of *Survive or Thrive: 6 Relationships Every Pastor Needs*

"Some books you read for fun; some books you read to stay current in your field. But how many books have you ever read because it's a matter of life and death? If you're a pastor, that's why you need to read this book—your destiny is hanging in the balance. You may think I'm just being dramatic, but Tom Nelson—with more than three decades of experience as a pastor—shows how the hazards of your occupation are liable to squeeze the life right out of your soul unless you learn to abide in the intimate watchcare of the Great Shepherd."

Bill Hendricks, executive director for Christian leadership, the Hendricks Center at Dallas Theological Seminary, and president of the Giftedness Center

"Tom Nelson has given pastors and all Christian leaders a diagnostic tool and prescription for effective leadership in this insightful book."

C. Jeffrey Wright, CEO of UMI (Urban Ministries, Inc.), Chicago

"With surprising candor and humility rooted in an honest spirituality that seriously wrestles with the Word and the world together, this is a window into the mind and heart of someone who longs for the reality of an integral life for himself and for all of us. Every pastor I know would be graced by this apprenticeship in print."

Steven Garber, author of *The Seamless Life* and senior fellow for vocation and the common good with the M. J. Murdock Charitable Trust

"Tom reminds us of the vital role of hands in the formation of the heart, which enables pastors to comprehend that the greatest influence of Jesus' apprentices does not rely on grandiose achievements but rather on the condition of their hearts. Begin a new journey carrying Jesus' yoke of apprenticeship as you are enlightened by this timeless book."

Fernando Tamara, pastor of Hispanic ministries at Orange County First Assembly of God and regional development representative for Made to Flourish

"An apt subtitle for Tom Nelson's desperately needed book could have been *What They Didn't Teach You in Seminary*. With no hint of hubris, Tom quietly moves into the way of the Good Shepherd, guiding fellow clergy to rediscover, refocus, and restore their call to a healthy ordained ministry."

David W. Miller, director of the Princeton University Faith and Work Initiative

TOM NELSON

THE
FLOURISHING
PASTOR

Recovering *the* Lost Art *of*
Shepherd Leadership

Foreword by Chris Brooks

An imprint of InterVarsity Press
Downers Grove, Illinois

InterVarsity Press
P.O. Box 1400, Downers Grove, IL 60515-1426
ivpress.com
email@ivpress.com

InterVarsity Press® is the book-publishing division of InterVarsity Christian Fellowship/USA®, a movement
of students and faculty active on campus at hundreds of universities, colleges, and schools of nursing in the United States
of America, and a member movement of the International Fellowship of Evangelical Students. For information
about local and regional activities, visit intervarsity.org.

Scripture quotations, unless otherwise noted, are from The Holy Bible, English Standard Version,
copyright © 2001 by Crossway Bibles, a division of Good News Publishers. Used by permission. All rights reserved.

While any stories in this book are true, some names and identifying information may have been changed
to protect the privacy of individuals.

Cover design and image composite: David Fassett
Interior design: Daniel van Loon
Images: green leaves: © filmfoto / iStock / Getty Images Plus
        gold leaf background: © Katsumi Murouchi / Moment / Getty Images
        wood grain texture: © sankai / iStock / Getty Images Plus

ISBN 978-1-5140-0132-5 (print)
ISBN 978-1-5140-0133-2 (digital)

Printed in the United States of America ∞

InterVarsity Press is committed to ecological stewardship and to the conservation of natural resources
in all our operations. This book was printed using sustainably sourced paper.

Library of Congress Cataloging-in-Publication Data
Names: Nelson, Tom, 1956- author.
Title: The flourishing pastor : recovering the lost art of shepherd
    leadership / Tom Nelson.
Description: Downers Grove, IL : IVP, [2021] | Includes bibliographical
    references and index.
Identifiers: LCCN 2021030830 (print) | LCCN 2021030831 (ebook) | ISBN
    9781514001325 (paperback) | ISBN 9781514001332 (ebook)
Subjects: LCSH: LCSH: Pastoral theology. | Clergy—Religious life. | Christian
    leadership. | Discipling (Christianity) | Church work. |
    Clergy—Appointment, call, and election.
Classification: LCC BV4011.6 .N45 2021 (print) | LCC BV4011.6 (ebook) |
    DDC 248.8/92—dc23
LC record available at https://lccn.loc.gov/2021030830
LC ebook record available at https://lccn.loc.gov/2021030831

P   25   24   23   22   21   20   19   18   17   16   15   14   13   12   11   10   9   8   7   6   5

Y   39   38   37   36   35   34   33   32   31   30   29   28   27   26   25   24   23

This book is dedicated to the two women
who have most shaped the contours of my life and work.
MY MOM, DELIGHT,
who modeled for me a life of apprenticeship to Jesus,
AND MY WIFE, LIZ,
whose Christlike love and timeless wisdom
are grace gifts beyond measure.
I am eternally grateful.

CONTENTS

FOREWORD

CHRIS BROOKS

Pastors aren't superheroes! This was a tough lesson for me to learn. Growing up, I loved reading the stories of Iron Man, Captain America, and Superman. They were perfection personified. Physically invincible, morally uncompromising, endowed with unparalleled intellect, and always clear minded concerning their purpose and life mission (or so it seemed to me as a child). The amazing saga of their lives played out right before my eyes in each new edition of their comic books or episode of their cartoon series. In my daydreams and playdates with friends I would make believe that I was one of these men of renown. My only disappointment was knowing they were merely characters on a page whom I would never meet in real life.

So you can only imagine the overwhelming joy I felt as a young thirteen-year-old when I walked into the youth meeting at my childhood church and met what felt like my first real-life superhero. His name was Eugene Broadway. He didn't wear a cape or a mask, but I swear he was just as incredible as any of the characters in my comic books. He was a youth pastor who to me seemed just as invincible, uncompromising, wise, and clear minded about his purpose and mission as Captain America or Superman. He had awesome superpowers. He could mesmerize a group of teenagers with the passion of his preaching. His prayers transformed human hearts. He offered wise counsel to my deepest problems at the drop of a hat, in a way that astonished my parents. He even had this cool green car, kind of like his own Batmobile, that he would drive around town picking up teens for church so they could experience the transcendent love of Christ-centered community.

From the day I met Eugene Broadway, I wanted to emulate him. In my heart I determined that I wanted to be a ministry superhero just like him. I began to study my Bible like him, pray like him, and I even developed a preaching style that was just like his.

But a strange thing happened the older I got and the more time I spent with him. I began to see how human he was. There were times when he grew tired, was afraid, didn't have answers to tough questions, prayed prayers of lament, and even seemed unclear about the direction of his life. And then one day the inconceivable happened; he got sick and, shortly after, passed away. I was bewildered and confused. It was only after his death that I came to grips with the hard truth that as great of a man as he was, Eugene Broadway was no superhero. And sadly, this meant neither was I.

Over the years, I have struggled to accept my own humanity. Maybe you can relate. After all, it is hard to admit that I am often anxious, frequently uncertain, and even emotionally immature at times. The good news is that, through the years, friends like Tom Nelson have helped me to see that I don't have to pretend to be Superman. Ordination certificates don't come with capes and pastors aren't superheroes. But, praise God, we serve a sovereign Savior. My flourishing does not depend on my superpowers, and neither does yours. *The Flourishing Pastor* is a joyful reminder that we are products of the supernatural grace of God expressed through the victory of the cross of Christ and the triumph of the gospel in our lives.

The wisdom in the pages you are about to read shows us a better way to flourish than pretending to be superheroes. We can be vulnerable if our faith is in Jesus and our anchor is in the Scriptures. We can lead our churches when we accept that our wholeness is in Christ alone. We are his apprentices, learning from our master how to live fully integrated lives. My friend Tom has done research in the lab of real-life ministry. God has used him to show many pastors how the gospel gives us power for work and worship for Sundays as well as Mondays. Ultimately the apostle Paul was right, "his strength is made perfect in our weakness" (see 2 Cor 12:9). This means we can take off the mask and stop measuring ourselves by attendance numbers, offering totals, and the amount of likes on our social media posts. In my life, Tom has been a wise sage whose humble wisdom comes from allowing the Lord to truly be his shepherd. I trust that you will find him worth listening to as well, because the godly guidance found in these pages will not only encourage your heart but also will allow you to finish well. So take off your cape, put on God's grace, and let the journey begin!

INTRODUCTION

Life can only be understood backwards;
but it must be lived forwards.

Søren Kierkegaard

These words of nineteenth-century Danish philosopher Søren Kierkegaard continue to be wise and welcome companions in my journey of faith. When I look back at over thirty years of pastoral leadership, my heart is filled with gratitude for the vocational calling God has entrusted me to steward.[1] I am also reminded of the rugged, invigorating, and changing terrain I have traversed in my pastoral calling, often to my great surprise.

Some of my earliest memories encompass the sights, sounds, and smells of the hard church pews in the sanctuary of our rural Minnesota country church. Here, in the remote obscurity of time and space, the transcendent triune God of the universe revealed himself to a scruffy, disheveled boy. At an early age, I was given a most precious grace gift, to passionately love the One in whom I lived and breathed. In his mysterious grace, Jesus the crucified and risen Savior invited me to a life of apprenticeship, to know him and be known by him, and to learn from him the joyful contours of the good, true, and beautiful life both now and for all eternity.

I recall many Sunday mornings from when I was around eight years of age, sitting in church next to my mother, listening to the sermon. While I heard the pastor speaking, it was not uncommon to be distracted by an inaudible voice I kept hearing in my mind. The message was tender in tone, crystal clear in direction, and remarkably consistent: "I want you to do this someday." While I realize not all who are called to the pastoral vocation experience what I experienced, my vocational calling came to me at an early age, progressing with growing conviction into adulthood.

After four years of rigorous study at a prominent evangelical seminary, my wife, Liz, and I landed in Kansas City as pioneer church planters with sincere hearts, high ideals, and hopeful faith. With greater insight from hindsight, we now look back on those early years of pastoral ministry and realize how unprepared and woefully equipped we were for the vocational calling we had embraced. An impoverished theological vision, inadequate spiritual formation, and faulty pastoral praxis placed us on a perilous personal and vocational trajectory. We knew the sizable risk and high failure rate of pioneer church planting, but we did not grasp how much we were at risk in our own flourishing.

The pastoral vocational calling is a wonderful privilege, but it is also fraught with many perils. In addition to our own weaknesses and sinful proclivities, we face spiritual opposition, difficult dynamics in our family systems, and very demanding leadership roles. Pastors share the joys and heartaches of many, stewarding the care and spiritual formation of congregants. In addition, we foster the ongoing health of the local church as an enduring institution. In aggregate, the weighty and complex stewardships pastors carry often feel exhausting and overwhelming. The pastoral calling is a very challenging vocation.

So how are pastors doing today? When we survey the landscape of contemporary pastoral leadership, we find many pastors are not flourishing.[2] What we uncover behind professional Sunday smiles is pastoral isolation and burnout; struggles with relational, emotional, physical, and spiritual health; increasing expectations of congregations; conflicts with governing boards as well as the increased complexity of the pastoral vocation. Added to these challenges, pastors face strong cultural headwinds in an increasingly secular context. In this cultural milieu, pastors are often marginalized, at best seen as a kind of quaint cultural anachronism and at worst oppressors of human freedom. I believe the pastoral vocation is increasingly at risk, and the ramifications for the vitality of the local church community and its mission in the world are hanging on a more precarious leadership thread. Pastoral leadership matters more than we may realize. When pastors flourish, congregations flourish, and when congregations flourish, communities flourish.

For the last two decades I have had the privilege of working with many younger pastors fresh out of seminary who join our local church's two-year immersive residency program. At a favorite coffee shop, I have had many heartfelt conversations as young pastors wrestle with whether they should be pastors, whether they can truly flourish over a lifetime in the pastoral vocation. Many young pastors have seen way too many discouraging examples of pastors who have melted down personally and professionally and way too few examples of pastors who continue to flourish over the long haul of pastoral leadership. While I admit there are many perils in the pastoral vocation, into this growing cynicism I want to scream from the rooftops the hopeful truth that the One who calls pastors will provide the wisdom, guidance, strength, and empowerment to flourish and finish well.

Even though I have served in a pastoral vocation for over three decades, I continue to stay passionately curious, joyfully grateful, and hopefully expectant. Clearly I have not arrived, nor do I claim superior wisdom, but, transparently, my understanding of the pastoral calling is vastly different now than it was when I first picked up the mantle of pastoral leadership. As I have sought greater faithfulness, fruitfulness, and flourishing, I have been on a steep learning, unlearning, and relearning curve. This has caused me to see the primacy of shepherding as the paradigm for my vocation. Psalm 78:72 has illumined my understanding, formation, and practice of the pastoral vocation. The psalmist speaks of Israel's King David. "So he shepherded them according to the integrity of his heart and guided them with his skillful hands." In this inspired text of Holy Scripture, those called to the pastoral vocation are given wisdom that is both timely and timeless, concerned with both the inner person and the outer work.

Recapturing Scripture's calling for pastoral shepherding has meant embracing a more robust biblical theology—a greater canonical coherence that reframes exegesis and language to adhere to the entire biblical witness of Holy Scripture—with the gospel centrally speaking into every nook and cranny of human existence. I've grown in breadth of pastoral formational skills, moving into classic spiritual disciplines, interpersonal neurobiology, and attachment theory. My pastoral practices—from liturgy to discipleship to pastoral care—have adopted a more integral approach, equipping congregants for their Monday vocational worlds. Pastoring the whole life of a disciple now includes the integration of faith, work, and economic wisdom; that is, a primary work of the church is the church at work.

In the pages that follow, Psalm 78:72 will serve as an inspirational framework for our exploration and reflection. Pursuing the lost art of shepherding leadership, we will examine a shepherding leadership paradigm, probe integral spiritual formation, and share pastoral practices that fuel pastoral flourishing and leadership effectiveness. If you are considering the pastoral vocation, my prayer is that this book will offer insight and hope that pastoral leadership is a calling where joyful flourishing is truly possible. If you are presently serving in a pastoral vocation, I pray this labor of love from an imperfect pastoral colleague will give you some helpful insight and be a booster shot of encouragement to live well and pastor well. If you are not in pastoral leadership but desire to encourage your pastoral staff, I trust this book will prove a gift of loving encouragement to your pastor and assist you in better understanding, supporting, and praying for those who serve you and your local church.

I am grateful for the many friends who have encouraged me to share these pastoral leadership loaves and fishes. May Jesus bless and multiply them, encouraging and nourishing your heart, mind, body, and soul.

PART ONE

THE

SHEPHERD

So he shepherded them . . .

Psalm 78:72 NASB

1

A CALLING IN CRISIS

*American pastors are abandoning their posts, left and right, at an
alarming rate. They are not leaving their churches and getting other jobs.
Congregations still pay their salaries. Their names remain on the church
stationary and they continue in pulpits on Sunday mornings. But they are
abandoning their posts, their calling. They have gone whoring after other gods.*

EUGENE PETERSON, *WORKING THE ANGLES*

I met pastor Dave at a local coffee shop. One of Dave's congregants
had connected us, hoping that I might be of some encouragement
to his pastor. Though I had never met Dave before, I immediately
liked him. He greeted me with attentive eyes, a warm toothy smile, and
a firm handshake. After ordering our favorite bold coffee, we sat down
at a corner table searching for a bit of privacy, hopeful our words would
be muffled by the many conversations near us.

Right from the start as Dave shared his story, I thought, *What a great
guy.* My admiration only continued to build as Dave gave me a snapshot
of the many external evidences of pastoral success he was experiencing.
As I listened intently, the words that kept bouncing around in my mind
were, *Dave you are not only a great guy, you are a great pastor.* After
getting a warm-up of coffee, Dave's sunny disposition and enthusiastic

demeanor changed. It was obvious that something was on his heart, something important he wanted to share. Feeling safe with me, Dave ventured to take a risk to go below the surface, to welcome me under the waterline of his life. Dave looked me in the eye and said, "Tom, if truth be told, while my church is flourishing, I am smiling on the outside, but dying on the inside."

Dave's transparency initially took me by surprise, but it was not shocking. Dave is like many pastors I encounter. In one sense Dave is doing well. He is gifted for his pastoral calling. Dave does not have some disqualifying sin hiding in his closet. Dave has a good marriage, he is an involved dad, his church is growing in attendance, and the church budget is financially healthy. From all appearances, Dave would seem a poster boy for a flourishing pastor, but like so many of his peers, behind his pastoral gifting, diligence, and the many accoutrements of success lurks a less impressive world where often hidden forces threaten his well-being and longevity as a pastor. Dave knows that behind his Sunday smiles, he is in peril. He knows he needs to change, things need to change, but what does he do, where does he go, and whom does he seek out?

HOW ARE PASTORS DOING?

Pastors often experience demanding workloads, financial challenges, balancing family demands, exhaustion, and burnout. The Flourishing in Ministry research project funded by the Lilly Endowment completed a study of more than ten thousand pastors from twenty different denominations, representing a variety of racial ethnicities and including both male and female pastors.[1] Perhaps most compelling is the number of pastors who expressed serious concern about their daily well-being. "Almost 40 percent of all clergy report low satisfaction with their overall life. . . . And slightly more than 40 percent—41 percent of women and 42 percent of men—report high levels of daily stress."[2] Adding to the high levels of daily stress, pastors are now serving in a broader cultural context that is often less supportive and can be oppositional, even hostile.

Henri Nouwen summarized this changing cultural milieu and its effect on clergy. "In this climate of secularization, Christian leaders feel less and less relevant and more and more marginalized."[3] Under the cultural canopy of an increasingly secular age,[4] pastors are increasingly viewed by many people they encounter as a kind of mysterious, quaint cultural anachronism. At best, they are hopelessly irrelevant, except for perhaps marriage ceremonies and memorial services. The inconvenient truth is that many younger pastors and more seasoned pastors are hurting and ineffective. They are often inadequately trained, spiritually malformed, chronically discouraged, and woefully prepared to lead increasingly complex institutions and diverse faith communities. They often experience the gnawing fear of inadequacy deep within them.

While there are a host of external and cultural factors contributing to a lack of pastoral flourishing that require attention, perhaps more insidious and ultimately perilous are the internal dimensions navigating the pastoral calling itself. It is not just that many pastors feel over their heads and stressed out, many have lost their way.

LOST SHEPHERDS

I really enjoy officiating at weddings. I plan every detail carefully and meticulously, checking and rechecking the exact time and place of the wedding. Being late to a wedding is a nightmare I have revisited during restless nights. Recently that nightmare presented itself to me as I got in my car and headed to a wedding destination some forty miles away. The wedding venue seemed out of the way on the map, but it was not far from where I lived, so I thought I could navigate my way there with no problem. About halfway to my destination on increasingly remote back-country roads, I became more and more confused as to my location. I wasn't sure where I was, and I was even more confused as to where I should be going. I picked up my smart phone. Much to my dismay, I had no cellular service. I had no GPS, nor could I call the wedding venue. At that moment, a pit emerged in my stomach and anxious thoughts tormented my mind. I was lost. I looked at my watch. Would I be late for the wedding? What would the wedding party do? How would I explain my tardiness to the bride and groom? I pulled over on the side of the road and shot up a desperate prayer. A car soon approached, and thanks to its local driver I was given directions that got me to the wedding venue just in the nick of time.

As a pastor, being lost is not only unpleasant, it can be quite perilous. Being lost attempting to get to a wedding venue is one thing, but being lost in the pastor calling is more consequential. While the image of a lost sheep is rather common; less common in our social imagination is a lost shepherd. Sheep are not the only ones who get lost, shepherds do as well. Shepherds and the sheep suffer for it.

The Old Testament prophet Ezekiel speaks timeless truth across the terrain of time. In losing their way, Israel's leaders have abandoned their vocational stewardship to care for the sheep. Perhaps they lost their first love, faced their glaring inadequacy, were simply overwhelmed, or over time felt great fatigue. Whatever contributed to their getting lost, they clearly were neglecting their vocational stewardship and blatantly taking advantage of their positions of power at the expense of the people they had been called to serve. Ezekiel lays down the gauntlet of indictment, pointing to leaders who have lost their way:

> Ah, shepherds of Israel who have been feeding yourselves! Should not shepherds feed the sheep? You eat the fat, you clothe yourselves with the wool, you slaughter the fat ones, but you do not feed the sheep. The weak you have not strengthened, the sick you have not healed, the injured you have not bound up, the strayed you have not brought back, the lost you have not sought, and with force and harshness you have ruled them. (Ezek 34:2-4)[5]

While Ezekiel's literary imagery is embedded in an agrarian context, his prophetic message must not be missed for our time.[6] Confronted with our own inadequacies, exhaustion, and pastoral disillusionment, we can abandon our shepherding calling and get perilously lost. If you are willing to be brutally honest, perhaps the prophet Ezekiel's forceful words describe the painful reality of your heart. When shepherds become lost, neither they nor their flock flourish.

THREE PERILOUS PATHS

Pastors can get lost in their callings in many ways, but they often unwisely pursue three particularly common and perilous paths. I like to describe them as the celebrity path, the visionary path, and the lone ranger path. Let's take a closer look at the pastors who follow these paths.

The celebrity pastor. When I travel and speak, usually the first thing I encounter when I arrive at a conference venue is the green room. The green room is where pastors and musicians hang out before they go on stage. The green room has a good purpose—providing a quiet place for preparation without interruption—yet often the accoutrements of success and the exaggerated image of a celebrity brand lurk in its distorting shadows. In the green room there is often jockeying for prominence and the stroking of oversized egos. The green room culture regularly reinforces a distorted telos of pastoral success rather than pastoral faithfulness—much more about furthering a brand than furthering the kingdom, more about amplifying a person than exalting Christ. The green room often promotes a toxic celebrity Christian culture. Fame, applause, and celebrity status is a very intoxicating substance even for pastors, wooing them down a perilous path. A pastor's secure gospel identity in Christ is easily hijacked by the fickle applause of a crowd.

At the heart of the celebrity pastor is what Saint Augustine aptly described as disordered love.[7] Lurking behind a smiling stage presence is an inordinate narcissistic love of self at the expense of love for God and others. Instead of living before an audience of One, the celebrity pastor lives before an audience of many. Most on his or her mind is how well they are performing in the eyes of the crowd. The crowd need not be big nor the stage prominent for the celebrity pastor to emerge. Celebrity is not necessarily tied to the size of the audience, but rather the size of ego longing to be stroked. A megapastoral ego is not only found in some megachurch contexts. They can be found in all sizes of churches. Big frogs live in small ponds too. And with the advent of online services and social media, the reach of any pastor can be far and wide. The perilous path of the celebrity pastor now lurks online and in the virtual world of our interconnected global information age.

For many pastors, preaching to the gathered church is a highly important and significant aspect of their pastoral calling. I do not want in any way to undermine the high importance of stewarding well the weekly communication of God's Word to a congregation. Neither do I want to minimize the crucial importance in growing in the craft and skill in preaching if that is an essential aspect of a pastor's primary job description. As a pastor who has had the humbling privilege of preaching to a congregation for more than thirty years, I also know firsthand some of the unique heart temptations that pastors face in the preaching enterprise. At soul level, preaching puts the pastor in a very vulnerable space where our sense of self-worth can become closely connected to the affirmation or criticism of our Sunday listeners. While pastors can preach passionately about the peril of idolatry, ironically at the same time pastors can be wrestling with the idolatry of their own preaching. Pastors' hearts are idol factories too, and our preaching can become an idolatrous Sunday performance. The untold secret lurking inside the heart of many pastors is an ongoing struggle with envy of other pastors who have greater preaching skills and larger congregations. Pastors are often ranked internally and externally as successful by their upfront communication skills. Conference speaking opportunities and placement among plenary speakers along with sizes of honoraria also reinforce a success pecking order, stroking egos as well as eliciting envy from other pastors.

Many parishioners and faith communities encourage pastors down the perilous path of celebrity. I will never forget a particular time I was invited to speak at a multiday conference to be held at a church in another state. The church was both generous and gracious to pay for my family to join me. We arrived from the airport and pulled up to the church in our rental car. A big sign in bold letters greeted us. It read, "Let Tom Nelson Wow You!" At that point, my two children burst out in uncontrollable laughter. All of us in the car knew that the church congregation was going to be sorely disappointed. They had invited the wrong speaker. Transparently, I am anything but a "wower," yet I find that many well-meaning congregants and church leaders fuel the Sunday wow factor, reinforcing the perilous celebrity path. Is it any wonder that pastors' roller coaster mental and emotional state of being on Monday is inextricably linked to the comments—both positive and negative—surrounding their Sunday performance?

The disordered love of the crowd's applause is intoxicating and impairs pastoral flourishing. David French rightfully notes that celebrity pastors receive the "false blessing" that all celebrities do: "celebrity itself has its own charisma."[8] That is, people act differently around celebrities in exaggerated laughter, spellbound fascination with every word, and it produces a reality that is, "both exhilarating—as it feeds the ego—and exhausting."[9] And under the influence of this kind of applause, blurred vision hides the deceitfulness of the heart while bolstering the confidence in one's own virtue.[10] John the Baptist's maxim deteriorates into, "I must increase."[11] Though the disordered love of the crowd's applause produces an impressive celebrity platform, it doesn't take interest in compelling Christlike character. Equipping the church, then, inordinately focuses on the Sunday gathered church—the pastor's platform—failing to more fully equip the scattered church for their Monday world.

Jesus is interested in something different. His restorative and commissioning words to Peter calling for a reordering of heart loves are both timeless and timely, "Simon, son of John, do you love me more than these?" (Jn 21:15). A toxic celebrity culture is wreaking havoc in pastors' lives, their families, on the church, and on its witness in the world. The heavy weight of pastors' highly visible public platforms is much more than the depth of their ill-formed character can sustain. Jesus shatters any glimmer of celebrity leadership, reminding us the greatest among us will not be a celebrity, but a servant (Mk 10:42-43). Jesus does not offer shepherds a green room to pridefully bask in; instead he offers a cross to carry and a basin and towel to serve with.

The visionary pastor. "God has given me a vision!" These were the opening words declared by a Christian pastoral leader I knew as he began his persuasive appeal for a multiyear fundraising campaign. His vision was indeed grand, including the purchase of a large piece of pricey prime real estate and the early scale drawings of the magnificent buildings that would be erected on the land in the future. Many lofty words were uttered, how thousands of lives would be impacted for Christ in the city and around the world. Yet for that to happen, financial sacrifice and big faith would be needed for the entire faith community. A sense of excitement permeated the large room, trust was extended, financial pledges were made, but behind the visionary curtain more disturbing realities persisted. In an attempt to secure the pricey property, the nonprofit organization had overreached and overleveraged. Cash flow was on vapor. Employee benefits were cut. Payroll remained at high risk. Employee morale plummeted. The mission was being compromised, yet the leader's grand vision trumped normal board prudence and critical dissent. Eventually things imploded, leaving behind a painful trail of disillusioned faith refugees fleeing from one more toxic faith visionary environment.

In my early years of pastoring, I heard a great deal about the essential role of vision within the spiritual leadership enterprise. When I crafted the initial ministry blueprint for the church plant I was leading, I found myself overly influenced by hyperbolic visionary language animated by large congregational numbers—*a church of five thousand in ten years*—and an even grander change-the-world transformation exclamation. In my heart of hearts, way too much of the motivation behind my visionary rhetoric was not about the mission of God in the world, but that I would be a successful pastor and lead a successful church. I regret this and I have needed to take this to the Lord in a spirit of repentance.

The importance of vision was often tied to a particular translation of one part of a single verse in the Old Testament book of Proverbs. "Where there is no vision, the people perish" (Prov 29:18 KJV).[12] When we place the entire verse in view, we note that the idea presented here is not some human vision cast by spiritual leaders, but rather the truths of God's Word revealed to people. Later translations better capture the wisdom principle embedded in the text, framing the proper meaning as "revelation" or "prophetic revelation."[13] The last part of the verse points to the "blessedness or happiness" of a people when they keep the law, that is, the revealed word of God.[14] When a people do not have access to God's revealed word, they do "perish;" they do become "unrestrained." If we rightly apply the Proverbs principle to the shepherding pastoral role, then a primary role of spiritual leadership is to feed the sheep with the nourishing truths from Holy Scripture. Well-fed sheep are well-led sheep. The Proverbs writer is not advocating for spiritual leaders to conjure up a desired picture of the future, but rather to grasp the essential importance of the timeless truths of Holy Scripture for the flourishing of a community.

Tragically, not only has vision been misunderstood from a biblical perspective, there has been little reflection on the potential perils of vision both for the pastoral leader and the faith community. Ironically, pastors can too easily lose our way in our vision. Pastoral leadership training enthusiastically heralds the possibilities of vision but presents an eerie, deafening silence regarding the sizable downsides of the visionary pastor. Goal setting usurped by "visions" transform the power equation. A pastor friend of mine, who left a large and growing church with a self-proclaimed visionary leader, described the powerless position for those under the leader: the only person allowed to have credible, forward-thinking ideas is the visionary. Oversight boards can be hand-picked by visionary leaders and, instead of wisely stewarding the mission, they become enablers of the visionary. Visionaries become closed to true accountability and robust assessment; this inability to receive challenges often obscures their own embeddedness in contemporary values. Such a power differential flings open the door to abuse of power and reckless risk. Founding, entrepreneurial pastors are perhaps most in danger of potential abuse, but all pastors who embrace an impoverished visionary leadership paradigm are vulnerable. Of course, not all visionary leaders go off the rails or become toxic, but the strong propensity over time is to head toward that direction.

Martyred German pastor Dietrich Bonhoeffer experienced firsthand the destructive perils of visionary leadership in the rise of twentieth-century German nationalism and fascism. In his brilliant work framing the contours of a flourishing faith community, pastor Bonhoeffer points out the perilous path of the visionary pastoral leader:

> God hates visionary dreaming, it makes the dreamer proud and pretentious. The man who fashions a visionary ideal of community demands that it be realized by God, by others, and by himself. . . . When his ideal picture is destroyed, he sees the community going to smash. So he becomes, first an accuser of his brethren, then an accuser of God, and finally the despairing accuser of himself.[15]

Dietrich Bonhoeffer paints an ugly picture of pastoral visionary leadership driven by a vision of an idealized faith community. Pastors can easily fall into this trap, demanding a particular level of spiritual formation or a kind of utopian community that is devoid of a hopeful realism required for life together in the already, not-fully-yet moment of redemptive history. Visionary dreaming becomes more toxic when it moves beyond an idealized faith community to a grand future we strive to create—a grand future that is often fueled by cultural success norms in the bigger and the better, the more grand and spectacular, motivated not by the glory of God, but driven by the sizable ego and the glory of the visionary leader.

The rise and fall of Jim Bakker and the PTL ministry empire is one of the most tragic examples of visionary pastoral leadership that badly went off the rails. Much damage has been done to individual lives, to the church, and to our gospel witness; the damage continues to linger decades later. Analyzing the problems is not self-righteous finger-pointing but a lesson-learning exercise. A broken man, Jim Bakker was imprisoned in the Federal Penitentiary in Rochester, Minnesota, where he discovered the writings of Dietrich Bonhoeffer regarding the danger of visionary dreaming.

Jim Bakker, whose visionary dream became an unima nightmare, wrote from a prison cell:

> God had been showing me that one of my most tragic mistakes in life was allowing my vision of Heritage USA to become the focal point of PTL rather than keeping the gospel of Jesus Christ as our top priority. When I read Bonhoeffer's words, they seemed to leap off the pages at me.... Ouch! Bonhoeffer's words hit me right between the eyes. I did not like to see myself reflected on the pages, especially to think of myself as the destroyer of the very community I had hoped to build because of my love for my dream.[16]

Like so many, I looked up to a prominent leader and trusted him to be a person of integrity and impeccable Christian conduct. He was a gifted Christian speaker with a large, global vision of bringing Christian apologetics to an increasingly secular world. He had visited our congregation, equipping our faith community with the existential and philosophical underpinnings of our Christian faith. When I spent time with him, he would speak with great passion about the global vision his organization had to change the world. The author of several insightful books, I would often quote him in my sermons. I was most appreciative when he enthusiastically endorsed one of my books. When he died, I felt a sense of loss both personally and for the global church he had inspired and equipped. After he died, I wrote a tribute to him expressing my appreciation for what I truly believed was his well-lived life and impactful ministry. However, not long after his passing, reports increasingly came out that this visionary Christian leader had been living a duplicitous life, engaging in serious sexual misconduct and years of horrendous predatory abuse of women.[17] I was simply devastated not only by his shocking, heartbreaking, and unthinkable, evil actions, but also by the entire organization and its board, which enabled this visionary leader to live a life of unaccountability and fostered an organizational culture that chastised anyone who would raise questions about matters of moral and financial integrity. Clearly there were many factors at work in this toxic visionary environment, and it is a sober reminder for all of us who serve in spiritual leadership roles. The inconvenient truth is, visionary leaders and the environments cultivated around them are often seedbeds for a variety of abuses.[18]

The perilous path of the visionary leader is often paved with prideful distortion. Vision—with or without a "God told me" authority—can be deceptive. Vision can easily distort a pastor's sense of self-importance and often fans vocational arrogance. Pastors are highly vulnerable to embrace the distortion that their specific callings are more important and more consequential to God and to God's mission in the world than congregants' callings throughout the week. Vision can lead to mission drift and drain energy and resources away from the primacy of spiritual formation and the local church's primary disciple-making mission.

Jim Collins' insight on leadership and effective companies has and continues to shape a great deal of thought about the leadership enterprise in the world. He points out the limitations of what he describes as the ego-driven "genius with a thousand helpers" model of leadership.[19] Equally problematic in the nonprofit world is the visionary with a thousand parishioners. Unfortunately, this is often the profile of the pastoral leader that is held up as the model of effectiveness and faithfulness for other pastors to emulate.

Another problem often left unexplored is how burdensome the visionary model can be to the pastor who has embodied and embraced it as his or her leadership modus operandi. Creating a local church culture where the expectation of a faith community is to regularly receive a new and fresh vision of the future places enormous pressure on the visionary. Visionary pastors may not see themselves as needing to once again ascend Mount Sinai to receive the latest special revelation. However, the pressure-filled expectation of repeatedly discovering the new vision for the community is daunting and often a contributing factor for pastoral exhaustion, disillusionment, cynicism, and burnout.

As a pastor, I really enjoy my time with new people who are beginning to attend our local church. I love hearing the stories of their spiritual

journeys and how Christ is transforming their lives. One of my responsibilities in our newcomer gatherings is to articulate the mission and the
culture of our church family. Usually in one form or another I am asked
about the vision of our church. Though nuanced, my response is basically
that there are no visionary leaders in our church, no grand guiding vision
of a desired future. Instead, our vision as a faith community is the gospel
vision Jesus gives us in Holy Scripture of the abundant life of intimacy,
integrity, influence, and joy he invites us to experience as his apprentices.
If we are going to be pastoral visionaries, this is the kingdom vision we
must continually cast.

Rather than pursuing the perilous path of visionary leadership, a
wiser path is to become the lead servant in a faith community. The lead
servant seeks God's presence and future direction for a faith community
in the context of a plurality of gifted local church leaders. Wise planning
and taking bold steps of faith are a vital part of the pastoral leadership
calling, but the primary vision we are to cast is the vision of the gospel
life Jesus calls us to live in his kingdom reign, embodied within a local
faith community in the manifest presence and power of the Holy Spirit.
The vision pastors desperately need is not one of a humanized grand
future, but a growing vision of the glory of our triune God. A grave peril
for pastors is the seduction of accomplishment at the expense of
intimacy. While celebrity pastors lose their way in disordered loves and
visionary pastors in prideful distortions, lone ranger pastors get lost in
their own isolation.

The lone ranger pastor. One story reveals the crisis of the lone ranger
pastor. After I had finished speaking to a group of pastors on the dangers
of pastoral isolation, a pastor approached me with droplets of tears on
his face. His surfacing emotion and his transparent words immediately
connected us at the heart level. Standing before me was a seasoned
pastor who had faithfully served a local church for almost thirty years.
Yet at the overwhelming realization, he could no longer ignore his own
isolation. As I put my arms around him, words of heartache tumbled out
of his weary soul. "For thirty years, I have done this alone, keeping my

arm's distance from others. I am going to wither and die without community." Wiping tears from his eyes, he assured me that his next step would be to reach out to another pastor in his community and pursue a transparent friendship. Before departing, we paused to pray that God would honor his courageous pursuit and provide that safe place of human connection, to know and be known by others.

Few vocations are more social in nature and people focused than the pastoral calling. The dripping irony is that surrounded by many people, pastors are often intensely lonely and socially isolated. The lone ranger pastor is one of the most harmful ways pastors can get lost in their callings. Pastoral isolation is a toxic seedbed for burnout and scandalous behavior. The damage done to pastors, their families, congregations, and the collective witness of the church is beyond description.

Matt Bloom is a leading researcher on clergy well-being. Clergy isolation from other clergy and congregational members along with a lack of close friendships outside the church is a serious obstacle to pastoral wholeness, health, and longevity. Bloom's research points to the essential need for clergy social support, what he describes as "backstage support." He writes, "Studies conducted in more than forty countries around the world have found that positive, caring, nurturing relationships are among the most important conditions for wellbeing . . . the absence of strong social support can have devastating effects on our health and wellbeing."[20]

Extensive research by Rae Jean Proeschold-Bell and Jason Byasse regarding clergy health points to a corollary connection tying excessive stress to pastoral isolation. While these researchers avoid strong prescriptive pronouncements, they do point out that social isolation is highly detrimental and to be avoided at all costs. They offer wise words to all pastors, but particularly those who are in the early years of their calling. "It is essential to start cultivating friendships early, perhaps while you are in seminary or with people you knew 'before,' and then continue to nurture those friendships. Consider having an annual getaway with one or two friends."[21]

Donald Guthrie, Bob Burns, Tasha D. Chapman, and their research team have conducted in-depth studies on pastoral well-being and resilience. The research points to pastoral isolation as a main concern:

> We are saying that it is easy for pastors, fearing what people might think, to become isolated from others. By so doing, they fail to grow spiritually. As one pastor put it, "I have a longing to be shepherded by someone else, but a fear to actually ask someone into my life." Again the themes weave together: isolation is bad self-care and poor leadership as well.[22]

In a research study by the Barna Group, 52 percent of pastors say they have felt very lonely and isolated from others in a three-month period.[23] Clearly there is increasing evidence and a growing concern regarding pastoral isolation. For pastors to flourish over the long haul, pastors must move from the gravitational pull of relational and institutional isolation to greater relational connectedness. Yet another pernicious harm is lurking in the dark shadows of pastoral isolation— prideful self-sufficiency.

Consider the case of Alex Honnold. It may have been one of the most daring and courageous climbs in human history. On June 3, 2017, Honnold climbed El Capitan in the Yosemite Valley on the Freerider route without rope or protection. In three hours and fifty-six minutes, he ascended the three-thousand-foot granite wall, reaching the summit safe and sound.[24] It is hard not to be in dumbfounded awe of Honnold's historic feat. As someone who is afraid of heights, I shudder to think of standing on top of a three-thousand-foot precipitous drop, let alone climbing it like a human fly without any safety gear. Yet this image of the free solo climber speaks loudly to the self-imposed isolation of pastoral life and leadership. There is a pervasive and prideful self-sufficient paradigm of the pastor as a solo climber, untethered to other leaders, without the ground support and safety ropes of community. A documentary on Honnold revealed that he lived his life pretty much the same way he climbed, without important and life-giving relational connections with others. From his nonnurturing childhood to his isolated adulthood, Honnold often kept at arm's lengths others who longed to connect with him in a deepening relationship and friendship.[25]

Holy Scripture tells us God created each of us for relational connection with himself and others. God even declared it was not good for man to be alone (Gen 2:18). We cannot be well alone, or be truly joyful alone, nor can we work well alone. We are also redeemed with community in mind and are called to be a part of a local church community (Mt 16:18). Pastors are not only shepherds; they must always keep in mind they are sheep too. Pastors who flourish live before an audience of One, but they serve as chief servants among a community of many.

When we look into the New Testament, we get a powerful glimpse of flourishing and resilient shepherding leadership. There is not a hint of the self-sufficient pastor free soloing. Instead, we see a compelling picture of the essential importance of intimacy with God and the close relational connections with others.

The apostle Paul provided leadership not in self-sufficient isolation but in the context of and in collaboration with other leaders. In the book of Acts, Luke lists seven of Paul's closest traveling companions: Sopater, Aristarchus, Secundus, Gaius, Timothy, Tychicus, and Trophimus (Acts 20:4). We see not a hint of free soloing leadership isolation. Later in the book of Acts, Luke showcases, with almost a sense of literary amazement, the close relational connection and deep affection flowing in Paul's farewell address to the leaders of the church at Ephesus (Acts 20:17-38). It is not incidental that Paul's final greeting recorded in his second letter to pastor Timothy lists nine individual names of his dear friends: Prisca, Aquila, Onesiphorous, Erastus, Trophimus, Eubulus, Pudens, Linus, and Claudia (2 Tim 4:19-21). Paul teaches us by his life and words that spiritual leadership may at times feel lonely, but it is never a solitary enterprise.

Henri Nouwen speaks words of wisdom:

When Jesus speaks about shepherding, he does not want us to think about a brave, lonely shepherd who takes care of a large flock of obedient sheep. In many ways, he makes it clear that ministry is a communal and mutual experience. . . . I have found over and over again how hard it is to be truly faithful to Jesus when I am alone.[26]

Pastors can and do get lost in navigating their callings. All too often pastors pursue the perilous paths of the celebrity, the visionary, and the lone ranger. So how do lost shepherds find their way back home? This is where our attention must turn next.

2

FINDING OUR WAY HOME

*Jesus sends us out to be shepherds, and Jesus promises a life in which
we increasingly have to stretch out our hands and be led to places we
would rather not go. He asks us to move from a concern for relevance
to a life of prayer, from worries about popularity to communal and
mutual ministry and from a leadership built on power to a leadership
in which we critically discern where God is leading us and our people.*

HENRI NOUWEN, *IN THE NAME OF JESUS*

There are two things that really stress me out. Getting lost and asking
for directions. Perhaps that is why I am such a fan of GPS technology. Outside of the wheel, my vote for the greatest human
invention is the Global Positioning System. Whether I find myself in a
brand-new city or another country, I may be completely clueless about
where I am, but I am never lost. All I have to do is let my handheld
device know where I want to go, and then the best route and the time it
will take to arrive at my desired destination instantly appear on my
screen. Not only is the optimum route provided on my screen, I also hear
a very pleasant and always patient voice telling me when and where I am
to take the next turn. I simply cannot imagine traveling without GPS
technology to guide me.

Knowing where we are going and having confidence we will arrive at our desired destination is not only important when we travel, it is also crucial in navigating our vocational callings. Like many callings, the pastoral calling is hard to navigate, and the road ahead often seems murky and unclear. Every day is a new day. Every situation and context is unique. Every morning we get out of bed, we are above our pay grade. In every new role and phase of life we are rookies. The inconvenient truth is this: it is all too easy and common for pastors to lose their way. Even with the best of intentions, pastors can take wrong turns. Pastors can find themselves facing dead-end streets. Perhaps most unsettling is that many pastors do not realize they have lost their way until meltdown, burnout, or disaster strikes. The resulting collateral damage to themselves, their family members, and the faith community they serve has a long shelf life of pain, disillusionment, and heartache.

Getting lost is an ever-present danger throughout all stages of a pastoral ministry. How do pastors find their way back home again? Finding their way home again will require more than adopting a new philosophy of ministry or the latest church growth techniques. It will call for more than tweaking schedules and adjusting pastoral practices. What is needed is gaining greater paradigmatic clarity around the pastoral calling. To find their way, lost shepherds must embrace God's Positioning System, which first results in recalibrating life around its true north.

RECALIBRATING TRUE NORTH

Peering into a seemingly endless starlit night has always intrigued and inspired me. I remember as a young boy being enraptured as I stared into a crystal-clear summer sky. Lying on my back, feeling the residual warmth of the earth beneath me, seeing the unending world above me, big questions emerged within me. Where did all this come from? Where was it all going? What was my place in it? Did I really matter? How was I to live my life in light of it?[1]

Undergirding the vocational calling of a pastor are foundational existential questions each of us must address at the deepest level of our human experience. Questions regarding origin, destiny, knowing, suffering, meaning, and purpose confront every pastor as we seek to make sense of the world and live lives of logical consistency and integral coherence. If these existential questions are not satisfactorily answered, the pastoral calling—no matter how sincere and well-intentioned—will be built on a fragile and frail foundation. When the rains of life begin pouring down on pastoral life and work, we want to have the strength and resilience not only to endure intense difficulty, but to flourish in the midst of it. So where do we begin?

The pastoral calling begins with God and his good-news story, our true north. A. W. Tozer makes the salient point that our deepest existential questions must begin with God. Tozer writes:

> What comes into our minds when we think about God is the most important thing about us. The history of mankind will probably show that no people has ever risen above its religion, and man's spiritual history will positively demonstrate that no religion has ever been greater than its idea of God.[2]

Tozer rightly reminds us that our idea of God calibrates us. God's character and existence is the bedrock of all reality and must firmly anchor the pastoral calling. If there is intellectual wavering at this foundational level, the pastoral calling will in time run aground on the rocky shoreline of debilitating doubt, disillusionment, and despair. A pastor's heart, soul, mind, and body must first and foremost be firmly tethered to the faith proposition that God is real and has revealed himself to his created world. God's inescapable reality is the truest truth of the universe. Our understanding of the triune God is revealed through the created world, yet supremely through the sixty-six books of canonical Scripture and the story it tells.[3] This means we too are storied people and shepherd others into a great story unfolding in space and time that we participate in.

The four-chapter story. Against the backdrop of a great deal of biblical complexity and mystery, it is clarifying for pastors to see the God of Holy Scripture revealing himself through the coherent framework of a four-chapter story: original creation, fall, redemption, and new creation. The theological categories of the four-chapter biblical storyline recalibrate human existential categories. As a faith community, we like to translate the four chapters as the *ought, is, can,* and *will*.[4] The first chapter of "original creation" portrays the world as it ought to be. The *ought* in our storied lives reflects God's perfect desire and design for his good world and it points us to the truth that we live not in a nihilistic universe, but rather a moral universe. The second chapter, which we refer to as "the fall," portrays the world as it now is. The *is* in our story reflects the brokenness of our lives and world we experience on a daily basis as a result of sin and its disintegrating effects in our relationships and all dimensions of reality. The *is* plays a foundational role in the difficult matter of theodicy, providing pastors a coherent understanding of evil and suffering in the world. This framework is essential for pastoral care as parishioners encounter a great deal of suffering in their lives. Pastors also must understand that a part of the *is* is not only the painful reality of our fallen human nature, but also the reality of a personal evil one who hates God and seeks to deceive and destroy the world God designed and loves.

The third chapter of "redemption" brings good news to the world as it portrays the world as it can be. The *can* in our story reflects God's desire and loving commitment manifested preeminently through the sending of his Son, Jesus, as an atoning sacrifice for sinful humanity, rescuing us from sin and death and making possible new-creation life. Even in the midst of the most agonizing crucibles of suffering and injustice, pastors can be oracles of soul-transforming hope. For God has not abandoned his good yet broken world, but he is redeeming it, bringing his kingdom reign to the world through Jesus the crucified and risen king. The fourth chapter of "new creation" or "consummation" is the final chapter of the biblical story, and it portrays what *will be* one day, our telos. New creation brings great hopefulness to the world. We know that the God of history is moving history forward to an ultimate good end of judging evil and restoring perfect intimacy and fellowship of humanity with the triune God. We will eternally dwell with him in the new heavens and new earth.

A gospel centrality. Yet we must see that this four-chapter story is centered in a person, the person of Jesus. He is the truest truth. Truth is a person. Metaphysical reality is ultimately rooted in a person. That is, pastors are not recalibrating around just an idea or a story, but a person. From original creation to consummation, Jesus is the focal point of the story. And not only that, we have the soul-inspiring hope and historical confidence that Jesus also entered the story. Jesus left the heavenly throne room of the triune God, came to a sin-ravaged planet, taking on human flesh, living a sinless life, ushering in the reign of God, and laying down his life on the cross as an atoning sacrifice for our sin. Jesus defeated death, bodily rising from the dead, ascending into heaven, and he will return one day to this earth to set things right again. Embracing Jesus in repentance and faith, not on the basis of any merit of our own, we experience forgiveness of sin and a new-creation life here and now in his already, not-fully-yet kingdom.

The pastoral calling emerges out of the context of this biblical storyline, providing a coherent understanding of our world, our place in it, and the hope of the gospel at the center of our lives and work. At the very heart of the pastoral calling is our indwelling of this ongoing and unfolding story about Jesus—living, loving, breathing, and sharing the good news. Human and redemptive history marches on and the pastoral calling walks in step with a triune God, dwelling outside of time, who is accomplishing his sovereign purposes within time for his ultimate glory and praise.

If the gospel is about a person, then pastoral calling is deeply relational. The Christian faith we affirm and proclaim is not merely a moral system or set of doctrinal beliefs (as important as they may be), but rather a person we know and are known by. From original creation to consummation, the good-news story has a constant theme of relational intimacy with God and others. The pastor has a lifelong quest not merely to know about God, but to know God personally and to be known by God intimately. In his brilliant gospel-centered letter to the Galatians, the apostle Paul points us to a growing intimacy with God. "But now that … you have come to know God, or rather to be known by God" (Gal 4:9). Our present intimacy with Christ and the indwelling presence of the Holy Spirit is an appetizer of what is to come. In his poetic description of love, Paul writes, "For now we see in a mirror dimly, but then face to face. Now I know in part; then shall I know fully, even as I have been fully known" (1 Cor 13:12).

Starting with why. Not only do pastors orient their vocational callings within the framework of God's personal good-news story, they must also have and maintain clarity around their ultimate purpose. Our telos must be recalibrated. Simon Sinek reminds us that we must start everything we do by first asking the big why question. "By why I mean, what is your purpose, cause or belief? Why does your company exist? Why do you get out of bed every morning? Why should anyone care?"[5] All too often the pastoral calling focuses on what we are to do and not why we do what we do. When the "why" of our calling gets fuzzy, erosion of passion and drift of mission are inevitable. The Westminster Catechism asks first the big why question: What is the chief end of man? The answer: to glorify God and enjoy him forever.[6] While this is true for all followers of Jesus, the pastoral calling builds on this purposeful foundation to include why the church they serve exists. In addition to the Westminster Catechism, as a pastor of a local church, I add Jesus and his church being the hope of the world. The big why that animates my pastoral calling, what gets me out of bed every morning and compels me to bring my best to the work God has called me to do, is I believe with every fabric of my being that the local church as God designed it is the hope of the world. For over thirty years of pastoral ministry, maintaining clarity around the big why of my calling has allowed me to thrive on both the highest mountaintops and deepest valleys that come with serving a faith community.

Our time horizon. As a church-planting pastor one of the most important questions I had to consider from the very beginning was what time horizon would animate the architectural design and mission of the church we were launching. While we had the timeless horizon of eternity as our ultimate aim, the timely horizon of an enduring institution that would serve multiple generations and outlast our lives was paramount. Whether we are building a company, an organization, or a life, having a longtime horizon in view is crucially important for any pastor. The pastoral calling embraces a longtime horizon, knowing God's view of time is vastly different from ours. The apostle Peter, hopeful that Jesus would return in his lifetime, puts it this way: "But do not overlook this one fact, beloved, that with the Lord one day is as a thousand years, and a thousand years as one day" (2 Pet 3:8). Though we anticipate the day when God will close the curtain of time in human history, if our vocational calling is limited to something that can be accomplished merely in our lifetime, the scope of our thinking is woefully inadequate. On the other hand, we recognize the brevity of our temporal journey and the importance of stewarding time well. The psalmist not only points us to an endless eternal time horizon but also a short temporal horizon. "So teach us to number our days that we may get a heart of wisdom" (Ps 90:12). With the strong tug of eternity in our hearts, we seek to embody wise lives in the here and now. Many pastors experience burnout because of a faulty time horizon. When we start with our own time horizons, often focused on immediacy, our lives and ministries become perilously frenetic, resulting in burnout or compromise through one of the three faulty leadership paradigms. We are called to live before our audience of One, causing our time horizon to be recalibrated by the eternal God in his temporal plan for us.

From the story we believe we occupy, to our new time horizon, recalibrating our true north redirects everything about who we are as pastors and what we do in our vocations. All reality is encompassed in a personal triune God made known in his clearest revelation, Jesus Christ. By this true north, lost shepherds are found. By this reorientation, we can rightly follow God's guideposts.

FOLLOWING THE GUIDEPOSTS

When I first turn on my GPS, I have to begin moving for it to calibrate which cardinal direction my car faces. Until that point, any direction it gives doesn't make sense. The previous section set us on track to face true north, and from here, we are able to make sense of the guideposts God has given for our pastoral calling moving forward.

Psalm 78 provides a guiding text that brings clarity and guidance to our calling to help us navigate the challenging terrain of pastoral life and work. The psalmist says:

> He also chose His servant David
> And took him from the sheepfolds:
> From the care of the ewes with nursing lambs He brought him
> To shepherd Jacob His people,
> And Israel His inheritance.
> So he shepherded them according to the integrity of his heart,
> And guided them with his skillful hands. (Psalm 78:70-72 NASB)

Showcasing Israel's King David as an exemplar model of shepherding leadership, five timeless truths emerge, assisting lost shepherds to find their way back home to a place of wholeness and flourishing.[7] I like to think of these five truths as navigational guideposts; the signs along the road to help keep us going the right way. The five navigational guideposts for the pastoral calling journey are these: trust in a sovereign God, heed the shepherd's calling, embrace obscurity, pursue an integral life, and cultivate leadership competency. Let's take a closer look at Psalm 78 and explore these guideposts further.

Trust a sovereign God. Psalm 78 is framed in a historical genre recalling God's sovereign faithfulness to his covenant people, encouraging and guiding new and emerging generations to trust his loyal love. The God who made the world is active in his world. The psalmist reminds his readers that despite the past failures and faithlessness of his covenant people, God has remained faithful and is worthy to be trusted completely. The literary crescendo of Psalm 78 is captured in verses 70-72, showcasing King David as a timeless exemplar of God-honoring shepherding leadership.

Placing our trust in a sovereign God who is active in the shepherding leadership enterprise is the first navigational guidepost for the pastoral calling. The psalmist employs three strong verbs heralding providential intervention in the leadership journey of King David. First, God "chose" David his servant. Second, God "took" David from the sheepfolds. Third, God "brought" David to shepherd Jacob his people.

Like King David, it is crucially important for pastors to grasp that the primary actor in their lives and work is God himself. It is not that pastors do not have the responsibility of faithful and courageous agency; it is that God is ultimately the guiding light, empowerment, and force orchestrating circumstances and resources to accomplish his purposes. Pastors can and must anchor their lives and work, trusting in a sovereign triune God who is not only always with them, but goes before them. We not only walk by faith and lead by faith; we also rest in that faith, knowing that a sovereign God is actively involved in the myriad of details, circumstances, and responsibilities that await us each and every day.

I have often been reminded that God is the one really in charge and not me. I was presented with the opportunity to lead a new and frankly overwhelming ministry initiative. My wife, Liz, and I entered into a season of prayerful discernment. The more I thought and prayed about this new opportunity, the more I felt a suffocating weight on my shoulders. The amount of work and the sizable challenges that lay ahead simply overwhelmed me. It was exhausting just thinking about it. The time drew near for making the decision. One night as I was climbing into bed, God's inaudible voice spoke softly to my heart. "Tom, I am in this and I want you to do this. I have prepared you to do this. I will not only be with you, I will go ahead of you. I will put the team together to do this and provide the resources. Now watch me and trust me. Let's do this together."

In my pastoral calling, hearing God's inaudible voice in such a dramatic and clear fashion is not the norm. The necessary guiding navigational norm is a daily trust and confidence not only that a sovereign God has called pastors, but that he is the one providentially guiding us each step of the way. Properly understood, faith in a sovereign God is not the last resort we look to for guidance, it is the primary way we see and navigate reality. We live our lives looking forward, but we understand them looking backward. Through the clarifying lens of hindsight, we see God's wise orchestration of circumstances, relationships, and resources all for our ultimate good, the advancement of God's kingdom, and for his glory and praise. A dear friend of mine regularly reminds me, "Tom, you don't have to make it happen. God's got this." And indeed he does.

Heed the shepherd's calling. The second navigational guidepost for the pastor is to heed the shepherd's calling. The psalmist frames King David's leadership calling "to shepherd Jacob his people, / Israel his inheritance" (Ps 78:71). Here in Psalm 78 and throughout Holy Scripture, the guiding model we are given for pastoral leadership is one of a shepherd (see Jn 10:11-16; 21:15-17; Acts 20:28-30; 1 Pet 5:2-4.).

I have never shepherded sheep, but I grew up on a Minnesotan dairy farm. Even though I was young and didn't really grasp many aspects of farm life, my youthful eyes could see that caring for animals required constant attentiveness and a ton of hard work. Farm animals needed to be watered and fed. They needed to be sheltered from the cold and protected from danger. Farm animals required extra care when giving birth and medicine when sick.

Many of us who are called to be pastors do not live in an agrarian context, let alone a Middle Eastern Bedouin culture.[8] Yet if we are going to navigate well our pastoral calling, we are wise to extract timeless principles shaping the shepherding paradigm of leadership and apply them to our unique gifting and ministry context. Timothy Laniak, who has lived and studied in a Middle Eastern Bedouin culture, is one of the leading scholars of the shepherding culture. He mines the rich depths and variegated contours of the shepherding metaphor, pointing out three primary leadership roles. The call of the shepherd leader is to provide, protect, and guide.[9] While the shepherd leader is clearly entrusted with a compelling mission (Mt 22:37-40; 28:19-20; Eph 4:11-13), the calling is highly relational. Faithful stewardship of the shepherd's calling is faithful presence with the sheep and attentiveness to the sheep. Shepherding leadership flows out of and in the midst of a faith community. A dual-oversight role emerges, with the goals of individual well-being as well as communal flourishing. Shepherding leaders nourish both individual growth and institutional health. The shepherd leader is a highly relational calling. If people are not your thing, then pastoring should not be your thing.[10] It is not about whether we are more of an extrovert or an introvert; it is about how widely and deeply we love the people entrusted to our care.

Jesus placed his leadership calling within the shepherding paradigm. Jesus not only referred to himself as the Good Shepherd, he also made the point that he knew each of his sheep by name and they knew his voice (Jn 10:3). Yet Jesus raises the bar on shepherding leadership to one of ultimate sacrifice, a willingness to lay down our lives for those under our shepherding care and stewardship. Jesus said, "I am the good shepherd. The good shepherd lays down his life for the sheep" (Jn 10:11). Of course, our Lord will literally shed his innocent blood on the cross, paying the penalty for our sin, but the guiding principle of self-sacrificial and not self-serving leadership is embedded in Jesus' life and teaching.

Pastor Larry Osborne rightly observes how Jesus' words radically reframed the shepherding leadership paradigm to include more than provision, protection, and guidance, but also self-sacrifice. "He (Jesus) said they lay down their lives for the sheep. If those words mean anything, one thing is crystal clear. When it comes to being a New Testament shepherd, it's all about the sheep, not the shepherd."[11]

The pastoral calling is not only a calling requiring self-sacrifice, it is all about the sheep. We must never forget whose sheep we shepherd and whose church we serve. The psalmist reminds us that David's calling as a shepherd leader was not one of ownership, but one of stewardship. David was called to shepherd God's people. Not only were the sheep God's people, they were also God's inheritance. The language of inheritance suggests the extremely high value God places on his covenantal image bearers. As pastors we are entrusted to protect, provide, guide, and nourish what God cherishes and values most. Pastors must never forget that the sheep belong to God and that we are accountable for leading them well.

Embrace obscurity. The third navigational guidepost animating the pastoral calling is to embrace obscurity. Pastoral obscurity is all too often seen as a limiting impediment rather than a God-sized opportunity. For in the crucible of obscurity, God does some of his most transforming work. The psalmist notes that God chose and prepared David in obscurity before putting him in a position of visibility. "He chose David his servant and took him from the sheepfolds" (Ps 78:70). What a compelling picture we are given of young David's faithful heart and tender hands, faithfully carrying out his assigned duties in complete obscurity in the wilderness with only his audience of One observing. God's path of obscurity often makes its way through rugged terrain of the wilderness. The wilderness is a major motif in the biblical story. Ironically, the wilderness can be both a place of deprivation and delight, a place where we can lose our bearings as well as find renewed direction. The wilderness of obscurity is often God's path for the preparation and formation of shepherd leaders. Timothy Laniak writes, "Biblically, the wilderness is a place of dependent, disciplined, purifying solitude where God must be trusted. Deserts bring people quickly to the end of their self-sufficiency and independence."[12]

The Holy Scriptures provides more narrative texture around the defining moment of David's shepherding leadership calling in the wilderness of obscurity. As Jesse's youngest son, David is shepherding the family flock. David is so out of the picture that he is not even thought of or considered as a candidate to be Israel's next king. When Samuel comes to Bethlehem to look for the next king, all of Jesse's sons are paraded before the prophet, yet not one of them passes the grade. Even the prophet Samuel is surprised. David's brothers looked really good on the outside, but something essential for shepherding leadership was missing at the heart level. The Lord speaks to Samuel, instructing him to see the future king through a new paradigmatic lens, one focused not on the externals of appearance but the internal reality of the heart. "But the

LORD said to Samuel, 'Do not look on his appearance or on the height of his stature, because I have rejected him. For the LORD sees not as man sees: man looks on the outward appearance, but the LORD looks on the heart'" (1 Sam 16:7). All of a sudden the biblical narrative presents a surprising twist. "Then Samuel said to Jesse, 'Are all your sons here?' And he said, 'There remains yet the youngest, but behold, he is keeping the sheep.' And Samuel said to Jesse, 'Send and get him, for we will not sit down till he comes here'" (1 Sam 16:11-12). Summoned from the wilderness of obscurity, a young David is anointed by Samuel, filled and empowered by the Spirit for what will prove in time to be a very visible shepherding leadership calling.

David's story reminds us that shepherding leaders are forged on the anvil of obscurity and refined in the crucible of visibility. I encounter so many pastors who lament their "small" ministries and the obscurity of their lives. The chafing rub of comparison with other more visible pastors and larger churches erodes their joy, confidence, and contentment. Over time, many pastors get lost in the suffocating fog of bitterness toward God and the congregation they serve. The New Testament writer James reminds us that where there is jealousy and selfish ambition there is disorder and every evil thing (Jas 3:16). One of the great antidotes to toxic selfish ambition and jealousy is leaning in to the refining and formational grace found in pastoral obscurity. The greatest challenge to the pastoral calling is not serving in obscurity, rather it is navigating the seductive perils that visibility often brings.

In my midtwenties I was privileged to lead a college parachurch ministry. My position of leadership placed me in a very visible role not only on the Southern Methodist University campus, but also in the city of Dallas. Having so much visibility at such a young age afforded me exposure to outstanding leaders. I am very grateful for these years in my life. Transparently, the limelight was ego stroking and exhilarating, but I found myself being confronted by a growing dissonance. There was an increasingly unsettledness in my spirit when I paused long enough to slow down from my adrenaline-driven lifestyle and take inventory of my life. In my heart I knew I desperately needed greater personal maturity and spiritual depth under the visible waterline of my hauntingly shallow inner world. What I needed most was not more vocational visibility, but rather greater obscurity.

Seeking more obscurity meant, for me, leaving a highly visible role in Dallas and moving to Kansas City to pioneer church plant. God knew his perfect plan for me was learning to faithfully serve in obscurity. Over the years, I have made decisions to be less visible in my pastoral calling, choosing less-known places and spaces of obscurity. As pastoral shepherds, there are times God places us in visible roles and on visible stages, but we must embrace these stewardships with great prayer and multiple layers of accountability. If God wants you to be more visible, it is wise and protective to your soul to let him put you there in his way and in his perfect timing.

I like to think of my shepherding pastoral calling like a turtle on a fencepost. I am reminded regularly that no turtle gets to the top of a fencepost on its own. Someone has to put the turtle there. This is true for every pastoral leader. However low or high your pastoral ministry fencepost, make sure you are not trying to crawl to the visible top on your own. If God wants you there, let God unmistakably put you there.

For many pastors who find themselves in a place of visibility, their depth of character, spiritual formation, and intimacy with Christ is not enough to sustain the heavy weight of the pressures of visible success. They have needed more time in the wilderness of obscurity. A great peril awaits pastors when the light shining on them is far brighter than the light shining from within them. If we find ourselves in places of visibility without enough formational ballast under the waterline of our life, what do we do? We have to first be in touch with the true state of our inner world. This accurate self-reflection flows from extended time alone with the Lord in study and prayer as well as inviting a few wise people to speak raw honesty into our life. We must cultivate the discipline of inviting others to offer critique and insight even if it is initially hard to hear. Visibility can be perilous to our souls and our relationships in all seasons of our life and phases in our pastoral leadership. In the last few years, with the counsel of my wife, Liz, and others close to me, I have intentionally reduced my amount of travel and have been more selective regarding speaking invitations outside my local church. I continue to need spaces of obscurity for the well-being of my soul, creativity in my ministry, and increasing depth in my relationships with those closest to me. Obscurity is a good place to be, and pastors are wise only to step into greater visibility if the Lord is clearly calling them to a larger ministry stage.

Pursue an integral life. The fourth important navigational guidepost for the pastoral calling is to pursue an integral life. After framing the shepherding leadership paradigm, the psalmist says, "So he [David] shepherded them according to the integrity of his heart" (Ps 78:72 NASB). Integrity of heart is foundational to the shepherding leadership enterprise. The biblical understanding of integrity is more than mere truth telling or an external conformity to an ethical standard.[13] While those each matter, what matters most is the transformed inner world of the shepherding leader. Shepherding leadership flows from an ever-increasing, integral inner world moving outward to an integrated life. The shepherd leader lives, loves, and leads out of the overflow of an integral life, a wholeness of soul. This integrity of heart is manifested in deepening spiritual formation, increasing wisdom, growing emotional maturity, greater virtue, and the fruit of the Spirit.

Since I was young boy, the lyrics of one of my favorite gospel hymns of the church captured my deepest heart longings for an integrated life. "What can wash away my sin, nothing but the blood of Jesus, what can make me whole again, nothing but the blood of Jesus."[14] The good news of the gospel not only brings forgiveness to our sinful lives; it also brings the hope of an integral wholeness to our lives and pastoral calling. Shepherding leaders live from an integral heart, pursue integrated lives, and experience a joyful, seamless fabric of faithfulness.[15]

Cultivate leadership competency. The fifth important navigational guidepost for the pastoral calling is to cultivate leadership competency.

The psalmist not only affirms the importance of leadership integrity but also shepherding leadership skill: David "shepherded them according to the integrity of his heart, / And guided them with his skillful hands" (Ps 78:72 NASB). Shepherding leadership done well requires an ongoing growth in leadership competency.

One of the most common pastoral care conversations I have with congregants is around their agonizing struggle in the workplace with incompetent superiors. As a pastor, I too have found myself in contexts where leadership competency is woefully lacking and brutally intolerable. One of the inconvenient truths of the nonprofit world is how often leadership incompetency is tolerated, even promoted in the context of superficial niceness and familial loyalties. The local church needs the highest level of leadership competency for it to become more beautiful in its expression and more effective in its mission.

The challenge and complexities of pastoral leadership have increased greatly in modern times. A researcher on pastoral resilience puts it this way: "The responsibilities of leadership and management are rarely discussed in theological training. Indeed pastors are generally surprised by how much leadership and management is involved in their work. And they must learn it on the job."[16] I have experienced, and continue to experience, what research is telling us about the competency needed for pastoral effectiveness. Leadership competency—relationally, emotionally, organizationally, and technically—is a crucial component of a nourishing organizational culture and oversight effectiveness. I am intentional in seeking opportunities for continuing education and leadership-sharpening experiences. Growing in our leadership competency is not an option; it is a vital stewardship of our calling. The shepherding leader must embrace a teachable attitude; a growing curiosity; and an eagerness to learn, unlearn, and relearn the increasing competency their calling requires, which means spending time and money to stay up to date.

Faithful and fruitful shepherding leaders continue to pursue greater competency in leading their congregations toward increased spiritual formation and missional impact. The more years we are called to be a pastor, the greater our leadership ability, insight, and capacity ought to grow. Yet we must never confuse pastoral adequacy with leadership competence. Our adequacy is always anchored in the triune God, in his continual presence, guidance, and power. The apostle Paul speaks a great deal about spiritual leadership in his second letter to the church at Corinth. Paul reminds us of the source of leadership adequacy. "Such *is the* confidence we have toward God through Christ. Not that we are adequate in ourselves *so as* to consider anything as *having come* from ourselves, but our adequacy is from God" (2 Cor 3:4-5 NASB).

FINDING OUR WAY HOME

It is not only sheep that get lost; shepherds get lost too. Yet set against the bleak backdrop of lost shepherds, the prophet Jeremiah provides hope that God will provide shepherds who find their way home again. "And I will give you shepherds after my own heart, who will feed you with knowledge and understanding" (Jer 3:15).

Finding our way home, we must establish a firm existential foundation of our faith, clarity of our purpose, and the time horizon that animates our lives and work. We pursue our pastoral calling by embracing a gospel centrality, cultivating intimacy with God, and living fully into the reality of God's unfolding story. As we navigate the often confusing and perilous pastoral calling, we are wise to keep our eyes on five guideposts given to us in Psalm 78. May we trust in a sovereign God, heed the shepherd's calling, embrace obscurity, pursue an integral life, and cultivate leadership competency. And finally, in finding our way home, shepherding leaders must not only learn to shepherd well, we need to be shepherded well. This is where we now turn our attention.

3

THE LORD IS MY SHEPHERD

*We have reflected often on being shepherd leaders,
but the Twenty Third Psalm is a reminder that we are both
shepherds and sheep. Biblically, leading begins with being led.*

TIMOTHY LANIAK, *WHILE SHEPHERDS WATCH THEIR FLOCKS*

I call him "Coach." Actually, his name is Bill, but referring to him by his common name somehow dilutes his importance in my life. Bill is a seasoned life coach who comes aside leaders in a variety of callings, helping them gain greater clarity regarding how God has wired them, how best they can add value to the organizations they serve, and how they can personally flourish over the long haul. Drawing from years of experience and the finest evaluative tools available, my coach knows me very well. Coach Bill has poked and prodded my deepest thoughts, the stirrings of my heart, the mysterious reaches of my imagination and hopes, and the longings of my soul, and he has walked me through the rugged terrain of my past. We have talked openly and candidly about early childhood trauma, family of origin dynamics, motivational patterns, and personal strengths and weaknesses. Coach Bill rigorously assessed my personal well-being, my marriage, and my leadership effectiveness.

At times the level of personal vulnerability with my coach has felt uncomfortable, but I am learning that being truly known by others and knowing oneself requires peeling back the many protective layers I have accumulated along the way. Working with Coach Bill, I have gained greater clarity as to who I am and what I am to do. I have also gained a wise, safe, and trusted friend who really knows me and desires the best for me. I know Bill is just a text or phone call away. His wise leadership in my life is helping me to take seriously the stewardship of self-care and to better lead others. I simply cannot imagine leading well without his guiding wisdom and attentive presence in my life.

OUR LIFE COACH

As good and great as the grace gift of Coach Bill is in my life, there is a more important life coach essential to pastoral flourishing. In our prideful self-importance we all too often live as if pastoral leadership is a solitary, self-sufficient enterprise. The painful irony is that we speak to others about cultivating intimacy with God while we neglect our own intimacy with God. Pastoral leadership can be a very exhilarating calling, yet it can also be a perilous journey for us individually, for our families, and for those we serve. Immersed in the context of a local faith community, we live, love, and lead out of the overflow of whose we are, who we are, and who we are becoming. Resilient and flourishing leadership over the long haul demands one thing above all other things, growing in intimacy with the greatest lover of our soul. Everything else in our lives rests on and revolves around our ultimate life coach, our triune God, who is our shepherd before whom we are completely safe, truly known, and greatly loved. To lead out of a shepherding paradigm, we need to receive God's loving shepherding first.

The secret sauce. Kansas City is a great place to live—and to eat. The city I call home is known for many things, but perhaps most for the best barbecue in the country. There is no greater appetizer of heaven than the sight and smell of a heaping plate of beef burned ends appearing at your table. Every year Kansas City hosts the largest barbecue contest in the nation. In the world of culinary greatness, the coveted prize of barbecue champion is tops. If you ask the award-winning chefs what sets their barbecue apart, they will inevitably point to their special sauce. They will also tell you that the recipe for their award-winning sauce is a well-guarded secret.

What is true in award-winning barbecue is also true in flourishing pastoral leadership. I believe there is a secret sauce to pastoral wholeness, well-being, resiliency, effectiveness, and fruitfulness. The secret sauce of pastoral leadership is not in learning to lead well—as important as that may be—but rather learning to be led well. Pastors' leadership ceiling is not ultimately how well they lead, but how well they are being led. Pastors not only must have integrity of heart and skillful hands, they must cultivate an intimate friendship with the shepherd of their lives, increasingly knowing him and being known by him. Pastoral leaders who lead well are well led.

A long resilience in the same direction. Pastors who flourish navigate well both the external and internal challenges that inevitably come with leading a faith community. Flourishing pastors are marked by a long resilience in the same direction. Larry Osborne makes the point that pastoral leadership is anything but easy, an ever-increasing challenge in our fast-changing culture. "Let's be honest. Spiritual leadership isn't easy. It's hard work. Always has been. Always will be. And sometimes it's more difficult than it is at other times. We live in one of those times."[1] While there are many external challenges facing pastors, the most perilous challenges are those that lurk in the pastor's inner world. Less so than the challenging circumstances around us, the churnings within us prove most dangerous to pastoral leadership.

At soul level we experience many fears, temptations, and deep longings. Worries and anxieties stalk our minds and interrupt our sleep. Doubts and discouragements become downdrafts draining our emotional energy. Confusions, conflicts, and perplexities greet us daily in the complex people-intensive texture of local church life. In addition, we face a relentless enemy. The evil one seeks to deceive, distract, disrupt, and destroy our lives and the bride of Christ we serve. The insightful words of the great Protestant reformer Martin Luther speak profoundly to the pastoral calling. "For still our ancient foe, doth seek to work us woe, his craft and power are great and armed with cruel hate, on earth is not his equal."[2]

During my seminary days, I attended a wonderful church and got to know the senior pastor well. Or at least I thought I knew him well. One unforgettable Sunday morning my world was shattered. Standing on the stage was my senior pastor surrounded by two elders of the church. One of the elders stepped forward to the podium and said, "Our pastor has an important announcement to make." Immediately the sanctuary became pin-drop silent. With a trembling voice and shaky hands, our pastor read a written statement confessing to his marital infidelity, expressing regret at the pain it was causing to his family and the church. Informing the congregation that he had tendered his letter of resignation effective immediately, he walked out the side door. I do not recall anything the elders said to the stunned church, but I do remember the suffocating ache in my heart and the nauseous pit in my stomach.

As a seminary student preparing for the pastoral calling, I not only felt deeply betrayed, I was shaken to the core of my being. Would I along the way compromise my integrity? Would I find myself living a lie? Would I sacrifice my family on the altar of vainglory and success? Was it really possible to flourish as a pastor not just for months or years, but also for decades? Who would I look to for help and encouragement? Would I finish well or fade in the stretch?

While pastors can and do experience dramatic moral meltdowns, over the years I have come to the conclusion that a more common peril and ever-present threat are the slow burnouts and insidious corrosion that occur slowly at soul level. When the initial vocational honeymoon period recedes, pastors soon encounter the hard realities of pastoral life and leadership. Ministry idealism is shattered, and lurking in the dark shadows of the soul is a quiet desperation, a dulling disillusionment, and a corrosive cynicism.

Eugene Peterson speaks poignantly to the lack of pastoral flourishing and resilience in our time:

> This widespread loss of what in healthier times was assumed leaves the pastor in enormous, though usually unnoticed peril. And the wreckage accumulates: we find pastors who don't pray, pastors who don't grow in faith, pastors who can't tell the difference between Christ and culture, pastors who chase fads, pastors who are cynical and shopworn, pastors who know less about prayer after twenty years of praying than they did on the day of their ordination, pastors with arrogant, outsized egos puffed up by years of hot-air flattery from well-meaning parishioners: "Great sermon Pastor. . . . Wonderful prayer, pastor. . . . I couldn't have made it through without you, Pastor."[3]

The pastoral calling is exhilarating and agonizing, truly glorious and very difficult. Our callings are anything but a hundred-yard dash. Pastors need to embrace a long view, knowing they sign up for an often thankless and arduous marathon. It is not how we start, but how we run the race and finish that really matters. Wherever we find ourselves in the pastoral journey, we need to come to grips with the truth that faithfulness, fruitfulness, and resiliency is not ultimately determined by how well we lead, but about how well we are led. Not how well we shepherd others, but first, how well we are shepherded.

Rediscovering Psalm 23. Job reviews are part of a healthy and well-organized local church culture and institution. In the local church I serve, every year employees go through a rigorous review. Job reviews primarily focus on job performance and much less on personal wholeness. A primary question of assessment is usually "Am I leading well?" Of course this question is of high importance, but I believe an even more crucial question ought to be considered, namely, "Am I being well led?" If as pastors we see ourselves as primarily leading rather than first following, it is all too easy to gain a prideful exaggerated sense of self-importance and nurture an untouchable spirit of unteachability. Instead, we are wise to view our calling through the dual lenses of both leading and following, of being both a sheep and a shepherd. The greatest lessons of leadership arise in the process of followership—both when we follow others well and ultimately when we follow our shepherd well. The first call of pastoral leadership is to draw near to and follow our Good Shepherd in tender intimacy, daily obedience, and a lifestyle of joyful worship. The affirmation of David's shepherding leadership in Psalm 78:72 is embedded in his experience of being shepherded by the Lord. Let's expand our view of shepherding leadership from Psalm 78 by rediscovering the timeless words of David, the shepherd king of Israel in Psalm 23:

> The LORD is my shepherd; I shall not want.
>   He makes me lie down in green pastures.
> He leads me beside still waters.
>   He restores my soul.
> He leads me in paths of righteousness
>   for his name's sake.
>
> Even though I walk through the valley of the shadow of death,
>   I will fear no evil,
> for you are with me;
>   your rod and your staff,
>   they comfort me.
>
> You prepare a table before me
>   in the presence of my enemies;
> you anoint my head with oil;
>   my cup overflows.
> Surely goodness and mercy shall follow me
>   all the days of my life,
> and I shall dwell in the house of the LORD
>   forever.

Since my earliest memories, the words of Psalm 23 have been regular companions of my soul. It was not until much later in my life that I began to realize that Psalm 23 was also a foundational biblical text for pastoral leadership. Psalm 23 continues to open my mind and nourish my heart to the transforming reality of the triune God whose intimate fellowship energizes, inspires, comforts, and guides my daily pastoral calling. It is time we see Psalm 23 as a formative and transformative pastoral leadership lifeline. Eugene Peterson rightly connects the Psalms to the calling of spiritual leadership. "For men and women called to leadership in the community of faith, apprenticeship in the Psalms is not an option, it is a mandate."[4]

The primary theme of Psalm 23 is revealed in the opening verse. "The Lord is my shepherd, I shall not want." Here we find one of the truest truths of the universe. The bedrock reality of the self-sustaining eternal triune God who has no lack is the source of and provision for a human life where there is no lack. Dallas Willard rightly asserts, "The experience of a life without lack depends first and foremost upon the presence of God in our lives, because the source of this life is God himself."[5] The spiritual formation and empowerment necessary for pastoral leadership is firmly anchored in and dependent on the reality of the eternal triune God, our Creator, Redeemer, and Sustainer. Most important for pastoral leadership is our own life with God, our Great and Good Shepherd, our most important life coach.

King David draws from his own experience as a shepherd boy and frames his entire psalm around the shepherding metaphor. David describes the with-God life, where there is no lack, through this metaphorical lens. David experiences God as a shepherd in a very personal, intimate way. Throughout, the psalm overwhelmingly and repeatedly emphasizes the first person singular. David repeatedly speaks of "my" shepherd, of God leading "me," of God being with "me," of God comforting "me." David's intimate and very personal relationship with God, his very own shepherd, is a distinctive mark over the entirety of Psalm 23.

For David, the eternal triune God is his Good Shepherd who is in charge of everything, who is always with him and constantly there for him. As a leader David is experiencing the with-God life where there is no lack. David looks to God to lead him as he leads others. David knows on an experiential level that his shepherd gets him, knows what he is going through, and is there with him when he is going through it. David has a transparent, safe, and secure relational attachment with God. In the context of his own sinful heart and fallen world, David is being well led. The Good Shepherd's sufficiency and infinite resources are accessible and available to him. David knows he is never alone.

Memorizing and meditating on Psalm 23 has become one of the most important and life-giving spiritual disciplines in my life and leadership journey. Over the years Psalm 23 has become the last words that come to my mind as I lay my head on the pillow at night and the first words that come to my mind when I awake in the morning. When I roll out of bed, each new day greets me with an undeniable truth. I was never designed to live within the suffocating confines of the puny resources of my own finitude. As my feet touch the carpeted floor, I recall Psalm 23, remembering who I am, whose I am, and who is with me. I was designed in original creation to live the with-God life, enjoying his intimate presence, drawing on his infinite wisdom, and tapping into his divine empowerment. I look to my shepherd to lead me well. I know him, and he knows me. I am deeply loved by him. He is my shepherd. I am well led.

FOUR REASSURING REALITIES
FOR PASTORAL LEADERS

In Psalm 23, King David weaves together a beautiful poetic tapestry describing his flourishing life. David expresses his full trust and confidence in God who is his shepherd. We do not know the specific context or circumstances of David's life or even his emotional state as he penned Psalm 23.[6] David's reference to the "valley of the shadow of death," may well indicate that he found himself in a very dark, perplexing, and fearful place. David's inspired words are not only a strong affirmation of bedrock theological truth, but also an encouraging reminder of how revealed truth informs and shapes the everyday life of pastoral leadership. In Psalm 23 we find four reassuring realities for pastoral leaders. Flourishing pastors are well led by the shepherd's attentive presence, wise guidance, abundant provision, and hopeful encouragement.

My shepherd's attentive presence. As David reflects on his Good Shepherd, what repeatedly reassures his heart is the attentive presence of the one who leads him. Throughout Psalm 23, David remembers the attentive presence and constant awareness of his shepherd. In Psalm 23:4, David explicitly declares, "you are with me." Yet throughout Psalm 23, the attentive presence of his shepherd is implicitly evident in a multitude of ways and contexts. David's shepherd is right there with him in the lush green pastures as well as the fearful dark valleys. His shepherd's attentive presence is there with him to restore his soul, to anoint his head with healing oil, and to comfort his anxious mind and fearful heart. His shepherd's presence is always there to guide him.

One of the common struggles of pastoral leadership is the sense of loneliness we feel. The past and present pain we experience, the shame we feel, often leads us to hide from others. Safe places to be completely ourselves—as well as safe friends who will love us for who we are and journey with us no matter what—can be hard to find (and keep). The difficult decisions we have to make for the good of the organization can often lead to being misunderstood, resulting in the alienation of relationships. The larger and increasingly complex organizations we lead, the fewer peers we have who can relate to the particular leadership challenges we face. These factors and more often contribute to a chronic kind of loneliness pastors can experience.

While we need to take steps to avoid pastoral isolation and pursue peer friendships, most important is to cultivate intimacy with the shepherd who is always with us and is always attentive to us. The most perilous pastoral isolation is a self-imposed one driven by spiritual neglect or relational distancing from the Good Shepherd himself. Flourishing pastors cultivate a constant awareness that they are never ever alone, that their Good Shepherd is right there with them, eager to share their burdens. Henri Nouwen puts it this way:

> The mystery of God's love is not that he takes our pains away, but that he first wants to share them with us.... The truly good news is that God is not a distant God, a God to be feared and avoided, a God of revenge, but a God who is moved by our pains and participates in the fullness of the human struggle.[7]

Facing perilous and uncertain times, the Old Testament prophet Isaiah pens words of comfort to God's covenant people. Isaiah points them to God's attentive presence in their lives. The one true God is not only there with his people; he is also actively intervening on behalf of them. Isaiah writes, "Fear not, for I am with you; be not dismayed, for I am your God; I will strengthen you, I will help you, I will uphold you with my righteous right hand" (Is 41:10). Isaiah's inspired words describe God's always alert and increasing attentiveness to us not only as pastoral leaders, but also as his beloved children.

When my daughter was a young toddler learning how to walk, she would attempt to come down the carpeted stairs from her upstairs bedroom. Since we were both early risers, Sarah's early morning bold adventure led me to camp myself at the bottom of the stairs. Sensing her lack of stability, I would climb up near her should she lose her balance. Increasingly as Sarah gained strength and confidence, she would increasingly make it down the flight of stairs without my assistance, but not without my presence. Once in a while Sarah would start to wobble. I would take her hand and help her as she made her way down the stairs. When Sarah did lose her balance and start to fall, she knew her dad was right there with his loving and strong arms, eager to hold her and get her safely down the rest of the way. As Sarah's dad, I was not only there with her; I was also there for her.

This is a similar picture the prophet Isaiah paints in regard to God's attentive presence in our lives. Our Good Shepherd is always there with us, ready and eager to intervene in our lives in increasing ways as we may have need. Sometimes as pastoral leaders all we need is the reassurance of his presence. Other times we need an extra dose of his strength to lead when our strength is failing. There are also challenges we face when we find ourselves needing resources way beyond what we possess. Then and there, our Good Shepherd is ready to actively assist us. We also experience times of despairing grief and numbing perplexity where we need our Good Shepherd to simply hold us with his loving and strong hands. Both Isaiah and King David point us to the attentive presence of our Good Shepherd as a foundational priority of God-honoring and God-sustaining pastoral leadership. Just prior to his ascension, Jesus, in commissioning his disciples to their disciple-making mission, reminds them of the primacy of his own presence with them. Jesus ends his instructions by reminding his fearful apprentices of his attentive presence. Jesus says, "I am with you always, even to the end of the age" (Mt 28:20)—that is, until the end of time.

Pastoral leaders who flourish firmly cement in their minds and hold closely in their hearts the reassuring reality of God's attentive presence in their lives and leadership calling. The bedrock reality that the triune God is with them always makes it possible for pastoral leadership to weather any storm, navigate uncharted territory, avoid corrosive cynicism, remain relational, and finish well. We are never on our own and never, ever alone. Our Good Shepherd is with us and for us.

My shepherd's wise guidance. One of the primary roles of the shepherd is to provide directional guidance for the flock. It is not surprising that a repeated, prominent theme of Psalm 23 is David being led and guided by his Good Shepherd. David says of his shepherd, "He leads me beside still waters, . . . He leads me in paths of righteousness for his name's sake" (Ps 23:2-3). Three Hebrew verbs capture the multifaceted guiding role of the shepherd, two of which are employed here in Psalm 23.[8] In Psalm 23 David emphasizes the very personal and tender guidance necessary for a flock to flourish. David recognizes and depends on his shepherd to guide him along a path of righteousness, which connotes a wisdom motif.

There are few things the pastoral calling needs more on a daily basis than wisdom. Like all leadership, pastors face a great deal of volatility, ambiguity, complexity, and uncertainty.[9] In addition to the challenging external environment, pastors walk the rugged terrain of their own weaknesses and frailties. The encouraging news of grace is that, paradoxically, pastoral weaknesses can become pathways to strength. God's power is often manifested in our weaknesses. So in that sense, when we are weak we are strong (see 2 Cor 12:9-10). While there are spiritual gifts of leadership, and leadership gifts can be developed to some degree, many of us are not exceptionally gifted in all the dimensions leadership requires. Often we have not had extensive pastoral experience. Even if we have a good deal of pastoral experience, in many ways each year we lead feels like a rookie season. All this combines to present any pastor with a formidable challenge.

Recognizing that the wise shepherd is there to guide me through his revealed Word and indwelling Holy Spirit is essential to leadership. We must nurture the necessary spiritual receptivity that makes possible leading a congregation with humility and confidence. We also must have the heart conviction as a pastoral leader that immediate access and great power are available to us through prayer. The New Testament writer James gives hopeful words of encouragement as to the efficacy of prayer. "If any of you lacks wisdom, let him ask God, who gives generously to all without reproach, and it will be given him" (Jas 1:5). It is often in the pastor's closet of prayer where the still small voice of God's shepherding guidance is best heard. The wise writer of Proverbs instructs us not only as individuals, but also as leaders to fully trust the One who is there to guide us. "Trust in the LORD with all your heart, and do not lean on your own understanding. In all your ways acknowledge him, and he will make straight your paths" (Prov 3:5-6).

As a pastoral leader I completely trust my Good Shepherd because I am confident he knows the best way for me to go. I know my Good Shepherd is not only with me, I know he goes before me. I am confident he is already steps ahead of me. Though I do not always know the way, I know he knows the way. My shepherd knows which way to go. I will follow him as I lead the flock.

My shepherd's abundant provision. The comforting theme of our shepherd's abundant provision repeatedly surfaces throughout Psalm 23. David speaks of lush green pastures, refreshing still waters, restoration of his soul, a rod of correction, a staff of protection, a lavish table of provision, healing oil on his head, and his life as a cup overflowing with God's tender care and good provision. There is not a hint of divine indifference or a trace of human scarcity in Psalm 23. Set against the backdrop of our human frailty, fragility, vulnerability, and dependence, David points us to a life of joyful security in God, our ultimate source of provision.

As pastoral leaders we face on a daily basis our own need for God's provision, whether that be physical, spiritual, emotional, relational, or financial. In addition to our own needs, we feel a heavy weight of the myriad of needs of the flock we serve. Sometimes the weight of the yoke of leadership feels exhausting and overwhelming. If we are going to flourish, we must look to our Good Shepherd to provide for us as well as the flock, knowing he will take care of us.

Mrs. Johnson led our first grade Sunday school class. Her love for a ragamuffin class of energetic and curious youngsters filled the musty air of the country church basement room she was assigned. Mrs. Johnson was big on cementing in the minds of small children the timeless truths of Holy Scripture. One of the biblical passages most on her pedagogical radar was from the first epistle of Peter. "Casting all your care upon Him, for He cares for you" (1 Pet 5:7 NKJV). After having her class repeat several times Peter's inspired words of exhortation, Mrs. Johnson would break out in her toothy smile and say, "Children, God who loves you will take care of you." Then Mrs. Johnson would sing the refrain of a hymn she loved:

> God will take care of you,
> through every day, o'er all the way;
> He will take care of you,
> God will take care of you.[10]

The simple yet profound words Mrs. Johnson etched in my mind and poured into my soul continue to be a pastoral leadership lifeline for me. Facing new and larger challenges and taking larger steps of faith, knowing my Good Shepherd will take care of me has given me joyful resilience in the midst of overwhelming leadership challenges. Looking back, I can see how God has abundantly taken care of me as well as the local church congregation I love and serve. In Psalm 23 David recalls how God has and will abundantly take care of him, therefore he has nothing to fear. As the shepherd king, David can face the tasks of each day with confidence and the uncertainty of the future with buoyant hope. So can you and I.

Dallas Willard captures the heartbeat of Psalm 23. "Unlimited in resources, just as he is unlimited in love, he is the Good Shepherd who generously provides for our every need."[11] As pastoral leaders we will face overwhelming needs and seemingly impossible obstacles. This comes with the rugged turf of leadership. Few things are more vital to our effective leadership and personal flourishing than to hold closely to our heart our Good Shepherd's abundant provision. My shepherd is there to protect and provide for me. I can cast my daily cares on him, knowing he cares for me. When I feel most overwhelmed and find myself worried and anxious about the leadership realities facing me, I often say to my Good Shepherd, "Lord, you've got this." While this posture is not a license for passivity, and we are always called to do our part, we must often remind ourselves that he's got this. Whether we face a great need, an overwhelming challenge, or a broken relationship, we can place it in his loving, caring, and very capable hands.

My shepherd's hopeful encouragement. The pastoral calling is often a crucible of disappointment and discouragement. A shepherd carries a unique and heavy grief when sheep walk away. The spiritual growth and transformation of congregants can be painfully slow. Church budgets have shortfalls, capital campaigns prove disappointing, marriages melt down, interpersonal conflicts hinder unity, and people often resist needed change. Congregants we have loved and invested our lives in for years without explanation suddenly disappear and begin attending another church. For pastors to flourish, they need daily doses of divine encouragement.

The crescendo of Psalm 23:6 brings to our hearts life-giving words of hopeful encouragement. Our Good Shepherd not only leads us, he pursues us impassioned by his covenantal and tender love directed toward us. Eugene Peterson paraphrases David's words conveying an intensity of hot pursuit. "Your beauty and love chase after me every day of my life. I'm back home in the house of God for the rest of my life" (Ps 23:6 *The Message*).

My Good Shepherd is with me, goes ahead of me, and follows behind me. My Good Shepherd always has my back. Nothing can sneak up on me that my shepherd does not know or care about. My shepherd is watching out for me and cheering me on as I lead. No matter whether I experience agonizing failure, mediocre results, or stunning success, I am completely safe and secure in his sovereign love. The apostle Paul declares that because of the good news of the gospel, nothing I am facing or will encounter in the future will ever separate me from love of God in Christ Jesus our Lord (Rom 8:35-39). My Good Shepherd makes possible a joyful present and a hopeful future. With humble and expectant confidence in his Good Shepherd, David declares, "You make known to me the path of life; in your presence is fullness of joy; at your right hand are pleasures forevermore" (Ps 16:11).

Psalm 23 reminds us of four reassuring realities for pastoral leaders. Flourishing pastors are well led by the shepherd's attentive presence, wise guidance, abundant provision, and hopeful encouragement. Psalm 23 looks with anticipation to the ultimate Davidic king who would come, Messiah Jesus our Lord, Savior, and Good Shepherd.

JESUS MY GOOD SHEPHERD AND MY CLOSEST FRIEND

With Psalm 23 in the backdrop, Jesus points to himself as the Good Shepherd, the one in whom we experience a life without lack. The Gospel writer John presents a dynamic portrait of growing intimacy with Jesus as our Good Shepherd. Jesus our Good Shepherd is attentively present to us. We "hear his voice, and he calls his own sheep by name and leads them out" (Jn 10:3). Jesus our Good Shepherd wisely guides us. "He goes before them, and the sheep follow him, for they know his voice" (Jn 10:4). Jesus our Good Shepherd abundantly provides for us. Jesus says, "I came that they may have life and have it abundantly" (Jn 10:10). Jesus our Good Shepherd gives hopeful encouragement. Jesus our Good Shepherd sacrifices his very own life for us. Jesus declares, "I am the good shepherd. The good shepherd lays down his life for the sheep" (Jn 10:11).

On a rugged Roman cross, Jesus our Good Shepherd laid down his life for his sheep. The sinless Son of God took our place, making an atoning sacrifice, offering forgiveness from sin, and providing a new-creation life for us in his already, not-fully-yet kingdom. Jesus our Good Shepherd has made it possible for us to experience a life with no lack now and for all eternity.

Jesus also calls us friends. On the night before his crucifixion, Jesus gathers his fearful disciples around him. Jesus invites them to a life of growing intimacy with himself. Jesus invites his followers to be his closest friends. "No longer do I call you servants, for the servant does not know what his master is doing; but I have called you friends; for all I have heard from my Father I have made known to you" (Jn 15:15).

Flourishing pastors cultivate a growing and increasingly intimate friendship with the Good Shepherd of their lives, increasingly knowing him and being known by him. There is no greater personal joy or leadership priority than this. Pastoral leaders who lead well are well led. They follow the Good Shepherd, their very best friend in whom they experience an abundant life without lack. Lonely, lost, and hurting shepherds can find their way home to the Good Shepherd. They can flourish and finish well.

Now may the God of peace who brought again from the dead our Lord Jesus, the great shepherd of the sheep, by the blood of the eternal covenant, equip you with everything that you may do his will, working in us that which is pleasing in his sight, through Jesus Christ, to whom be glory forever and ever. Amen. (Heb 13:20-21)

PART TWO

INTEGRITY

OF HEART

*So he shepherded them according
to the integrity of his heart . . .*

PSALM 78:72 NASB

4

THE INTEGRAL LIFE

His good heart made him a good shepherd;
he guided the people wisely and well.

PSALM 78:72 *The Message*

His name was Humpty Dumpty, a plump egg-shaped fellow who shaped my imaginative world as a young boy. Humpty Dumpty was the most memorable character from my seemingly magical book of nursery rhymes. Little did I know at the time how profoundly the catchy and rhyming words of Humpty Dumpty would speak into my human experience and pastoral calling:

> Humpty Dumpty sat on a wall.
> Humpty Dumpty had a great fall.
> All the king's horses and all the king's men
> Could not put Humpty together again.

The Humpty Dumpty nursery rhyme captures the visceral awareness of my human brokenness as well as my deep longing for wholeness. The broken person that I am, I deeply long to be "put back together again."

As pastoral leaders we encounter on a daily basis a myriad of broken, Humpty Dumpty worlds. We find ourselves immersed in the messy middle of broken, Humpty Dumpty friendships; Humpty Dumpty marriages; Humpty Dumpty families; Humpty Dumpty illnesses, Humpty Dumpty addictions; Humpty Dumpty workplaces; and Humpty Dumpty finances. We feel the heavy heartache of so much human brokenness. We hear the heart cries of congregants who long to be put back together again. At the same time, we proclaim a glorious gospel message that Christ will not only forgive but bring healing and new-creation life now in his already, not-fully-yet kingdom. Yet if we are willing to be transparent, we often do not experience the transformation from brokenness to wholeness we so deeply long for in our own lives and leadership. Our lives are often much more like Humpty Dumpty than we care to admit.

HUMPTY DUMPTY PASTORS

Just a few years into my pastoral ministry, I faced an existential crisis of faith. My crisis of faith was not because I began to question the coherence and consistency of the Christian faith. My crisis was centered in the undeniable and painful lack of evidence of spiritual growth and transformation in the lives of my parishioners. The biblical truth I was passionately preaching and teaching to my flock was informing them but not changing them. Yet what troubled me most was my own lack of transformation from my brokenness to increasing wholeness. I was feeling a lot like a Humpty Dumpty pastor. I may have looked good on the outside, but I knew not all was well on the inside. My soul was in anguish, struggling to continue to believe that somehow I could be put back together again.[1]

My heartfelt conversations with many other Humpty Dumpty pastors have convinced me I am not alone in my experience. In this deep struggle with our own lack of spiritual formation, some pastors simply throw in the towel and leave their vocational callings. Other pastors continue on serving a faith community resigned to a professional politeness and a comfortable life, seeking distraction from the growing numbness of their souls.

As seen in the last few chapters, pastors have lost their way. Corrupt paradigms of the pastoral vocation prevent flourishing shepherds, pastors shepherded by God. And yet, having the correct paradigm isn't the full picture either. David shepherded *by the integrity of his heart.* The authenticity and effectiveness of our pastoral calling over the long and arduous terrain of local church leadership will require not only faithful service but also experiential, recognizable spiritual formation in our lives. Is the biblical truth we proclaim so passionately in our preaching informing and transforming our own lives? Under the waterline of our visible pastoral duties, are we becoming increasingly whole, or are we living in the dark and murky depths of our brokenness? Are we masking our own spiritual impoverishment under a thin veneer of nice and pleasant-sounding professionalism? Are we deceiving ourselves as well as others that our inner worlds are well and our lives are really together? Are we simply faking it? Flourishing as pastors demands that we deal with these questions.

In his farewell address to the church leaders at Ephesus, the apostle Paul offers sober words of warning. "Pay careful attention to yourselves and to all the flock, in which the Holy Spirit has made you overseers, to care for the church of God, which he obtained with his own blood" (Acts 20:28). While paying close attention to the well-being of the congregations we serve is vitally important, the apostle Paul's primary emphasis is on the integral wholeness of our hearts and well-being of our lives as leaders. Paying close attention to ourselves is multifaceted in its dimensions, but of primary importance is our own self-care. Properly understood, self-care is not selfishness; it is essential to our ongoing spiritual formation and a primary stewardship of pastoral leadership. Our own spiritual formation is job one. The next chapters devote themselves to this job of shepherding by the integrity of our hearts.

THE LIFE WE LONG TO LIVE

I believe the American writer Henry David Thoreau was on to something when he described the human condition as one of quiet desperation.[2] No matter our age, gender, life circumstances, or present vocational calling, each one of us confronts the discomforting truth there is a gnawing gap between the life we long to live and the life we presently live. Jesus offers hope to broken, Humpty Dumpty hearts and lives; he has come that you "may have life and have it abundantly" (Jn 10:10). Jesus invites you and me to experience the true life we long to live at the very core of our created being.

I am convinced we will never experience the life we long to live if our pursuit is focused on our own self-sufficiency or the accoutrements of pastoral success, brand recognition, ecclesial power, and material comforts. Os Guinness rightly points out the dripping irony of the impoverishment of so many of our lives today. "The trouble is that as modern people we have too much to live with and too little to live for. . . . In the midst of material plenty, we have spiritual poverty."[3] So often as pastors we lament the spiritual apathy and impoverishment of congregants, when our first order of lament ought to be our own woeful lack of spiritual formation in true Christlikeness. Is it any wonder why so many of our sermons lack authenticating spiritual unction, when our lives reflect such spiritual impoverishment? James Davison Hunter speaks insightfully to spiritual leaders about the temper of our times:

> The late modern world is deeply confounding, and its spiritual consolations are few. Like everyone else, Christians are hungry for authenticity, coherence, and depth, and yet the ways these are pursued fail to respond fully to those longings. The need for an alternate vision that is at least a little more adequate to the temper of our times is palpable.[4]

We must respond to the deep brokenness and heart longings of our own lives, and there is a wise path forward from spiritual impoverishment to authenticity, coherence, and wholeness. The good news of the gospel is that Jesus, our Creator and Redeemer, makes it possible for us to live the integral and whole life we so long to live. Our new-creation life, made possible by Jesus' atoning death on the cross and his death-defeating resurrection, is now available to us in his glorious kingdom. The quiet desperation we so often feel can become a joyful delight in the integrity of heart we experience each and every day as we walk in the power of the Holy Spirit. Our hearts can be formed in increasing Christ-likeness. Humpty Dumpty lives can be made whole again. As leaders we can experience what the psalmist describes as integrity of heart.

INTEGRITY OF HEART

In Psalm 78:72, the foundational building block of King David's leadership is framed around the phrase "integrity of heart." Two important Hebrew words, *heart* and *integrity*, emerge as central to any spiritual leadership enterprise. The human heart in Holy Scripture is not referring to an essential physical organ located inside our body, but rather a comprehensive reality that makes up our inner world of feeling, perceiving, willing, and thinking.[5] Through the dual lenses of both biblical and philosophical reflection, Dallas Willard sees the human heart as the very center of our lives. "When I speak of our heart, I refer to that center or inner core of our being from which all our actions flow."[6] Curt Thompson insightfully brings together rigorous biblical reflection, centuries of spiritual wisdom, as well as more recent interpersonal neurobiology research. Thompson offers a clarifying summary of the human heart. "The heart—our deepest emotional/cognitive/conscious/unconscious self—is manifested most profoundly at the level of the prefrontal cortex."[7] However we define it, the human heart is at the very heart of who we are as embodied beings. Good hearts make for good shepherds.

More than ethics. When we hear the word *integrity*, we are prone to think of conformity to a set of rules, being honest with others, or even being true to ourselves. While integrity has a component of ethical consistency, the idea—presented to us in Psalm 78 describing King David—is not primarily an ethical construct, focusing on actions like promise-keeping, honesty, and candor. Rather, integrity is an ontological reality.[8] Integrity is first and foremost something we are at the core of our being and not merely ways we externally conform our behavior to an ethical standard lived out in our daily lives. Integrity is not sin management.

When my wife, Liz, and I go shopping for fine furniture, we want to know about the quality of the product we are considering purchasing.

One of the questions we want to know is whether the furniture has true integrity. Is the furniture we are considering a solid piece of fine wood such as a dark-grained walnut or mahogany, or is it a thin veneer covering a wood composition core? The integrity of the wood matters. While we are willing to pay a good price for solid wood furniture, we do not want to pay solid wood prices for a veneer-covered piece of furniture. In a similar way, human integrity is more than a nice-looking external ethical veneer. Integrity goes to the core of a flourishing person whose entire life from inside to outside, from top to bottom, is remarkably whole, consistent, and coherent. We may even describe a person of integrity as "solid" or "the real deal." Integrity is not merely truth telling, it is truth living.

THE *TŌM* LIFE

The Hebrew word for integrity comes from the *tōm* / *tamim* word group and can be translated "wholeness," "blamelessness," or "uprightness."[9] The Old Testament Scriptures often employ this word group to describe a flourishing person in the context of worship, wisdom, and suffering,[10] and the term is also associated with an individual walking with God. Early in the book of Genesis, against the bleak backdrop of humanity's wickedness, Noah emerges as a bright luminary against a dark sky. The Genesis writer says of Noah, "Noah was a righteous man, blameless [*tōm*] in his generation. Noah walked with God" (Gen 6:9). A few distinctions need to be made. Unlike other notions of flourishing, *tōm* focuses on an individual's inner being. Though it typically appears in connection with ethically wise choices, and integrity is lived out as such, *tōm* is not about moral perfection. In Psalm 26, David cries out, "Vindicate me, O LORD, for I have walked in my integrity, and have trusted in the LORD without wavering" (Ps 26:1; see also Ps 7:8; 78:72). This is a state of being, not just an ethical way of life. *Tōm* is the transcendent connection of the inner world of a person with God—a connection with God that connects the parts of self, which is wholeness.

The grand crescendo of the Abrahamic covenant appears in the opening verses of Genesis 17. "When Abram was ninety-nine years old the LORD appeared to Abram and said to him, 'I am God Almighty; walk before me, and be blameless [*tamim*], that I may make my covenant between me and you, and may multiply you greatly'" (Gen 17:1-2). While God had already promised Abram many things—including a new land, a great name, and a multitude of descendants—God now invites Abraham to experience the flourishing life he had been designed to live: an integral life lost in the Garden of Eden, when sin and death entered God's good world, and one day yet future forever secured on a Roman cross by the atoning shed blood of Jesus. This integral life is not based on any merit of Abraham but offered to Abraham as a grace gift received through faith (Gen 15:6). Three seamless threads of thought make up God's gracious invitation to Abraham: a life of intimacy, integrity, and influence. Intimacy grounds the transcendent connection with God, which cultivates an integral life that results in true influence. These are God's gracious invitations to you as well.

INTIMACY WITH GOD

In Genesis 17:1, God reveals himself to Abraham, inviting Abraham "to walk before me."[11] God's gracious invitation to Abraham paints a compelling picture of a moment-by-moment lifestyle immersed in a face-to-face encounter, in the very presence of the all-powerful Creator God. Described here in a tone of loving tenderness is an intimacy of close proximity and presence. The very foundation of the integral life is the cultivation of intimacy with God. Without this ongoing relational pursuit, the integral life is impossible to experience. Out of a life of intimacy with God, an integral life is formed and emerges. In a pastoral leader, intimacy with God comes before integrity of heart.

In Christian spiritual formation there is no more important pursuit than the cultivation of intimacy with Christ. Out of the rich treasure trove of church history, Brother Lawrence describes walking before God as practicing the presence of God. "The most holy and necessary practice in our spiritual life is the presence of God. That means finding constant pleasure in his divine company, speaking humbly and lovingly with Him in all seasons, at every moment, without limiting the conversation in any way."[12] As image bearers of a relational triune God, we were created with relationship in mind, first with God and then with others within the loving boundaries of safe community. Knowing God and being known by God are, first and foremost, an intimate relational construct. You were made for God. You were designed to walk before God, to live, love, and breathe in his presence and enjoy continuous communion with God.

As a pastoral leader, the most foundational reality of your entire existence is that God knows you. God understands you. God gets you. He knows every nook and cranny of your life, every joy, every disappointment, every fear, every grief, and every failure. Forgiven and adopted into God's family, you are loved by Jesus with the very love which the Father loves Christ (Jn 15:9). Redeemed in Christ, you can truly experience a watchful and caring triune God attending to you with the deepest devotion and most tender affection. God takes great pleasure in you. You are God's beloved, the love of his heart. Imagine the impact on your life, your relationships, and your leadership if you were continually aware of God's presence with you throughout the day. You would lead with bold faith, humble confidence, hopeful realism, and contagious joy.

Practicing his presence. King David, who is described as having integrity of heart, is also the one who models so beautifully practicing the presence of God in his own life. In Psalm 139, David repeatedly affirms God's omnipresence, describing his own deep intimacy with God, who deeply knows him and is always near to him. In praise to God, David declares:

> O LORD, you have searched me and known me!
> You know when I sit down and when I rise up;
>   you discern my thoughts from afar.
> You search out my path and my lying down
>   and are acquainted with all my ways. (Ps 139:1-3)

In a burst of praise, David recalls that there is no place he can ever go where God is not with him and where God is not there for him. While David can lose his mindfulness of God, he knows experientially that God is always mindful of him. Curt Thompson points out David's clear sense of God's mindfulness of him:

> David feels searched, perceived, sought out, and protected. He senses the complexity and intimacy in which he was made—and that God was there when he made him. He senses himself in God's mind and senses God's thought toward him. Like a child who, when faced with adversity, pictures his mother thinking of him with comforting, assuring thoughts, so David does with God.[13]

Knowing he is safe and secure in God's attentive love, David ends Psalm 139 opening his heart to deeper intimacy with God. David longs to be more fully known by God. He cries out:

> Search me, O God, and know my heart!
> Try me and know my thoughts!
> And see if there be any grievous way in me,
>   and lead me in the way everlasting! (Ps 139:23-24)

Many of us fear or are anxious at the thought of God knowing all the secret, broken places of our hearts. At first, coming out of hiding is uncomfortable, but it is only there where we can be fully known and loved.

My deep, gnawing early-ministry faith crisis began with the recognition that many of my congregants had a great deal of Bible knowledge yet lacked in spiritual formation and growing intimacy with Jesus. So many were going through the external motions of nonintegral, stagnant faith. I realized that the congregation reflected my own lack of spiritual formation and intimacy with Jesus. Even though my brain was crammed full of Bible information and knowledge, I painfully had to confront a big disconnect between my mind and my heart. I began to realize that I had placed a primacy on the pursuit of ideas about Jesus at the expense of intimacy with Christ. And this became my real, troubling, soul-level crisis. The shame I was carrying around, the insecurities and past struggles of my life, had led to my fearful reluctance of being truly honest with God. A friend of mine said to me one day, "Perhaps you should read the Gospels again as if you have never read them." For the first time in my life, I truly began looking at them first through the prayerful lens of intimacy rather than ideas or actions. In God's mysterious providence and the work of the Holy Spirit, my eyes of faith were opened as I reread the Gospels. I now saw Jesus' precepts and practices as the pathway for deepening intimacy with Jesus, of knowing and being known. For the first time in a long time, I began to experience the intimacy with Jesus that my heart so longed for and my pastoral leadership truly required. It felt really good, right, and integral that I was now increasingly walking my talk and talking my walk. I was now shepherding my congregation with greater authenticity, freedom, and joy.

Walking before God, daily dwelling in his presence and experiencing intimate communion with God is the sweetest, most joyful, and happiest life imaginable. In Christ, this intimate, integral life is available to you. If we are to practice the presence of God, obedience to God must become a nonnegotiable in our daily lives.

The path of obedience. Walking before God entails wholehearted obedience to God and his word. Jesus reminds his followers that obedience to God is the faith pathway to cultivating intimacy with God. Jesus says, "Whoever has my commandments and keeps them, he it is who loves me. And he who loves me will be loved by my Father, and I will love him and manifest myself to him" (Jn 14:21). Many times I hear pastoral leaders say they long to experience deeper intimacy with God. Yet when we explore together at heart level, we often discover the greatest barrier to cultivating intimacy with God is an unwillingness to wholeheartedly obey God's word. It is all too easy and convenient to embrace partial obedience, but we must realize partial obedience is the most deceptive disobedience of all. No matter how we slice it or dice it, partial obedience is simply disguised disobedience. Our willful disobedience to God will always be a formidable barrier to deeper intimacy with God. Pastoral leaders who desire to have integrity of heart must regularly address with repentance areas of willful disobedience in their lives. Seeking out a spiritual director or a safe pastoral colleague is invaluable in healing confession and life-changing repentance at heart level in the spirit of James's words, "Therefore, confess your sins to one another and pray for one another; that you may be healed" (Jas 5:16).

Living before an audience of One. When God says to Abraham "Walk before me," he invites Abraham to live his life before an audience of One, namely, God himself. Pastors with integrity of heart live *coram Deo* (before God). Living before an audience of One means not only the ongoing cultivation of intimacy with God, but also the daily realization of our accountability to God. As creatures of the Creator God, we are accountable to the One who created us in his image. One of the truest truths of the universe is this: all that we are and have is a stewardship for which we will one day give an account to God.[14] Nothing we ever think, say, or do escapes God's loving but watchful attentiveness. The wise writer of Ecclesiastes concludes his passionate quest for the good and wise life with a bottom-line assertion. "The end of the matter; all has been heard. Fear God and keep his commandments, for this is the whole duty of man[kind]. For God will bring every deed into judgment, with every secret thing, whether good or evil" (Eccles 12:13-14). The writer Jeremiah also reminds us, "I the LORD search the heart and test the mind, to give every man according to his ways, according to the fruit of his deeds" (Jer 17:10).

When we walk before God, we are aware that God is aware of us and that he will examine our lives and reward us for the wise stewardship of our lives. We are wise to live each day cultivating the conscious awareness that God alone will give us our ultimate final exam. The apostle Paul reminds followers of Jesus they too will face the judgment seat of Christ. For true Christians, this judgment is not related to their salvation, but to the faithful or unfaithful stewardship of their lives. "For we must all appear before the judgment seat of Christ, so that each one may receive what is due for what he has done in the body, whether good or evil" (2 Cor 5:10).

I have repeatedly observed with a painful heart several pastoral colleagues who have melted down, walked away, faded away, or simply become slothful in their vocational callings. While many factors have contributed to wandering, disillusioned, or cynical hearts, high on the list is a rejection of the truth of being held accountable by a loving yet holy God. One of Satan's greatest deceptions is that we are not accountable to God for our lives. Martyred German pastor Dietrich Bonhoeffer made the poignant observation that when we fall into the grip of temptation, God becomes unreal to us.[15] Temptation often shrouds the fear of God in our lives. Perhaps Satan's greatest fear is not that we would stop loving God, but that we would stop fearing God. While the bedrock gospel truth of unmerited grace must not be minimized or lost, neither must a proper fear of God be minimized or lost. Integral shepherd leaders not only love God deeply, they also fear him properly.

A proper fear of God. C. S. Lewis rightly grasped both the grace of God and the fear of God. In his literary classic *The Lion, the Witch, and the Wardrobe*, Lewis brilliantly describes Lucy and Susan's anticipation of meeting the great lion Aslan, the Christ figure. The rich dialogue between Lucy and Mr. and Mrs. Beaver bring timeless truth not only to imaginative children but also to pastoral leaders:

> "If there's anyone who can appear before Aslan without their knees knocking, they're either braver than most or else just silly."
>
> "Then he isn't safe?" said Lucy.
>
> "Safe?" said Mr. Beaver. "Don't you hear what Mrs. Beaver tells you? Who said anything about safe? Course he isn't safe. But he's good. He's the King, I tell you."[16]

The triune God we love, serve, and worship with our entire lives is anything but safe, and we dare not treat him or his word trivially.

When we encounter in Holy Scripture the phrase "fear of God," we are tempted to hear it describing an angry God, one we must cower from in sheer terror. It is also tempting to quickly dismiss the fear of God as having no place for those who know gospel grace. Properly understood, to fear God is to live in graceful and wise obedience with a worshipful attitude of dependence, knowing that a loving God is watching and will require an accounting for the stewardship of our time, words, attitudes, actions, relationships, and resources. The Wisdom literature of the Old Testament contrasts the wise and foolish life around a proper fear of God. The writer of Proverbs declares, "The fear of the LORD is beginning of knowledge; the fools despise wisdom and instruction" (Prov 1:7). The apostle Paul makes the strong case that fearing God is a vital component of grace-empowered spiritual formation. Paul writes, "Since we have these promises, beloved, let us cleanse ourselves from every defilement of body and spirit, bringing holiness to completion in the fear of God" (2 Cor 7:1). The New Testament writer James, with a tone of great soberness, reminds spiritual leaders they will be judged by God with greater strictness (Jas 3:1).

Challenged by visibility. As pastoral leaders we often find ourselves in front of people, sometimes lots of people. Being on stage in the limelight and feeling the applause of a crowd can be a very intoxicating and seductive reality. The inspired words of the prophet Jeremiah are crucial for us as leaders to remember. "The heart is deceitful above all things, and desperately sick; who can understand it?" (Jer 17:9). One of the ways we can monitor the motivations of our heart is to ask ourselves if we are the same person at heart level when we are in front of a crowd as we are one-on-one with others. If we are immersed in spiritual community and have a close-knit group of spiritually minded friends, we can without defensiveness invite others to observe and probe the motives and intentions of our hearts.

After giving a sermon one Sunday morning, a friend of mine later pulled me aside and pointed out some egocentric language I was using. He wondered if perhaps at heart level, I was seeking to make myself look good, or in some way, was I seeking to impress others about my accomplishments? Was I longing too much to receive the praise of my congregants? Who was the audience I was ultimately addressing? He kindly suggested some other, less egocentric language I could use and encouraged me to take some time alone and reflect on what my heart was saying under the words I was speaking. Initially I felt inside a bit of defensiveness, but his insightful words led me to the needed heart examination, where I discovered that lurking in my heart was a trust in my own strength, a love for my own ego. I also needed change in the language of my public speaking. One of the most helpful litmus tests of the true condition of the heart of a pastor is what true motivations are fueling the speaking and public persona of his or her leadership. On the front page of my sermon or talk manuscripts I now write, "My Audience of One." This phrase helps me to remember my most important audience and has become a conscious moniker informing my daily life and pastoral leadership.

The good news is that pastors can experience integrity of heart and live integral lives. When we are in Christ and live before our audience of One, we have nothing to fear, nothing to hide, and nothing to prove. Our faith is not neutralized by fear, intimacy with Christ is not sabotaged by shame, and our work is not hijacked by ego. All the energy of our soul is focused on loving, honoring, and serving Jesus; this intimate loving is the integrating principle of our soul. As we love others well and live in joy, we live out our vocational callings in the world; shepherding by the integrity of our hearts becomes possible.

PURSUING INTEGRITY IN ALL OF LIFE

In Genesis 17:1, God not only invites Abraham to walk before him but also to experience a *tōm* or integral life.[17] We must not miss the sequential order of God's invitation. The integral life Abraham longs to live will emerge from the relational intimacy he is invited to experience. In the rich relational womb of a growing intimacy with God, Abraham will discover increasing integrity in all dimensions of life. Following God's invitation to Abraham, God reassures Abraham of the gracious life of blessing now and forever. Abraham is given a new name, a new identity, and the covenantal promise of a new land and great fruitfulness.[18] Abraham is invited by God to experience the flourishing life he was designed to live, the life he longed to live.

I still remember my ordination exam for my ecclesial credentialing as a young pastor. I had written an extensive paper outlining my doctrinal convictions as well as my sense of pastoral calling. During a three-hour interview by a team of seasoned leaders, I was asked many questions regarding theology and pastoral leadership. What I remember most from that day was the departing word lovingly spoken to me by a seasoned pastor. He pulled me aside and affirmed my calling then he left me with these words to ponder. "Tom, walk what you talk and talk what you walk. Don't talk what you don't walk and don't walk what you don't talk." Over the years, I have tucked those words of wisdom in the deepest recesses of my mind and heart, reminding me that the pastoral calling is an invitation to live an integrated life.

One of the great perils of the pastoral calling is the temptation to compartmentalize our lives rather than live integrated lives. It is all too easy for us not to walk our talk. Perhaps one of the greatest vocational hazards for pastors is that we are good at talking. In fact many of us are paid to talk well. We often call others to live lives we ourselves are not leading. We declare the gospel speaks into every nook and cranny of human existence. Yet all too often the gospel we love and proclaim is not speaking into every nook and cranny of our own existence. Our new life in Jesus' already, not-fully-yet kingdom pushes back the insidious perils of convenient compartmentalization and dichotomous thinking, like the division between "sacred" and "secular." Charles Spurgeon expounds:

> To a man who lives unto God nothing is secular, everything is sacred. He puts on his workday garment and it is a vestment to him. . . . He goes forth to his labor, and therein exercises the office of the priesthood. . . . He lives and moves in the divine presence. To draw a hard and fast line and say, "This is sacred, and this is secular,"

is, to my mind, diametrically opposed to the teaching of Christ and the spirit of the gospel.[19]

The transforming truths of the whole counsel of God revealed in Holy Scripture must be allowed to speak into and shape every dimension of our lives—our thoughts, desires, relationships, sexuality, money, and daily work. Not a square inch of our lives must be off limits to the Spirit's healing grace and transforming truth. We can and must model transparency, pursuing whole-life discipleship and all-of-life integration in the context of our faith community. The greatest sermon we ever preach is the integral life we live before God and those around us.

The more we grow in Christ, the deeper our communion is with him and the greater our desire to be an integral leader. When we pursue integrity, all of life comes into greater harmony. That which is disconnected becomes connected. The disordered loves of our idolatrous hearts are reordered. Our priorities are properly arranged. We experience well-kept hearts and become virtuous people. Steven Garber describes well the coherent and comprehensive nature of the integral life. "To see the whole life as important to God, to us, and to the world—the deepest and truest meaning of vocation—is to understand that our longing for coherence is born of our truest humanity, a calling into the reality that being human and being holy are one and the same life."[20]

Making sense of suffering. While the gospel speaks into every nook and cranny of human existence, the integral life is forged and formed in every nook and cranny of everyday life, including suffering. The Hebrew word *tōm* is closely connected to a way of being and a manner of life in the midst of suffering.[21] The Old Testament book of Job is an ancient theodicy that presents the person of Job, in the crucible of unimaginable suffering, as a person of integrity. Though the raw winds of adversity and calamity blow with hurricane force, Job's integrity remains intact. Job himself declares his integrity and even his wife—who wants Job to throw in the towel, to curse God and die—declares her husband as possessing an integral life. Even more importantly, God himself proclaims to Satan that his man Job was an integral person.[22]

It is not incidental that in the crucible of suffering, Job is presented as living an integral life. Job's life suggests to us as pastoral leaders that integrity of heart is a quality of soul that adversity and suffering often uniquely reveal. For the follower of Christ, suffering—though unpleasant—should not be surprising, neither should it be devastating, but rather seen as hopeful in the transformation of our lives into greater Christlikeness. The apostle Paul declares, "Not only that, but we rejoice in our sufferings, knowing that suffering produces endurance, and endurance produces character, and character produces hope" (Rom 5:3-4).

As pastoral leaders we will not only encounter adversity and suffering that is common to all, but also specific kinds of suffering tied to vocational faithfulness. We will feel the sting of wounding criticism. We will hear the disapproval of unfulfilled expectations. We will be ambushed by grief. We will look failure in the eyes. We will be misunderstood, misread, and mistreated. We will face the fierce loathing of the evil one whose demented hatred for the bride of Christ will be aimed directly at those who shepherd God's flock. Let us take up our cross and follow our Lord who suffered. Let us lean into the wind of adversity knowing that the integral life and leadership is hammered out on the anvil of suffering.

Seeking wisdom. Few biblical texts speak more about the integrity of life than the Old Testament book of Proverbs (see Prov 1:12; 2:7, 21; 10:9, 29; 11:3, 5, 20; 13:6; 19:1; 20:7; 28:6, 10, 18; 29:10.). While the biblical view of the integral life is more than mere ethics, how we live and lead others in our daily lives reflects the integrity of our hearts.[23] In Proverbs, we read:

> He stores up sound wisdom for the upright;
> he is a shield to those who walk in integrity,
> guarding paths of justice
> and watching over the way of his saints. (Prov 2:7-8)

The writer of Proverbs highlights the importance of wise living in the matters of justice and caring for the vulnerable. Proverbs portrays the integral life as displaying wisdom in our work and economics. Proverbs also emphasizes the importance of sexual purity, right relationships with our neighbors, managing our economic resources, and caring for our physical bodies. The integral life God calls us to live and empowers us to lead brings wise choices in very down-to-earth places.

Jesus tells us that our faithfulness or lack of faithfulness in the very earthly treasures of this world is tied to our access to the spiritual treasures of his kingdom (Lk 16:11). The apostle Paul reminds us as spiritual leaders that our qualification to lead in the church is directly tied to our effective management of our homes (1 Tim 3:5). The wise, integral life necessary for pastoral leadership in the church is first seen in the home. One of the most visible and telling indicators of integrity of heart is how pastors steward their personal finances. Pastoral financial fitness, emotional health, and physical discipline not only bring resiliency and longevity, but also reveal a life of integrity. While there is not a square inch of the universe that doesn't belong to Christ, there is not a square inch of our lives where wisdom is not needed and where integrity does not matter.

LEADING A LIFE OF INFLUENCE

God's gracious and life-altering invitation to Abraham was not only an invitation to intimacy and integrity, but also to a life of influence. Genesis 17 paints a picture of the great fruitfulness of Abraham's life and lasting legacy. The cultural mandate given to Abraham and to each of us in original creation calls us to lives of fruitfulness (Gen 1:28). Jesus reminds us that a life of fruitfulness indicates his disciples and that our heavenly Father is glorified when we bear much fruit (see Jn 15). A life of fruitfulness flows from our intimate abiding with Jesus. This is the life we were created to live, the life we long to live—a life of fruitfulness in intimacy, integrity, and influence.

We are meaning-seeking creatures and part of that quest for meaning is in the work we are called to do and our contribution to the world.[24] As leaders we not only long to be different, we long to make a difference. And yet undergirding a life of influence is a recognition that our ultimate value as pastoral leaders does not lie in what we do, but in who we are and whose we are. What is most influential is not the size of our accomplishments but the condition of our hearts. An integral life redefines what an influential life is.

Pastor Harold Bishop never became a household name, nor did he achieve great notoriety, but over thirty years of local church ministry, he maintained a well-kept heart, modeled an integral life, and influenced many for Christ. I met Pastor Bishop while I was on staff with a college ministry at the University of Kansas in the town of Lawrence, Kansas. During the two years I lived and worked in Lawrence, I was given the rare privilege of being part of the local church congregation Harold Bishop so faithfully and capably served. I saw firsthand Pastor Bishop's love for Christ and his flock. My wife, Liz, and I were privileged to have Pastor Bishop officiate our wedding.

I will never forget the morning of our wedding, when I stopped by the church sanctuary to pick up an item. Peeking in the sanctuary door, there was Pastor Bishop all by himself vacuuming the brown carpet at the front of the church, making sure everything was just right for our wedding that night. Harold Bishop was no Humpty Dumpty pastor. He lived an integral life before his audience of One, and like his Lord, he led with a basin and towel in his well-worn hands. Pastor Bishop led well because he was well led. Because he had an integral heart, he was a good shepherd leader.

5

APPRENTICESHIP WITH JESUS

By watching the master and emulating his efforts in the presence
of his example, the apprentice unconsciously picks up the rules of the art,
including those which are not explicitly known to the master himself.

MICHAEL POLANYI, *PERSONAL KNOWLEDGE*

Those who teach us shape us. Bob was my high school business teacher. During my freshman year in high school, Bob introduced me to the vast and intriguing world of business and commerce in a free market economy. As eye-opening and engaging as my classroom experience was, outside the classroom was where Bob taught me most. In addition to being a high school business teacher, Bob also owned and managed a very successful and highly profitable Dairy Queen restaurant.

During my freshman year, Bob pulled me aside and asked if I would like a job working at his Dairy Queen. Little did I know it, but that seemingly ordinary day would prove to be a watershed moment in my life. For the next eight years, my boss would profoundly instill wise business acumen and shape my understanding of leadership. Bob opened his heart to me, believed in me, affirmed me, and often communicated his love for me. In the live laboratory of a thriving small business, Bob verbalized words of wisdom, but most of what I learned about life and leadership was unspoken, tacitly transferred to me in the incarnational embodiment of a close friendship and day-to-day apprenticeship.

Looking back at those eight formative years in my life, I now realize that the most important lessons I have learned about leadership did not occur in a classroom, but rather in my apprenticeship with Bob managing a Dairy Queen restaurant. I am immensely grateful for my formal educational training. As a pastor, I believe seminary education is important and of great value. In the classroom, my seminary professors equipped me with exegetical tools for a lifetime of learning propositional knowledge, but inherent to this pastoral preparation model was a deficiency of tacit knowledge acquired in an apprenticeship context. During my four years of seminary, I was entrusted with much theological information without the relational attentiveness necessary for personal transformation. After seminary when I began my pastoral work, I discovered how woefully prepared I was to lead a local church faith community. What was missing in my spiritual formation and leadership training was an apprenticeship model of learning immersed in the live laboratory of everyday local church life. Who Bob was to me in a business context is what I needed in a local church context, but it was hauntingly absent.

AN APPRENTICESHIP MODEL

If pastors are going to lead well, they must first learn to follow well. The lost art of shepherding leadership needs the recovery of apprenticeship because it is primarily calibrated around a person, not a leadership strategy. Integrity of heart and skillful hands emerge out of a relationship-rich apprenticeship where tacit knowledge is transferred life-on-life. Jesus, the greatest leader ever to walk on this sin-scarred planet, embraced and taught an apprenticeship model. Jesus noted the unique power of the apprenticeship model to not only shape, but also transform lives. Jesus put it this way: "A disciple is not above his teacher, but everyone when he is fully trained will be like his teacher" (Lk 6:40). While pastors need to be in apprentice relationships with other leaders, which I will touch on later in this chapter, our primary transforming apprenticeship is with Jesus, the Good Shepherd. There is no substitute for our most important apprenticeship. When we apprentice ourselves to Jesus—the most brilliant and integral being in the universe—with time, training, discipline, and the indwelling power of the Holy Spirit, we become increasingly like Jesus. In our apprenticeship with Jesus, we experience the deepest intimacy our hearts long for and learn an integral life through imitation, which produces the most important qualification of pastoral leadership: whether we are truly becoming like Jesus. But what does this integration journey look like with Jesus as our apprentice?

A paradoxical journey. Apprenticeship with Jesus takes place in the rugged and paradoxical terrain of the flourishing life Jesus offers us in his already, not-fully-yet kingdom. Jesus communicates to all who would become his disciples a consistent apprenticeship pattern of invitation, metaphor, and paradox. In the Gospel of Mark, Jesus invites his apprentices to take up their cross and follow him. Jesus says, "If anyone would come after me, let him deny himself and take up his cross and follow me. . . . but whoever loses his life for my sake and the gospel's will save it" (Mk 8:34-35). Jesus' invitation to follow him and experience true life is framed in the metaphor of a cross. In the first century, a cross was understood as an instrument of death. Embedded in the metaphor of the cross we discover a kingdom paradox: in dying we find life. By its very design, apprenticeship with Jesus will involve an ongoing dying to self, but in dying to ourselves, we will find true life. Dietrich Bonhoeffer captures the very essence of Jesus' invitation to apprenticeship when he says, "When Christ calls a man, he bids him come and die."[1] Henri Nouwen describes the costly cross-path of apprenticeship for the Christian leader. "The way of the Christian leader is not the way of upward mobility in which our world has invested so much, but the way of downward mobility ending on the cross."[2] Francis Schaeffer, who faced a great crisis of faith around the lack of personal transformation in his life as well as in other Christians, speaks wisely. "The moment we accepted Jesus Christ as our Savior, we were justified and our guilt was gone once for all. That is absolute. But if we want to know anything of reality in the Christian life, anything of true spirituality, we must 'take up our cross' daily."[3]

In addition to the metaphor of the cross, Jesus points all who would become his disciples to the metaphor of the vine. In the Gospel of John, Jesus invites his apprentices to a fruitful life of joyful intimacy with himself. Jesus says, "Abide in me, and I in you. As the branch cannot bear fruit by itself, unless it abides in the vine, neither can you, unless you abide in me. I am the vine; you are the branches. Whoever abides in me and I in him, he it is that bears much fruit, for apart from me you can do nothing" (Jn 15:4-5). A grapevine was a metaphorical picture of vibrant, organic life and flourishing fruitfulness. Apprenticeship with Jesus will lead us to an intimate relationship with Jesus, a relationship of secure attachment and life-giving joy. Yet embedded in the metaphor of the vine is the paradox of pruning (Jn 15:2). When a plant is pruned, some vibrant growth is removed to make way for increased growth to occur. The kingdom paradox is that while pruning initially takes away, pruning eventually gives more back. Wise and disciplined pruning produces more fruitfulness. Apprenticeship with Jesus will inevitably involve saying goodbye to some good things in our lives to make way for better things. A person increasingly whole can let go of what the Lord chooses to release.

In the Gospel of Matthew, Jesus invites all who would be his apprentices to a life of rest as we learn from him. Following his same pattern of invitation, metaphor, and paradox, Jesus employs a metaphor of the yoke. Jesus says, "Take my yoke upon you, and learn from me, for I am gentle and humble of heart, and you will find rest for your souls" (Mt 11:29). In the first century, the yoke was a picture of forced submission, coercive enslavement, and dehumanization. Embedded in the metaphor of the yoke, Jesus communicates a stunning paradox. In his yoke of submission, his apprentices will find true freedom and experience what it means to be fully human. In his yoke, Jesus' disciples will experience true rest. Those who become his apprentices will joyfully embrace a life of comprehensive submission and wholehearted obedience to Jesus.

We must not miss that apprenticeship with Jesus as he walks us down the path of paradox. Heeding Jesus' call on our lives entails following him, abiding in him, and learning from him. For us to lead well, we must be yoked to Jesus. One of the most glaring ironies of our time is that so many pastors who teach and talk about discipleship have not themselves entered into apprenticeship with Jesus. Their pastoral vocation is a barrier to intimacy with Jesus. When pastors choose the green room, free soloing, and a compartmentalized life, they leave themselves only with a tragic, buffered existence. Lack of spiritual formation into greater Christ-likeness in many pastoral leaders today is alarming evidence of a lack of apprenticeship with Jesus. Many pastors have not personally responded in faith and obedience to the Great Invitation Jesus has extended to them.

Rediscovering the Great Invitation. Many years ago, my wife, Liz, and I received an invitation that stands above all the rest. The day it arrived in our mailbox, we rushed to open it. The invitation was from the White House, boldly stamped with the gold lettering of the official presidential seal. Holding the beautiful invitation in our hands, our hearts skipped a beat. We were being invited to a large banquet, a formal gala affair in a five-star Washington hotel. When we received the invitation, we looked at our busy schedule and thought, "Oh, we don't have the time for this," right? Like a piece of junk mail, we tossed it into the trash, right? No! This invitation was different. Why? Because of who sent it. Holding the presidential invitation in our hands, our eyes and hearts were firmly set on Washington, DC. Nothing was about to deter us.

Invitations matter a great deal in our lives—depending, of course, on who invites us and what they are inviting us to experience. Invitations can be future memories made; they can also prove to be watershed moments in our lives. Jesus, the Prince of Peace—not just the president, not the leader of the free world, but the Creator of the whole world— offers each one of us the most remarkable invitation imaginable. Jesus, who is the King of kings, the Lord of all, graciously extends to you and me the amazing privilege to become his intimate apprentice, to know him, to be known by him, to be loved by him, to learn from him. If we desire to be shepherding leaders with integrity of heart, we must in expectant faith and joyful obedience embrace his Great Invitation.

For many years as a pastor, I missed the essential importance of Jesus' heart-skipping, jaw-dropping, and transformational invitation to become his yoked apprentice. I knew Jesus' teaching on the Great Commandment was important.[4] Loving God and one's neighbor is at the heart of the Christian faith. I also knew the Great Commission was important.[5] Making disciples of all the nations was foundational to the church's global gospel mission. What I did not comprehend was how both the Great Commandment and the Great Commission were in peril without embracing Jesus' Great Invitation. This may seem shocking, but here is why this is such an inconvenient truth: if we seek to live out the Great Commandment without being apprenticed to Jesus, the Great Commandment becomes the Great Setup. We simply cannot love God and our neighbor as we ought to without Jesus teaching and training us how to do this very thing in the dark murkiness of our deceptive hearts and the rough-and-tumble of everyday life in a fallen world. If we seek to obey the Great Commission to make disciples without first becoming an apprentice to Jesus ourselves, then our disciple-making efforts, no matter how sincere or noble, will prove anemic and impoverished. When we embrace the Great Commission without embracing the Great Invitation, the Great Commission becomes the Great Omission.[6]

Much is at stake in our lives and pastoral leadership if we miss one of Jesus' most important teachings. A. W. Tozer insightfully pointed out the great importance of rediscovering what he astutely called "bedridden truths." Bedridden truths are those often-familiar words that "lose all the power of truth and lie bed-ridden in the dormitory of the soul, side by side with the most despised and exploded errors."[7] Tragically, I believe for many of us, Jesus' Great Invitation has become a bedridden truth. Like God's gracious invitation offered to Abraham—to experience a life of intimacy, integrity, and influence—Jesus also extends a gracious invitation to experience the abundant, integral life we were originally designed to live. Let's take a closer look.

A CLOSER LOOK AT THE GREAT INVITATION

The Gospel writer Matthew reveals Jesus' words of invitation in the context of Jesus' prayerful intimacy with the Father:

> At that time Jesus declared, "I thank you, Father, Lord of heaven and earth, that you have hidden these things from the wise and understanding and revealed them to little children; yes, Father, for such was your gracious will. All things have been handed over to me by my Father, and no one knows the Son except the Father, and no one knows the Father except the Son and anyone to whom the Son chooses to reveal him. Come to me, all who labor and are heavy laden, and I will give you rest. Take my yoke upon you, and learn from me, for I am gentle and lowly in heart, and you will find rest for your souls. For my yoke is easy, and my burden is light." (Mt 11:25-30)

What a beautiful and compelling picture we are given of the intimacy of the Father and the Son delightfully communing together in the breathtaking mystery of triune love. We are also reminded of who Jesus really is as the Messianic prophet, priest, and king. Jesus the very Son of God expresses to the Father his prophetic role of revelation, his priestly role of mediation, and his kingly role of authority. In this preamble to the Great Invitation, it is important for us to see the stunning "who" of the invitation placed before the "what."[8]

Pause for a moment and reflect on who is extending you the invitation to become his apprentice. This is Jesus, Creator and Redeemer, the one of whom the apostle Paul speaks with such breathtaking eloquence. "For by him all things were created, in heaven and on earth, visible and invisible, whether thrones or dominions or rulers or authorities—all things were created through him and for him. And he is before all things, and in him all things hold together" (Col 1:16-17). Paul continues reminding us that Jesus, the incarnated sinless God-man, has made it possible for sinful creatures like you and me to be forgiven, redeemed, regenerated, and reconciled through his atoning death on the cross.

"For in him all the fullness of God was pleased to dwell, and through him to reconcile to himself all things, whether on earth or in heaven, making peace by the blood of his cross" (Col 1:19-20). Only through the cross of Christ can we enter the yoke of Christ. The unmerited grace of gospel faith opens the door and paves the way for our apprenticeship with Jesus. Grace makes possible, empowers, and forges our intimate apprenticeship with Jesus. Rightly, the cross of Christ must remain at the heart of our faith, but tragically, the yoke of Christ has become for many merely a tangential curiosity.

Come to me. Jesus' Great Invitation to apprenticeship begins with the tender and loving words "come to me." Jesus does not invite us to a set of religious rules, a particular philosophy of life, or a system of theology. Instead Jesus invites all who would follow him to know him and be known by him in an ongoing intimate relationship; that is Jesus' "what." Dietrich Bonhoeffer rightly observes that at the very heart of the call of discipleship is Jesus' gracious invitation to himself. "When we are called to follow Christ, we are summoned to an exclusive attachment to his person. The grace of his call bursts all the bonds of legalism. It is a gracious call, a gracious commandment."[9]

As pastoral leaders we must grasp that Jesus sets our true-north compass setting for apprenticeship as one of intimacy and not one of accomplishment. The primary aim of our apprenticeship with Jesus is not to accomplish great things for Jesus, but to enjoy a growing intimacy with Jesus. So many pastors are spiritually malformed and lose their way because from the very start of pastoral ministry, their life and leadership compass setting is off true north. As leaders, our ubiquitous temptation is to focus the energy of our lives on accomplishing great things for Jesus rather than first growing in greater intimacy with Jesus. Let's be honest: much of the visible things we strive so hard to accomplish are done out of our own insecurities, in our own strength, and for our own glory. This can prove perilous on many levels.[10] Institutional processes as well as individuals around us often reinforce our visible, measurable accomplishments for God. It is not that accomplishment and missional advancement does not matter, but often it matters too much, both within us and to those around us. For many pastors, performance reviews disproportionately focus on ministry accomplishment—evidences of visible success—and not on a growing Christlikeness of life. What we measure, we value, and what we value, we measure. The fruits of the Spirit are great evidence of our intimacy with Jesus: love, joy, peace, patience, kindness, goodness, faithfulness, gentleness, and self-control.

When we perceive we have accomplished great things for Jesus and have successful or highly visible ministries, the temptation for blinding pride is more than many of us can resist. When we conclude we have not done great things for Jesus or we have a more obscure ministry, or our gifting is less than our peers, the temptation to discouragement, bitterness, envy, and even despair is ever present. One of the most devastating and darkest realities lurking in many pastors' hearts is a bitter envy of pastoral peers who have greater visibility and larger ministries. But if as pastors our compass setting is firmly set on intimacy with Jesus, with a secure attachment of our new identity in Christ, whether we have a ministry viewed by others or ourselves as successful or not, our souls will be well and the people we lead will be served well.

Apprenticeship with Jesus makes relational intimacy with Jesus our highest priority and the focus of our mindfulness and attentiveness. Henri Nouwen speaks wisely to those called to shepherd God's flock. "The great message that we have to carry, as ministers of God's word and followers of Jesus, is that God loves us not because of what we do or accomplish, but because God created and redeemed us in love and has chosen us to proclaim that love as the true source of human life."[11] When we respond to Jesus' words "come to me," we experience our Good Shepherd's tender love for us, his delight in us, and his longing to be with us. When I hear Jesus' words "come to me," I often imagine Jesus walking into the room and looking for me, his eyes delighting in me and with a wide smile welcoming me into his arms. The words of the contemporary Christian song "Come to Me"[12] beautifully captures the tender grace of Jesus' Great Invitation:

Jesus there is waiting
Patiently for thee
Hear Him gently calling
Come O come to Me

When we say yes to Jesus' Great Invitation, we enter the with-Jesus life. When the Jerusalem religious leaders observe the boldness and brilliance of Peter and John, they are simply dumbfounded. All they can attribute this remarkable display of leadership to is that Peter and John had been spending time with Jesus. "Now when they saw the boldness of Peter and John, and perceived that they were uneducated, common men, they were astonished. And they recognized that they had been with Jesus" (Acts 4:13). Spending much time with Jesus is not an option for pastors; it is essential and the fountainhead of sustained and effective servant leadership. Those who serve with us will recognize that the most distinctive and persuasive quality of our lives and leadership is that we have been with Jesus. Dietrich Bonhoeffer writes:

> The yoke and the burden of Christ are his cross. To go one's way under the sign of the cross is not misery and desperation, but peace and refreshment for the soul, its highest joy. Then we do not walk under our self-made laws and burdens, but under the yoke of him who knows us and who walks under the yoke with us. Under his yoke we are certain of his nearness and communion.[13]

Jesus' Great Invitation is not only an invitation to intimacy, but also an invitation to learn from Jesus how to live our lives like Jesus would if he were us. Learning from Jesus means we enter his yoke of apprenticeship.

Take my yoke. After Jesus invites us to a relationship with himself, he then invites us to take his yoke. The yoke was a rabbinical way of describing the rigorous and transformational learning-by-example process offered to their students or apprentices.[14] The metaphor of the yoke was drawn from an agrarian context where domesticated animals like two oxen would be harnessed together for the purpose of plowing fields or pulling a wagon. The yoke looked like the McDonald's golden arches turned upside down with a wooden beam across the top. Entering the farmer's yoke meant submission to their master. The oxen gave up personal freedom to gain the master's guidance and instruction as well as to find their larger purpose in the world. Paradoxically, submission was not the path to enslavement and deprivation, but the path to true freedom and flourishing. This metaphorical picture of domestic animals under the master's yoke is a revealing picture Jesus is painting for all who would enter his yoke of apprenticeship. The prerequisite for any aspiring apprentice of Jesus was not elite intellectual brilliance, but rather willful submission to the master teacher. Jesus' yoke of apprenticeship is truly open to all—to everyone who would submit fully to him as their master teacher—and is perfectly fitted uniquely for each person.

A pastor's lack of spiritual formation and anemic leadership are not in most cases a paucity of Bible information or superficial doctrinal reflection, but rather a lack of whole-life submission to Jesus. The greater and more comprehensive our submission and willful alignment with Jesus is in all dimensions of our lives, the greater depth and broader scope of our spiritual formation will be evident in the shepherding leadership enterprise we are called to live out in local church community. Hovering over the lives and leadership of so many pastors are Jesus' tearful and indicting words, "Why do you call me 'Lord, Lord' and not do what I tell you?" (Lk 6:46).

Understanding the empowerment of submission came to me during a family vacation to Minnesota. My children and I decided to go fishing at a spot where I grew up. The day was bright and sunny with puffy white cumulous clouds casting periodic, passing shadows on our path. The cool air was invigorating. We sloshed along as the stubborn dew clinging to the grass now drenched our soggy feet. Arriving at our fishing hole, we quickly baited our hooks and cast them into the water. I don't know what distracted my attention from fishing. Yet suddenly, over my right shoulder I saw a bald eagle swoop right over the small dam where we were fishing on the Rum River. It was as if the eagle was doing graceful touch-and-go landings on an aircraft carrier. I had never seen such precision and seemingly effortless grace. The eagle then began to circle in the clear blue cloudless sky above me. Higher and higher the eagle climbed, its strong wings propelling it even higher into the thinning atmosphere. Suddenly, the eagle stopped flapping its massive wings, locking them instead in a firm position. Effortlessly the eagle began to soar, caught up in the awesome power of atmospheric thermo currents thousands of feet above where I was standing. I was mesmerized by the beauty of the moment. Then I realized this majestic bird of prey was created not only to fly with the strength of its powerful wings, but also to soar on updraft currents far more powerful than its wings could ever muster. But to soar, the eagle had to stop relying on its own strength and rest on something much greater than itself. To soar, the eagle had to submit. In a similar way, when we take Jesus' yoke and embrace a life of submission, we learn we were not only created to fly on our own strength, but to soar on the powerful currents of Jesus' transforming grace and truth. In our yoked apprenticeship to Jesus, supernatural power is available to us, to experience what can only be described and explained as a supernatural life. Jesus' yoke of apprenticeship requires submission to him. There is simply no soaring without submission.

Learn from me. Jesus makes it explicit that the yoke he invites us to experience is a yoke designed for our training. Jesus says, "Take my yoke and learn from me." The agrarian-based metaphor Jesus uses captures the first-century reality that when a farmer wanted to train a new ox, he asked the village carpenter to custom make a yoke specifically for training. It is likely that as a carpenter, Jesus was quite familiar with yokes and probably crafted yokes with his well-worn hands. A good carpenter would measure the necks of the mature ox as well as the young ox that was about to be trained. The side where the mature ox would place its neck was larger and carried more of the weight than the side where the young ox would place its head. A properly designed yoke was custom fitted both for the mature master ox and the immature novice ox. When the time came for the young ox to be trained, the farmer would place the young ox in the training yoke next to the mature ox. Day after day, walking eyeball to eyeball with the mature ox, the young ox would learn from the mature ox, and with time the young ox would become just like the mature ox.

While Jesus' first-century listeners were familiar with animal yokes and how they worked, many of us are culturally far removed from the ancient agrarian world. Yet Jesus' metaphor contains a timeless truth we must not miss as it relates to how we learn from Jesus and are transformed by Jesus. For many of us the learning model we have been taught is one that is primarily the cognitive acquisition of propositional information, distanced from a relationship. While there are good and important things we learn in this common format, Jesus emphasized more the primacy of learning from someone and not just learning something apart from someone.

Michael Polanyi sought to bring needed correction to our often-distorted understanding of knowing, advocating for the importance of tacit knowledge. Tacit knowledge is the kind of knowing that is difficult to capture in propositional terms or categories, but that emerges in the context of a close relationship and in the imitation of another. Polanyi describes how tacit knowledge is transferred from one person to another. "By watching the master and emulating his efforts in the presence of his example, the apprentice unconsciously picks up the rules of the art, including those which are not explicitly known to the master himself."[15] Some things are best learned in the context of an ongoing master-apprentice relationship in the live laboratory of everyday life.

For many years my understanding of discipleship was impoverished because while I had paid close attention to the words of Jesus, I had not focused on the spiritual disciplines and rhythms of Jesus as he lived his sinless, incarnated life. When we apprentice our lives to Jesus, we imitate our master Jesus in a comprehensive manner. Dallas Willard opens our eyes to a more integral understanding of discipleship. Dallas writes, "The secret of the easy yoke, then is to learn to live our total lives, how to invest all our time and our energies of mind and body as he did."[16] In the easy yoke of Christ we learn the rhythms of grace embracing both Jesus' precepts as well as his practices. In his paraphrase of Jesus' Great Invitation, Eugene Peterson beautifully captures the life-altering apprenticeship available to us:

> Are you tired? Worn out? Burnt out on religion? Come to me. Get away with me and you'll recover your life. I'll show you how to take a real rest. Walk with me and work with me—watch how I do it. Learn the unforced rhythms of grace. I won't lay anything heavy or ill-fitting on you. Keep company with me and you'll learn to live freely and lightly. (Mt 11:28-30 *The Message*)

Growing in greater Christlikeness is the most important priority in pastoral leadership. Our yoked apprenticeship with Master Jesus will involve spiritual discipline. Writing to pastor Timothy, Paul urges his young protégé to "discipline yourself for the purpose of godliness" (1 Tim 4:7 NASB). The Greek word Paul uses here is the same word from which we get our English word *gymnasium*.[17] Paul is making a comparison: similarly to how our physical bodies need discipline to thrive, so do our spiritual lives. If we are going to run a marathon, we cannot just decide one day to go out and run twenty-six miles. No matter how hard we try to run a marathon, without the prerequisite of a disciplined and wise training regimen, we will simply not have the physical capacity and stamina to finish the race. An important parallel can be drawn as it relates to our spiritual growth and maturation in Christ. In our apprenticeship with Jesus, it is not merely trying harder, but training better that makes the transformative difference. We know how to be proficient in a foreign language, skilled in a musical instrument, or to excel in a sport; a great deal of practice is required. Proficiency does not come merely from trying hard, but from practicing well. Practice makes proficient. To lead well, we must train well. Integral pastoral leadership requires a disciplined life.

As apprentices of Jesus, we are wise to embrace the regular spiritual practices that our Master Jesus modeled. The pathway from saving faith in Christ to transforming obedience to Christ is empowered by the Holy

Spirit[18] and paved with spiritual disciplines. Not only were spiritual disciplines modeled by Jesus and the apostles as well as followers of Jesus for centuries, we are increasingly learning how transformational they are from an interpersonal neurobiology standpoint. Christian psychiatrist Curt Thompson makes this important point:

> Spiritual disciplines have been practiced in the life of deeply integrated followers of God for over three thousand years. Interestingly, they can facilitate the very things neuroscience and attachment theory research suggest are reflections of healthy mental states and secure attachment. Furthermore, these disciplines can strengthen the nine functions of the prefrontal cortex.[19]

While spiritual disciplines are not meritorious in any way, they are transformational in many ways.

While followers of Jesus have embraced many spiritual practices, five formative practices Jesus modeled were study, prayer, solitude, fasting, and service. I often refer to these formative spiritual practices as the "Five Smooth Stones."[20] I have incorporated these five practices into my leadership journey, and they have been embedded in our whole-life discipleship teaching at the local church I serve.

In the history of the church, spiritual disciplines have morphed into a toxic form of asceticism and legalism. For the pastoral leader, monitoring one's heart motivation for embracing the spiritual disciplines is vitally important. Satan can easily take something that is good and right, distort it and then deceive us away from the centrality of gospel grace. It is all too easy to slip into a self-righteous legalism that looks down on others who are less "disciplined" or to subtly buy into the prideful lie that we are somehow meriting God's acceptance of us in some way through our spiritual practices. But I believe pastors confront even greater peril today. This peril is not one of meritorious legalism, but one of licentious cheap grace. Because of the toxicity of legalism, it is all too easy to slowly slide into a perilous distortion of grace. While grace is opposed to human earning or merit, grace properly understood is not opposed to human effort and discipline. The good news of gospel grace is that Jesus has merited everything for us, that in Christ, because of his atoning work on the cross, we are completely forgiven, fully accepted, totally pleasing and unconditionally loved as a child of God. Grace—properly understood and applied—radically alters the motivation of our hearts to whole-heartedly obey Christ out of gratitude for what he has done for us.

Tragically, many pastoral leaders have thrown the spiritual-practices baby out with the toxic bathwater of meritorious legalism. Dietrich Bonhoeffer not only spoke to the church of his time, but speaks to the church in our time as well:

> Cheap grace is grace without discipleship, grace without the cross, grace without Jesus Christ, living and incarnate. . . . This cheap grace has been no less disastrous to our own spiritual lives. Instead of opening up the way to Christ, it has closed it. Instead of calling us to follow Christ, it has hardened us in our disobedience.[21]

You will find rest. In his Great Invitation, Jesus repeats twice a promise that we will find rest when we enter his yoke of apprenticeship. Jesus looks back to the Edenic garden and forward to a Roman cross. The first time the idea of rest appears in the biblical storyline is when God "rested" on the seventh day of creation (Gen 2:1-3). God rested not because somehow he was tired, weary, or bored, but rather because he delighted in the goodness of his creation. God's rest on the seventh day portrays the integral life God designed humans to live and frames the regular Sabbath rhythm his crown of creation must emulate to flourish. One day each week was set aside to cease from labor and to delight in God's goodness and abundant provision. Sabbath rest depicts the good and flourishing life God designed us to live. In his Great Invitation, Jesus' promise of giving true rest looks forward to his atoning work on the cross, which makes rest available to us. When we place our faith in Jesus' saving work, true rest is there for us to experience now and for all eternity.[22] In gospel faith we can enter rest, and we experience rest in our ongoing apprenticeship with Jesus.

As a pastoral leader, the most important question of self-examination besides embracing saving gospel faith is our response to Jesus' Great Invitation. Jesus' yoke is easy not because it is without effort or hardship, but because he designed it to fit us perfectly. The integral life we were designed to live and the integral leaders we long to be are found in our yoked apprenticeship with Jesus. In Jesus' yoke, we experience integrity of heart and we develop the skillful hands required for a life of effective pastoral leadership.

6

PURSUING WHOLENESS

But human beings that we are, there is something in us that cries out.
We do groan. We do sigh. We do protest. And sometimes, we long
for something more, maybe even for the way, "things are supposed to be."

Steven Garber, *The Seamless Life*

mong pastors of large churches in America, he was well-known for his gifted communication skills, "a rising star" in the megachurch world. Over the years, our lives briefly intersected at pastor gatherings and conferences. I very much appreciated my interaction with this fellow pastor, who was always gracious in his words and warm in his demeanor. I remember the sadness that came over me when I heard that he had been removed from the church he served because of a lack of integrity as well as abuses of leadership. I was encouraged that, rather than running from or denying the many struggles of his disordered internal world or minimizing the hurt he had caused to others, he had chosen to receive professional counseling, spiritual direction, and mentoring. I was also grateful he subsequently used his influential public platform to speak openly about his own internal struggles with the destructive pastoral celebrity culture and the sense of entitlement he had embraced. Yet at the heart of his pastoral implosion was something more perilous, perhaps subtler than even a sense of entitlement or a celebrity culture. He put it this way: "Over time, I had slowly stopped prioritizing my relationship with Jesus and made ministry my primary focus."[1] Ministry success and the accoutrements that often accompany it are not only very seductive; tragically, they can prove very destructive to pastors, their families, and the congregations they serve. How my heart broke when the news release about this pastor simply read, "He died from a self-inflicted gunshot wound."[2]

Someone taking their own life is always shocking and tragic, the result of a complex set of spiritual, psychological, emotional, social, and physical factors. However, when spiritual leaders take their own lives, the tsunami shock waves—not only to congregants, but also to other pastors—can be profoundly disorienting and massively devastating. With jaw-dropping disbelief, we wonder, How could this have happened? How are we to make any sense of it all? We look at our own lives, our own internal struggles, and wonder if this could also happen to us. A chilling fear stalks us; a disturbing dissonance confronts us. We too feel the daily challenges pressing in on us as well as the heavy burdens of others who confide in us the deepest secrets, the gnawing doubts, the agonizing disappointments, and the greatest longings of their souls. We are quick to seek the mending of others' wounds and at the same time often slow to pay attention to our own wounds. We know what it is like to dwell in the lonely and dark valley of fear. Though we are often seen as bulwarks of faith, we too find ourselves in the blinding fog of doubt. While the currency of our lives is joy, we often battle the storm clouds of discouragement. Not many days go by when we are not confronted with the rugged terrain of our own weaknesses. We can have sound doctrine and not be a sound person. We may be attentive to matters of the church and inattentive to the matters of our own soul. While giving deep theological answers we can be painfully shallow in our emotional and relational maturity. We may look impressive on the outside but may be withering away on the inside.

I was reminded of this truth when a tree outside of my office window was marked for removal. When I first heard the tree was going to be cut down, I was quite disappointed about it. I had grown fond of that tree. I appreciated the shade it brought and the birds it welcomed on its many branches. From my vantage point, the tree looked healthy, but the tree experts who kept the grounds looking beautiful saw something I did not see. A sense of lament came over me as I watched the tree being cut down. With unfeeling ease, the powerful chain saws ripped through the thick and stubborn trunk. Suddenly I saw what had been hidden on the inside of the tree. The life-giving center of the tree was rotting away! While the outside of the tree still looked fine, the tree was slowly dying, awaiting the next strong wind or lightning flash to send it crashing to the ground. The tree outside of my office window was anything but whole; it lacked integrity and I did not even see it. How true this can be in our own lives.

We've introduced the idea of wholeness in chapter four: having integrity is about having all parts of our lives well-integrated in God. Chapter five showed us that we are integrating around a person, Jesus Christ, who invites us into a learning apprenticeship by taking on his yoke. Now, we put the pieces together and discover how Jesus' Great Invitation extends to dimensions often overlooked in our lives; we realize that all parts of our lives may be wholly lived with, by, and through the most integrated Person. We will first begin by asking what truly is holistic life, then whether it is really possible, and most extensively, how this holism can reach every nook and cranny of shepherd leadership.

WHAT IS A HOLISTIC APPROACH?

Living and leading from an increasingly integral life is at the heart of being a flourishing and fruitful pastor. Yet if we are brutally honest, pursuing greater wholeness in our lives is often not where we expend our greatest energies. Whether it is a fallen pastoral colleague or a fallen tree, this may be a wake-up call that our own soul work is the first work of leadership. Your own soul care is of the highest importance, for you live and lead out of the overflow of your soul.

Anthony Hoekema makes this important observation:

> One of the most important aspects of the Christian view of man
> is that we must see him in unity, as a whole person. Human beings
> have often been thought of as consisting of distinct and sometimes
> separable "parts," which are abstracted from the whole. So in
> Christian circles, man has been thought of as consisting either of
> "body" and "soul," or of "body," "soul," and "spirit." Both secular
> scientists and Christian theologians, however, are increasingly rec-
> ognizing that such an understanding of human beings is wrong,
> and that man must be seen in his unity.[3]

Shepherd leader, all dimensions of your life matter to integral wholeness.
There is not any part of your life Jesus does not fully grasp or deeply care
about. Jesus wants to bring his transforming presence, power, and
wisdom to every relationship you have, to every decision you make, to
the work of your hands, and to every nook and cranny of your life. The
Great Invitation for rest and learning is not limited to spiritual life and
disciplines. When you are "all in" with Jesus, he is in all your life. Doug
Webster speaks of discipleship and its pursuit of an integral wholeness:

> Being a disciple is not a hobby. We are not disciples the way we are
> members of the Sierra Club or Rotary. One does not take up the
> easy yoke the way one takes up golf. The Christian life becomes an
> impossible burden when it is lived part-time or approached half-
> heartedly. Following Jesus requires everything else in life to be
> integrated with our commitment to Christ.[4]

Jesus invites everything we are and do to be brought into his yoke, his
burden. To keep him out of some parts of your life stagnates the
whole you.

THE POSSIBILITY OF A HOLISTIC LIFE

Seeing the struggles of fellow pastors as well as wrestling with our own
inner worlds, it is all too easy to question whether experiencing an

increasing wholeness of soul is possible for us. But as the apostle Peter, no stranger to failure and struggle, reminds us, transformational supernatural resources are available to us:

> His divine power has granted to us all things that pertain to life and godliness, through the knowledge of him who called us to his own glory and excellence, by which he has granted to us his precious and very great promises, so that through them you may become partakers of the divine nature, having escaped from the corruption that is in the world because of sinful desire. (2 Pet 1:3-4)

The apostle Peter declares we can have a proper confidence knowing the integral life we long to live is one we can truly experience because of the transforming power of the gospel. The good news of the gospel is not only that our sins can be forgiven and we can be reconciled to God, but also that we can be made new from the inside out. Our lives not only stand on the firm ground of God's promises; at the core of our being we have been given new-creation life, we have been made new (2 Cor 5:17). By experiencing the new birth we become partakers of the divine nature, a nature that is integral and whole (Jn 3:7-8; 1 Pet 1:3-5). In the same way original creation was integral, so too is our new creation in Christ. The integral life God has for us to experience now in his already, not-fully-yet kingdom is not a fleeting mirage of mere wishful optimism, it is at the very foundation of our hopeful Christian faith. The disintegration and compartmentalization so evident in sin-ravaged hearts can become integral and seamless. We can be healed and we can become whole.

As pastoral leaders we must look to Jesus the Great Physician, who can truly bring healing to the deepest depths of our very being. We don't have to hide our wounds or hold up a good-looking image or fake integrity. Our wounds can be healed, and we can truly find and experience an increasingly integral life. Henri Nouwen offers a poignant reminder that hiding our wounds is counterproductive in ministry. In fact, it is through our own suffering and healing that we are able to truly provide guidance to those who suffer. "The great illusion of leadership is to think that man can be led out of the desert by someone who has never been there. Our lives are filled with examples which tell us that leadership asks for understanding and that understanding requires sharing."[5] As leaders, we must acknowledge and embrace our wounds if we are ever to be able to shepherd effectively. It is only through the experience of our own healing through the power of Christ that we can offer that same hope to those we lead. As those who have been healed by Jesus, we can pick up the mantle of our shepherding calling and become wounded healers.[6] Soaking our lives in Holy Scripture, empowered by the indwelling Holy Spirit, we point others to Christ, the one who can truly heal the wounds and the brokenness within us and among us.

THE "HOW" OF HOLISM

A virtuous life. We begin the "how" by considering the role of physical, performative action toward holistic shepherding. The apostle Peter not only points us to the supernatural resources that are available to us in Christ, he also emphasizes our role and responsibility in growing as whole and virtuous persons. The integral life is a virtuous life. A virtuous life becomes in time an effective, fruitful life. The apostle Peter writes:

> For this very reason, make every effort to supplement your faith with virtue, and virtue with knowledge, and knowledge with self-control, and self-control with steadfastness, and steadfastness with godliness, and godliness with brotherly affection, and brotherly affection with love. For if these qualities are yours and are increasing, they keep you from being ineffective or unfruitful in the knowledge of our Lord Jesus Christ. (2 Pet 1:5-8)

Peter's strong admonition to grow in virtue must not be missed for those who would embrace the calling to become shepherd leaders of a local church congregation. Peter's use of the language of virtue reflects a long tradition from the ancient Greek philosopher Aristotle who articulates the truly good life as one whose outward actions consistently and coherently reflect a person's inward character. In the Aristotelian tradition, each day presented a fresh opportunity to practice virtue or vice. Cultivating virtue and shunning vice was seen as crucial to moral formation. This means complete formation goes beyond knowing; it requires doing. Hands have a vital role in forming the heart.[7] A truly virtuous life nourishes internal harmony, consistent coherence, personal integrity, and demonstrable external ethics.

In the Christian tradition, the virtuous life also includes faith, hope, and love and was modeled perfectly by Jesus. Jesus was the paragon of the virtuous life to be emulated by his followers in their apprenticeship with him. Rebekah DeYoung insightfully affirms Jesus as the role model of virtue. "Christ's life and ministry model the virtues for us, and we must rely on his grace and power of the Holy Spirit to make progress in our imitation of him."[8] Tragically the virtue tradition in the life of the pastoral leader has often been woefully neglected.[9] The acquisition of virtue is a vital aspect of spiritual formation, inherent in our apprenticeship with Jesus and foundational to effective pastoral leadership. The credibility and persuasive voice of pastoral leadership is closely tied to the virtuous or nonvirtuous life he or she exemplifies in the midst of the ebb and flow of daily congregational life. The pursuit of wholeness inevitably takes us down the path of an increasingly virtuous life. True leadership influence must be fueled by the virtuous life you are living.

Living relationally. The pursuit of wholeness or integrity was one of the heartfelt passions of King David. While King David failed at times, his life quest for personal wholeness never ceased. This is evident throughout Psalm 101, one of the most important soul companions to the life of any pastoral leader. Psalm 101 might rightly be called the integrity Psalm. Three times the Hebrew word for integrity appears.[10] King David anchors his integrity quest in his intimate and joyful relationship with God. David declares, "I will sing of steadfast love and justice; / to you, O LORD, I will make music" (Ps 101:1). David's heart is filled with joy overflowing in song when he reflects on the steadfast love he is experiencing. The Hebrew word David uses, translated "steadfast love," describes God's covenantal love for his people, but it also captures a sense of security and strong relational attachment.[11]

Marcus Warner and Jim Wilder capture this Hebrew word well. "*Hesed* is one of the most common words used in the Old Testament to describe God. You can translate it 'sticky love.' It is the sort of love you can't shake off. It sticks to you through every high and low, every success and failure, every malfunction and sin."[12] Through every high and low, David is experiencing God's secure attachment love. This attachment love will permeate the covenantal community he is leading as king. In his words, we hear the relational centrality of the integral life David lived out in community:

> I will look with favor on the faithful in the land,
>   that they may dwell with me;
> he who walks in the way that is blameless [integral]
>   shall minister to me. (Ps 101:6)

The quality and depth of our relationship with God and others lived in spiritual community is a reliable assessment barometer of our growing integral life. Regardless of personality and cultural differences, integral pastoral leaders live relationally and nourish communities where relational depth is highly prized and continually pursued. Jesus reminded his disciples that an authenticating mark of their loving relationship with him was their loving relationship with others. "By this all people will know that you are my disciples, if you have love for one another" (Jn 13:35). It is all too easy for pastoral leaders to lose sight of the primacy of close relationships in their own lives.

Pursuing the integral life is not a solitary enterprise. As leaders, we become more integral beings within a highly relational community. Our own spiritual formation into greater Christlikeness as well as effective leadership takes place within the context of spiritual community where we know and are known by others. If a pastor is married, there is no greater relational priority than to cultivate a growing intimate relationship with his or her spouse (see Eph 5:22-33; 1 Pet 3:1-7.).[13] A pastor who is single will need to nurture close spiritual friendships.[14] Whatever our life season or stage, remaining relational is vital for deepening spiritual formation and a life of wholeness. Marcus Warner and James Wilder encourage leaders to grow in emotional and relational maturity, keeping relationships bigger than problems. They wisely exhort leaders pursuing wholeness to cultivate curiosity, kindness, and appreciation in the communities they serve.[15]

As leaders, we have different personality types and propensities of introversion or extroversion. If we are going to experience an integral life, however, we will need to avoid at all costs the impoverishment of isolation and remain relational. This will require courage and intentionality, embracing a lifestyle with the margin of time and emotional energy required for deep relationships to thrive and grow. Living relationally with other broken and sinful image bearers will at times be painful and many times will be very messy. Pastoral leaders will most likely experience—at some point in their journey—the excruciating pain of betrayal from fellow staff members, lay leaders, or friends. Pastors and their families will feel the sting of criticism, some warranted and many times unwarranted.

When my children were young, they would remind me that although I spoke about living before an audience of One, they lived each and every Sunday before an audience of a thousand. While maintaining proper family and pastoral boundaries is important for well-being and longevity, developing and keeping close, transparent friendships is crucially important. One of the greatest and most perilous temptations pastors face is the temptation to turn inward and hide under a protective shell. Rather than emotionally or physically distancing ourselves from others, pursuing deeper relational connection is not only life-giving, it is essential. Friendships form us and unleash joy in our lives. Like a refreshing stream, the joy birthed and sustained in the grateful heart of an integral leader flows from the relationships cultivated and cherished over a lifetime.

Seeing seamlessly. It was a simple song I learned as a young boy in Sunday school:

Oh, be careful, little eyes, what you see,

For the Father up above

Is looking down in love,

Oh be careful, little eyes, what you see.

The wisdom embedded in these simple lyrics has guided me through the years in my pursuit of an integral life. What we focus our eyes on matters. The psalmist closely ties integrity of heart with discerning eyes:

I will walk with integrity of heart
    within my house;
I will not set before my eyes
    anything that is worthless. (Ps 101:2-3)[16]

Like the psalmist, Jesus emphasizes the importance of our eyes, metaphorically pointing out that they are windows into our inner worlds. "Your eye is the lamp of your body. When your eye is healthy, your whole body is full of light, but when it is bad, your body is full of darkness" (Lk 11:34).

As pastoral leaders our sensory perception of the world around us requires a disciplined focus and a vigilant discernment of evil. The apostle Peter describes the evil one as a prowling lion and exhorts us to be sober-minded and watchful (1 Pet 5:8). Martin Luther's hymnody rings profoundly true: "though this world with devils filled, should threaten to undo us."[17] What I often find in pastoral leaders whose moral lives and sound doctrine begin to slowly erode is a prior loss of discerning focus, an emerging murkiness of clarity regarding good and evil—right and wrong—and the evil one's ubiquitous presence. The psalmist expresses his intentional desire to live a life of purity and integrity by resolving to have heightened discernment regarding evil in all its locations and manifestations. "A perverse heart shall be far from me; I will know nothing of evil" (Ps 101:4). The psalmist portrays a disciplined eye, a discerning posture that avoids the negative influences of evil and evildoers. "I hate the work of those who fall away; it shall not cling to me" (Ps 101:3). As a pastoral leader are you seeing the world within in you and around you with discernment? Do not lose sight of your adversary. Keep an eye on your eyes. Pay attention to what you are paying attention to.

The integral life not only watches what it sees, it also sees the world in a seamless way. When we embrace the gospel and experience a new birth, we not only experience new hearts, but also new eyes. We are now able to discern evil clearly, but we also see God differently. We also see ourselves differently and we see the world differently. Seeing seamlessly means we see both nonmaterial and material reality as created and sustained by God. We see and delight in the goodness of God's created material world. While eternity beckons, the temporal world of time and space in which we now dwell truly does matter. As pastoral leaders pursuing the integral life, we must see through blinding and faulty dichotomization of the secular and the sacred. We must grasp the value of the eternal without devaluing the temporal. Jesus reminds us that although the lilies of the field and the birds of the air exist in short-time duration, God provides and cares for them. Though not given much time to live in the world, the birds and flowers are still of great value to God and should be of great value to us as well. Ravaged by sin and groaning under its weight, God's created material world is still good and to be highly valued. Hymn writer Maltbie Babcock helps us to see seamlessly in her brilliant hymn, "This Is My Father's World":

This is my Father's world,
And to my listening ears,
all nature sings, and round me rings,
the music of the spheres.
This is my Father's world.
I rest me in the thought
of rocks and trees, of skies and seas—
His hand the wonders wrought.[18]

When we see the world seamlessly, the very ordinary lives we lead on very ordinary days become extraordinary in meaning and purpose. Steve

Garber helps us to view our lives and calling in a seamless way. "To see seamlessly is the hope, perhaps even to see sacramentally, where we have eyes to see where heaven and earth meet—where *ora et labora* [prayer and work] become one—right in the middle of our ordinary lives, lived as they must be in ordinary places."[19]

Walking wisely. As pastoral leaders there are few things we need more than living wisely and leading wisely. In a culture where we are information rich and wisdom poor, few things are more urgently needed than the timeless wisdom available to us in the Wisdom literature of Holy Scripture. Whether it is in the area of time, work, money, relationships, or sexual purity, I continually seek the wisdom available to me in the books of Psalms, Proverbs, and Ecclesiastes.

I have discovered over the years that what is most timely in guiding my leadership decisions is that which is timeless. Sometimes that which is most relevant is irrelevant. I also cling tightly to the promise that supernatural wisdom is always available to me through prayer. "If any of you lacks wisdom, let him ask God, who gives generously to all without reproach, and it will be given him" (Jas 1:5). A carefully prayed-through decision allows me to have humble confidence in moving forward even in the most difficult leadership terrain. In addition to prayer, walking in wisdom requires leaning heavily on the presence and empowering resources of the Holy Spirit. Walking wisely also means that as a pastoral leader, I carefully consider the seasons of life and I am attentive to the condition of the soil of my soul.[20] Bivocational pastors must discover sustainable and healthy rhythms for growth and wholeness within their context and time constraints. And all pastors must address how they are continuing to grow in becoming a wiser pastoral leader. The rhythms of our daily lives are informed by walking wisely.

Self-care is not selfishness. One of the greatest grace gifts in my life as a pastoral leader was the provision of a wise and seasoned executive coach. My executive coach is not only a close and trusted friend, he continues to speak truth and wisdom into my life. I will never forget a conversation we had at dinner when I asked him how effective he felt

I was in my current leadership roles. I was hoping my coach would give me a high grade for effectiveness as I was working hard and seeing many evidences of missional advancement in the organizations I serve. How my coach responded stunned me. He said he would rate me at about forty percent effectiveness. Seeing the shocked look on my face, he then went on to say that I was not leveraged in my strength areas, where I should be focused, and I was not paying enough attention to my own self-care.

My coach's loving yet clear exhortation opened my eyes to a glaring weakness in my life and leadership. For many years, I had deemed my own self-care as selfishness rather than God-honoring self-love. I don't know how many times I had read and quoted the Great Commandment to love others as myself, yet somehow I missed the loving myself part. When I speak of proper self-love fueling proper self-care, I am not talking about a carnal narcissism or egocentric self-absorption. Nor am I suggesting there are not times for pastoral leaders to sacrifice in serving others and moving the mission forward. What I now realize is that proper self-care is not selfishness; it is a primary stewardship of God-honoring servant leadership. Without proper self-care, the integral life is not possible, and neither is effective leadership over the long haul of the pastoral calling. Looking back in time, I now believe more pastors melt down in their personal lives, marriages, and leadership effectiveness due to a perennial lack of self-care than those who do from anything else. Younger pastors often ask me what I would do differently if I were to start over again. It does not take me long to respond: I would take my own self-care more seriously. So what does proper self-care look like for a pastor? There will be differences based on culture, personality, and your season of life, but there are some common themes.

While it is of utmost importance as pastoral leaders to care for our souls, we must not neglect the importance of caring for our physical bodies. God designed us as embodied creatures and declared the great goodness of our material creation (Gen 1:31). Although our physical bodies are now corrupted by sin, the apostle Paul reminds us our bodies are now temples of the Holy Spirit and we are to glorify God in our bodies (1 Cor 6:19-20). Our bodies are one of our primary stewardships from God. Caring for our physical bodies means we take seriously the importance of getting our needed sleep. Not getting enough sleep is often an indicator that we are trying to do too much. While slothfulness is a very real and dangerous vice for pastors, so is the vice of workaholism. Sadly, pastors are often positively reinforced by church members and church boards for their destructive workaholism in the name of being fully committed to Christ and the church. In addition to sleep, eating nutritiously and maintaining a healthy weight also allows our bodies to function well. Regular medical checkups encourage healthy lifestyle patterns and can alert us to changes we may need to make in our lifestyles. When it comes to our overall well-being, our bodies keep score.[21] Regular physical exercise is an important means of self-care. One of the most important self-care disciplines of my life has been my regular running regimen. Few things in my life give me a greater sense of physical, mental, and spiritual well-being than my physical exercise routines. In addition to these benefits, I have discovered that my most creative cognitive ideation often takes place during my physical exercise. Cultivating your physical well-being may look differently. Yet taking good care of the body God has entrusted to you is a high stewardship of your pastoral leadership. Your physical strength and energy allow you to think well, love well, and lead well in both tranquil and turbulent times. It is said that fatigue makes cowards of us all, but what is not said is that fatigue makes fools of us all.

Running out of gas in my car and being stranded by the road is one of my irrational fears. So it is not surprising that one of the gauges on my car dashboard I keep my eye on is the level of fuel in my tank. Transparently, I seldom let my tank get below half full. While that may seem a bit overboard, the good thing is that my car has never run out of gas. While I have been vigilant about keeping my car fueled, as a pastor I have not been as diligent in keeping my emotional tank fueled. With so many people needs, expectations, and demands tugging at us from every direction, the calling of a shepherd is emotionally draining. My wife, Liz, has loved me enough to help me see my blind spots and has been invaluable in assisting me in developing wise boundaries and patterns that allow me to replenish my emotional tank.

One of the most important disciplines for your overall emotional and spiritual well-being is to build Sabbaths into your life. I grew up in a context that distorted the idea of Sabbath by placing it in a legalistic lens rather than a life-giving lens. In my earlier years as a pastor, I tended to minimize the importance of Sabbath, but the more I have studied Scripture, I realize God's original design for human flourishing included one day each week for rest and renewal. Building into your weekly schedule a sabbatical day is not a diversion from your calling; it is essential to your calling and a vital aspect of your self-care. In addition to a weekly Sabbath, taking yearly vacations reflects a broader Sabbath principle of the goodness of rest and renewal. In my local church context, we not only mandate yearly vacations for our pastoral staff, but also offer twelve-week sabbaticals every five to seven years. The sabbatical principle of rest and renewal nourishes physical, spiritual, emotional, and relational health in your life and models for others in your congregation the path to greater wholeness.

I will never forget the advice a wise executive gave me when I was a seminarian. Over breakfast he expressed his sadness at how many pastors he knew over the years had lost their marriages and had less-than-flourishing family lives. He pointed out to me that many of the pastors he knew neglected their family because they deemed their church work as more important. He then paused, looked me straight in the eye and said, "Tom, there are two things I want you to remember. First, never lose your family because of the ministry. Second, love where you go home to at night." What puzzled me was not his admonition to put my family before ministry, but what did he mean by loving where I live? So I asked him. He simply reminded me that our homes are a place of refuge from the world, a place of rest and renewal. These wise words have guided me over the years, and my wife, Liz, and I have invested time and treasure in making the place we live a place of rest and beauty, one conducive to hospitality.

As pastoral leaders we don't have to have elaborate homes, but within our budgetary capacity we are wise to invest resources in making our homes a refuge, a place of beauty and serenity. Creating beautiful, warm, and inviting spaces in our homes enhances the flourishing and joy of others who share with us times of celebration, laughter, and fun. Surrounding our lives with beauty is not only a way to minimize the corrosive effects of evil, it is also a way to bring joy and well-being to our lives and relationships. We were created to flourish in a beautiful garden, and even though we live in a fallen world, we are renewed when we encounter beauty. In addition to making our home a place of beauty, my wife, Liz, and I seek out beautiful places in nature that renews us. We enjoy walking in a park, hiking in the mountains, strolling along the ocean, working in a garden, visiting a museum, or listening to a symphony. Immersing our lives in beauty is an important aspect of self-care.

As pastors we are often more aware of our congregation's emotional and mental health needs than we are of our own. Growing in our own greater self-awareness is not the same thing as self-absorption. Gaining greater understanding of who we are builds into our lives increasing emotional and personal maturity. In their research Marcus Warner and Jim Wilder conclude that emotional maturity is vital for effective leadership. "I have become convinced that the number one lid on most leaders is emotional immaturity."[22] One of the most insightful experiences in gaining greater self-understanding was a meeting I had with a professional counselor whose expertise centered in family of origin. Other areas of fruitful exploration with a counselor are how stress negatively influences us with illness, irritability, forgetfulness, and relational depletion; how we experience and respond to grief, loss, and disappointment in our lives; and how we navigate both small and big life changes while spouses and close friends can help us grow in our psychological awareness, I have found that most pastors are wise to work with a professional Christian counselor to assist them in their emotional well-being and growth in personal maturity.

Beginning in a garden long ago, fallen human beings have experienced the disintegrating reality of shame (see Gen 2:25 and all of Gen 3). While human guilt reflects the experience of having done something wrong, shame conveys that there is something inherently wrong with us. Shame is a reality we feel deep within us, telling us, reminding us, we are bad, that somehow we are not enough. All of us wrestle with shame and its debilitating and destructive role in our lives and relationships with others. Ironically many pastors who proclaim the good news of the gospel, that in Christ our guilt and shame are removed, often struggle with shame in their own lives. Shame's corrosive effect on integral well-being and leadership effectiveness is now just being understood in a more comprehensive way. By its very nature, shame likes to hide and is often silent and subtle. The good news is we can find healing in the shame we experience. Curt Thompson points out the remedy. "Healing shame requires our being vulnerable with other people in embodied actions."[23] Perfectly secure and safe in the love of Christ, we can choose not to hide from others, but to live lives of transparency and vulnerability before others. As a pastor, I have found that the more vulnerable I am with the safe people around me, the more emotionally resilient I am and the more joy I experience even in times of difficulty and suffering.

Superheroes have always stirred my heart and fueled my imagination. Growing up my favorite superhero was Superman. I was inspired by his heroic goodness and stunning strength. Yet I soon learned that Superman was anything but super when he encountered kryptonite. Kryptonite stopped Superman in his tracks and rendered him weak and virtually useless. While pastors are far from superheroes with superhero strength, we can encounter forms of our own kryptonite that wreak havoc on our inner worlds and our relationships with others, rendering us ineffective in our leadership. While we may identify several forms of pastoral kryptonite, I believe the one most perilous is hurriedness of spirit.

The times I was able to spend time with and learn from Dallas Willard were some of the greatest grace gifts I have ever been given. One of the first times I heard Willard speak was a seminar he did for pastoral leaders on the topic of the sin of the hurried life. Willard pointed to the life of Jesus, who, although fully engaged in his redemptive mission, was never in a hurry. His conclusion was that our apprenticeship with Jesus will mean eliminating hurriedness in our lives. Equating hurry with sin was not only provocative to say the least; it also revealed a painful and inconvenient truth about my life. As a pastoral leader I was finding a false sense of worth, value, and self-importance in the crammed fullness of my schedule. Living a life with little time or thought margin meant I was often running on empty, continually distracted and not paying attention to what I should be paying attention to. It has been said that if the devil can't get us to sin, he will keep us busy. While this may be true, perhaps one of a pastor's most subtle yet deadly sins is a hurried spirit. A hurried spirit prevents us from loving God and others well. This is why Willard's now-famous words to pastors have found such resonance and soul-level traction. "Ruthlessly eliminate hurry in your life."[24]

PASTOR JOHN YATES SR.

Is it really possible over the long haul for shepherding leaders to live and lead out of the overflow of an increasingly joyful, hopeful, and integral life? The life and fruitful ministry of my friend and pastor John Yates Sr., declares a resounding yes. Pastor John has been in a pastoral role for over fifty years, and he served the same congregation in the Washington, DC, area for forty years. Over four decades, John and his wife, Susan, have faced the highs and lows of congregational life and leadership. Now in a new chapter of his life, John continues to stay curious, grow in deeper intimacy with Christ, and be generative as he seeks to encourage and mentor a new generation of clergy.

I asked John how he has pursued the wholeness and well-being in his life that has allowed him to lead with great effectiveness and joyful longevity. John responded by sharing three ongoing commitments in his life that are wise exhortations for all shepherd leaders who long to be fruitful and effective in their calling. First, stay wholeheartedly committed to regular Bible study and prayer that feed your soul. Second, be committed to and be vulnerable with a small group of friends who are not only cheerleaders of your life, but also challengers in helping you navigate the often dark and murky contours of your inner world. Third, make it a priority to get away from the responsibilities of leadership to rest and be renewed. John put it this way, "cultivate another life." Find a hobby or other activities—whether it is bird watching, golf, woodworking, or gardening—that are healing and joyful diversions from the heavy burdens of shepherding a flock. As an apprentice of Jesus, John Yates has led well a local church with integrity of heart and skillful hands. In the power of the Holy Spirit and in the gracious yoke of Jesus, we can do the same.[25]

PART THREE

SKILLFUL

HANDS

So he shepherded them according to the integrity of his heart,
And guided them with his skillful hands.

Psalm 78:72 NASB

7

A FAITHFUL PRESENCE

*In short, faithful presence in practice is the exercise of leadership
in all spheres and all levels of life and activity. It represents a
quality of commitment oriented to the fruitfulness, wholeness
and wellbeing of all. It is, therefore, the opposite of elitism and
the domination it implies. It is also the antithesis of celebrity.*

JAMES DAVISON HUNTER, *TO CHANGE THE WORLD*

Receiving critical emails from congregants is not an unusual experience for pastors. I remember opening an email from an upset congregant who felt like a recent sermon had implicitly endorsed parents sending their children to public school over a private school or homeschool option. The congregant finished the email saying, "I wouldn't send my dog to a public school." Transparently, I felt pretty defensive reading this email. In my sermon I had been very careful with my words. Recognizing each having strengths and weaknesses, I had never intended to communicate preference for one parental education pathway over another. In the past, I had heard strong and diverse opinions in my congregation regarding education, but never with such strident language. It was now painfully obvious this congregant had very strong opinions about how Christian parents ought to educate their children. What I deemed a parental gray zone requiring prayerful wisdom and freedom of choice, this congregant saw as a black-and-white issue of Christian faithfulness in an increasingly secularized culture.

As a younger pastor, I was ill-prepared for the challenges of navigating the fast-moving and ever-changing currents of the broader culture in which shepherding leadership takes place. Frankly, I was stunned, shocked, and disappointed when I quickly discovered sincere and well-meaning yet conflicted congregants at loggerheads with each other not over doctrinal differences but over differing political ideologies and views of broader cultural issues in everyday life.[1] A wide variety of life-style choices made by congregants around matters of education, entertainment, athletics, workplace ethics, social media, use of alcohol, political partisanship, and technology revealed the complex and often conflicting daily challenge of a fast-moving and ever-changing cultural context. Growing cultural diversity and complexity will increasingly require a discerning cultural intelligence for congregants to flourish in their Monday lives as well as promote unity within the local church. As shepherds, the cultural intelligence needed for leading a local congregation can simply seem daunting and overwhelming. Yet we can be confident that in our apprenticeship with the Good Shepherd, we will have the wisdom and courage to navigate our ever-changing world in a clear-minded way without the frenetic pace that often drives us to places of joyless impoverishment and disillusioning burnout. With skillful hands, shepherd leaders must equip congregants to live faithful, fruitful kingdom lives in an ever-changing world. When it comes to pastoral leadership, cultural intelligence is essential.

Shepherding leadership is not only about clarity of calling and living an integral life; it is also about leadership effectiveness. Serving under leadership in any organization that lacks the necessary leadership competence is frustrating, demoralizing, and demotivating, but this reality is all too common in the local church. Leadership researcher John Kotter presents a sobering picture of the leadership deficit across a wide range of profit and nonprofit entities. "I am completely convinced that most organizations today lack the leadership they need. And the shortfall is often large. I'm not talking about a deficit of 10%, but of 200%, 400%, or more in positions up and down the hierarchy."[2]

The Holy Scriptures speak a great deal about the importance of wisdom-infused competencies required for the multifaceted enterprise of spiritual leadership. In Psalm 78, King David is described as not only having integrity of heart, but also possessing skillful hands.[3] But what does leadership with skillful hands look like? What do "skillful hands" entail? The psalmist is describing not the five or seven steps to leadership effectiveness or merely technical competencies, but rather more of an art form that is highly relational, always dynamic, steeped in wisdom, and creatively adaptable.[4] In his classic book on leadership, *Leadership Is an Art*, Max DePree captures well what I believe the psalmist is describing when he speaks of the skillful hands of a pastoral leader. "Leadership is an art, something to be learned over time, not simply by reading books. Leadership is more tribal than scientific, more a weaving of relationships than an amassing of information."[5] One of the most important skills of shepherding leadership is insightful navigation of the broader contours of contemporary culture.

NAVIGATING AN EVER-CHANGING CULTURE

Shepherd leaders are wise to cultivate a dual perspective, one focused up close and the other further out—keeping a close eye on the internal processes of their church as well as observing the external forces of broader culture influencing the organization as it marches toward an unfolding future. It was said of the amazing Wayne Gretzky that what made him an extraordinary hockey player is he skated not where the puck was, but where the puck was heading. Pastoral leaders are wise to skate toward where the cultural puck is going. An essential aspect of shepherding is paying close attention to the world around them, watching for emerging trends, anticipating where the broader cultural currents are moving. Whether they are caring for sheep in a Middle Eastern Bedouin world or leading a local church in the high-tech Western world, skillful shepherds must be attuned to their external environment. Attentiveness to incremental as well as sudden changes occurring around them is not optional. Pastors need to understand their times.

Understanding our times. Tucked in what is often deemed a remote corner of Holy Scripture we find timeless leadership wisdom reminding us of the high importance of understanding our times. Describing to an exilic community Israel's remarkable historical ascendency as a nation, the writer of Chronicles highlights the cultural insight of the tribe of Issachar. "Of Issachar; men who had understanding of the times, to know what Israel ought to do, 200 chiefs and all their kinsmen under their command" (1 Chron 12:32). The sons of Issachar, seen through the lens of history, are commended not only for their insight regarding the broader ideas, technologies, and movements shaping their ancient world, but also how they provided wise guidance for an entire nation to flourish under David's kingship. While the sons of Issachar were a small tribe, they displayed exceptional cultural intelligence and as a result had an outsized influence. We might even say that while they were in touch with broader culture, they were not in tune with it. First Chronicles 12 gives no hint of capitulation to cultural accommodation or mindless conformity to cultural norms. At this point in the biblical narrative, they wisely avoided being cultural roadkill on the ancient cultural highway between the two superpowers of Egypt to the south and Mesopotamia to the north. Instead, the Issachar leadership walked attentively, seeking wisdom but with dependent, prayerful discernment in line with their covenant commitment to God.

As shepherd leaders, I believe we are wise to learn from the tribe of Issachar. It is often said of followers of Jesus that we are to be in the world but not of the world. If we are going to be in the world but not of the world, then we will need to be growing in our awareness and understanding of the times in which we live and lead. Discerning our particular times will require us to read historically and widely, listen attentively, and observe carefully shapers of the broader culture such as education, economics, media, movies, technology, art, and politics. As shepherd leaders we must read the Word and read the world. Looking through a biblical lens, we will need to be discerning about the positive components of emerging culture as well as the negative. Just about every culture and most cultural moments have a combination of both. A friend of mine who has a tight grasp on common grace regularly reminds me, "Tom, everyone gets at least a small part of the story right."

Our late modern world. Our late modern world contains formidable challenges to our Christian faith and worldview. In the Western world, we live in a time of increased secularity, making the plausibility of our faith for many an increasingly steep uphill climb. Charles Taylor has described this formidable secular canopy as the "immanent frame."[6] This immanent frame tends to reinforce in our daily lives that this material world and our temporal lives are all that is really real, all that is truly important. Taylor's insight that faith in God is no longer inevitable or even at times credible has important ramifications for us as pastoral leaders.[7] Set against the immanent frame of a God-absent world, our pastoral calling is anchored in a God-bathed world. Our brief temporal lives and daily work are immersed in the reality of a transcendent God and the glories of eternity. With our words and the work of our hands, we point others to a spiritual reality beyond this brief moment in time. As shepherd leaders we dare not forget we also face supernatural opposition that makes its way into the ideas and imaginations of a cultural moment where the kingdom of darkness and the kingdom of light seek influence.[8]

Chris Armstrong astutely presses into the immanent frame of late modernity, observing the blinding epistemic myopia of our times. "Our modern room is well lit by the bare bulb of science. But of what lies beyond we see nothing."[9] Peter Berger has pointed out the loss of plausibility structures, the lack of social institutions that reinforce strong and coherent beliefs.[10] Berger addresses an emerging challenge for faith communities. "Thus, the management of doubt becomes a problem for every religious tradition."[11] James Hunter echoes much of Peter Berger's thinking as he makes a strong case that the temper of our times is distinguished by difference and dissolution. By difference, Hunter points to pluralism, the ever-increasing presence of multiple cultures living in close proximity. In many ways this is a wonderful reality and a great opportunity for the church, but when confronted with a wide variety of faiths, belief, and unbelief, one's own faith and worldview may be more deeply questioned as an exclusive way to understand reality. Hunter also describes the temper of our times through the illuminating lens of dissolution. Dissolution deconstructs the most foundational assumptions of reality through emptying the meaning of words, often leading to an increased skepticism of one's true ability to objectively know reality or truth.[12] As late Western moderns, our minds are brimming with doubt—skeptical of authority, truth, history, and institutions, as well as just about everything associated with them, including the church. Almost every aspect of local church shepherding leadership is impacted by this cultural reality.

Cultural collisions. When we gain greater understanding of our times, we are reminded how differently so many of our fellow image bearers see life and the world. We regularly encounter others who have very different worldview assumptions; divergent historical and cultural experiences; and contrasting views of anthropology, gender, sexuality, politics, public policy, morality, and economics. Carl Trueman makes a compelling case that underlying much of our cultural conflict particularly around the sexual revolution is a radical reimagining and redefining of self. "In short, the sexual revolution is simply one manifestation of the larger revolution of the self that has taken place in the West and it is only as we come to understand that wider context that we can truly understand the dynamics of the sexual politics that now dominate our culture."[13] Confronting so much difference at such foundational societal levels often frays the fabric of civil discourse and shrouds common grace. These deep differences challenge Christian leaders who confront cultural and legal collisions over matters such as the sanctity of life and freedom of choice or personal religious liberty and LGBTQ+ rights.[14]

Luke Goodrich offers an important reminder to each of us and to the congregations we serve that in a late modern world we can expect marginalization, rejection, and at times even hostility to the Christian faith we cherish. While affirming the importance of preserving religious liberty for all as a high priority, Luke Goodrich rightly reminds us as apprentices of Jesus, "We're called not to 'win' but be like Christ." Rather than assume a cultural warrior posture, we can evidence a kingdom posture. Goodrich offers these important words of wisdom: "In short, we don't try to win a culture war; we try to glorify God by being like Christ."[15]

Cultural opportunities. As pastoral leaders we must recognize we face not only strong cultural headwinds, but also feel brisk tailwinds of opportunity to be the church and to move God's mission in the world forward. In many ways our twenty-first century is rather similar to the very pluralist first century, when the church flourished and the gospel spread throughout the Roman world. In our late modern world, when the exclusive truth claims we proclaim are harder for many to hear, the good deeds we do in the service of our fellow human beings speak loudly. Our call as church leaders is to make disciples, to care for the poor, be a voice for the marginalized, seek justice for the oppressed, do good work, and proclaim with words and deeds the gospel before a watching world—a world that is asking not primarily is Christianity true, but is it good? When so many have exhausted their quest for meaning, our Christian faith offers a hopeful message of forgiveness, of new life, of transformation, and joy both now and for all eternity.

A distinguishing mark of our cultural moment is a haunting loneliness. Never before in history have we been more connected to others through technology and the many tributaries of social media. At the same time so many feel so deeply alone and isolated. Loneliness is one of the greatest physical and mental health issues of our time.[16] The local church is uniquely designed to address the crying need for belonging and connection. As pastors we have the opportunity to lead a safe, spiritually empowered community where we know and are known; where we love and are loved; where we grow and help others grow. Truly these are opportune times to be the church in the world. Yet faithfulness and fruitfulness will require an extra dose of tender love, prayerful wisdom, and unwavering courage as we lead the church in our ever-changing and dynamic culture.

CHRIST AND CULTURE REVISITED

Growing up in my faith tradition, I was taught explicitly as well as absorbed implicitly a suspicious posture regarding the currents and practices of broader culture. Much of my faith identity and sanctification markers were wrapped around what I did not do that "those other people" did. When it came to my understanding of faithful Christian living in the world, I was taught a strong separatist posture toward culture. Over the years, I have experienced a greater dissonance of this view that rightly emphasizes the importance of purity yet often minimizes the biblical imperative to proximity and engagement within culture.

It was H. Richard Niebuhr who addressed the challenges of Christian faithfulness in light of the cultural context.[17] Niebuhr's five categories of Christ against culture; the Christ of culture; Christ above culture; Christ and culture in paradox; and Christ the transformer of culture have provided an intersectional language for thoughtful reflection on the differing postures Christians take in regard to the broader world around them. On one end of the spectrum is a strong separatism that embraces purity from culture, often taking a defensive stand against culture. On the other end of the spectrum is strong accommodation that embraces a cozy relevance to culture, often embodying contemporary cultural values and norms. Lying in between these two polarities are a range of intermediate postures. D. A. Carson offers a helpful and needed critique of Niebuhr's five categories that they lack theological depth and don't truly wrestle with the fact that each appeal to some level of biblical support.[18]

Jesus' compelling words that his followers are to be salt and light in the world are foundational in the ongoing challenge for wise cultural navigation. Jesus tells us that Christian faithfulness will involve close proximity to cultural context and that others will see the good works of the Christian community and glorify God as a result (Mt 5:13-16). Being salt and light in the world suggests to leaders of a local church community that we are called to walk a fine wisdom-line of maintaining purity distinctiveness from culture as well as staying in close proximity to culture.

Shepherding in exile. Pastoral leaders are wise to recognize that in many ways, as in the time of Jeremiah the prophet, we are shepherding our congregations in the context of exile. Writing to God's covenant people exiled to Babylon, Jeremiah frames faithfulness in terms of settling into their new land and seeking the good of pagan Babylon:

> Thus says the LORD of hosts, the God of Israel, to all the exiles whom I have sent into exile from Jerusalem to Babylon: Build houses and live in them; plant gardens and eat their produce. Take wives and have sons and daughters; take wives for your sons, and give your daughters in marriage, that they may bear sons and daughters; multiply there, and do not decrease. But seek the welfare of the city where I have sent you into exile, and pray to the LORD on its behalf, for in its welfare you will find your welfare. (Jer 29:4-7)

It must have been a surprise for God's people to hear these words from the prophet Jeremiah, yet they were the down-to-earth words they greatly needed for living faithfully in exile. Faithfulness would mean trusting in God's sovereignty; having a long-term perspective; living life in fruitful familial and economic ways; and being good neighbors, actively seeking the shalom of a pagan culture and city.[19]

Jeremiah's inspired words to the Babylonian exiles are wise words to us as pastoral leaders. There are many cultural landmines we can step on. We can undiscerningly embrace cultural accommodation and lose our distinctiveness. We can also unwisely embrace cultural separation and lose our witness. Or we can be seduced by the power of a winner-takes-all, cultural warrior mentality instead of embracing a sacrificial kingdom posture that seeks the good of all. James Hunter reminds us of our exilic context in the late modern world. "Ours is now, emphatically, a post-Christian culture, and the community of Christian believers are now, more than ever—spiritually speaking—exiles in a land of exile. Christians, as with the Israelites in Jeremiah's account, must come to terms with this exile."[20] Western Christians are living in a Babylonian context, yet we must also remember that the entire biblical storyline from Genesis 3 to Revelation 21 takes place in exile. One day yet future, our exile will end as the new creation emerges and "the dwelling place of God is with man[kind]" (Rev 21:3). Paul Williams presses into the implications for living and leading in an exilic context. "In the exilic paradigm, the explicit role of the people of God in relation to the world is threefold: to be a model or example, to be a channel of God's blessing, and to actively seek to reconcile all aspects of life to God."[21] Shepherding in exile will mean adopting a cultural posture not of monastic retreat, cozy cultural accommodation, or a cultural warrior mentality, but one of faithful presence.

A faithful presence. Few voices have shaped my thinking and approach to navigating the challenges of the late modern world more than James Hunter. On a small farm nestled in the Virginia mountains not far outside of Washington, DC, I was privileged to join a small group of pastors to interact and digest James Hunter's emerging work centered in what he deemed a faithful presence approach to cultural engagement. As one of the premier sociologists in our nation, James Hunter presented a powerful critique of several impoverished ways Christian leadership had been approaching cultural engagement. He also made a strong case regarding lasting cultural change, church renewal, and the importance of dense overlapping networks, including clergy networks.[22] The ideas embraced and the relationships formed in these intimate gatherings would prove transformational for me as well as the congregation I serve.

As it relates to Christ and culture, Hunter writes, "In opposition to the 'defensive against,' 'relevance to' and 'purity from' paradigms, I have suggested a model of engagement called 'faithful presence within.'"[23] Building on a robust theology of creation and incarnation, Hunter understands incarnation as a primary paradigm for followers of Jesus faithfully living their lives under the lordship of Jesus in the broader world. In a sense, faithful presence emphasizes the scattered church's mission, first and foremost, for all believers to bloom where God has called them. Hunter further elaborates a faithful presence approach, writing:

> I would suggest that a theology of faithful presence first calls Christians to attend to the people and places they experience directly. It is not that believers should be disconnected from, or avoid responsibility for, people and places across the globe. Far from it. Christians are called to "go into all the world," after all and to carry the good news in word and deed that God's kingdom has come. But with that said, the call of faithful presence gives priority to what is right in front of us—the community, the neighborhood, and the city, and the people for which they are constructed.[24]

The primacy of vocational discipleship. A faithful presence approach to cultural engagement will manifest itself in many ways in local church congregational life and mission. Leaders will place a primacy on the spiritual formation of church members within the transformational context of joy-filled, local church spiritual community. While the gathered church experience will be important, faithful presence pastors will also emphasize whole-life discipleship that equips congregants to be faithfully present in their various vocations and callings throughout the week. Paul Williams captures well a faithful presence approach and its implications for church leaders:

> God has so designed the church that faithful believers, scattered throughout society in all kinds of workplaces, neighborhoods, and communities are on the front line of missionary encounter. They do not need to "go" somewhere else to be missionally fruitful; they need to "go" into these places under the lordship of Jesus Christ. . . . Many church leaders spend a lot of time wondering how to reach a "secular society" and a lot of energy to start programs and initiatives, yet they fail to see that their congregants are already perfectly

placed to reach it, most of them in places that a church leader could never reach or be credible in.[25]

Emphasizing their Monday mission, I often remind my congregation God has sovereignly placed and empowered each one of them to be his salt-and-light witnesses through their paid and unpaid work in every nook and cranny of society. As pastoral leaders of faithful presence, we must grasp that a primary work of the church is the church at work.[26]

The peril of partisanship. One of the most perilous ways pastors are taken off mission is by identifying too closely with a particular political party. A faithful presence approach to cultural engagement will guard against the ubiquitous seduction of power, especially political power, embracing instead a posture of loving and sacrificial service for the good of all. Faithful presence emphasizes the goodness of the public witness of the church and avoids institutional capitulation to any political party or partisan ideology. In an increasingly polarized culture, many pastors feel like they are squeezed in a no-win tug-of-war by parishioners criticizing them both from left- and right-leaning ideologies. Parishioners all too often build their core identities around a political ideology, fueled by a particular media channel, much more than around their gospel identity. Pastors who embrace a faithful presence approach encourage individual congregants' civic engagement, but I believe wisely avoid political partisanship. A short-term partisan win for a pastor can lead to a long-term credibility loss in the community. Instead of building bridges, a pastor's partisan activities can build barriers with other faith communities who become more resistant to future common-good collaboration in a city or community. A shepherd leader does have a role in moral and justice advocacy but needs wisdom and discernment in the execution of this advocacy in the political and partisan realm. While pastors may have strong personal political or partisan views, I believe they must take great care if and when they bring them into the local church community. Congregational members can and often do have differing, polarizing political views and party loyalties. This can be a source of conflict and disunity or it can be a Spirit-filled opportunity for congregants to respectfully listen to each other's diverse perspectives and grow in humility, depth, and understanding.

Let's remember that Jesus' inner circle of disciples included both Matthew the tax collector, who was politically aligned with Rome, and Simon the zealot, who wanted to politically overthrow the government. Can you imagine the animated and perhaps at times heated conversations these two disciples of Jesus had around a Galilean campfire? Yet Matthew and Simon had a love and loyalty to each other that was unshakable, transcended by a higher love and loyalty to King Jesus and his kingdom. What an important model this is for us as pastors. As a pastoral leader in my culture and community context, I have made it a personal policy not to attend political party gatherings, place political bumper stickers on my car, or put political signs in my yard. While I encourage congregational members to seek public office, I do not explicitly or implicitly endorse any candidate, even ones in my congregation. Transparently, my commitment to avoid political partisanship has led to some painful criticism and even resulted in congregants leaving our local church. While it is painful to see some people leave the church over our nonpartisanship commitment, we have remained unified and have stayed on mission. You may choose to navigate the challenges as well as the opportunities for political and partisan engagement differently than I have in my shepherding role. However, I do believe the politicization of our Christian faith is often one of Satan's insidious strategies to co-opt our gospel identity and hinder our disciple-making mission.

FOUR PRACTICES OF FAITHFUL PRESENCE

Max DePree insightfully reminds us that effective leadership is not about following a list of things to do, but artful practices indwelled and modeled to others over time. DePree writes, "Leadership is much more an art, a belief, a condition of the heart, than a set of things to do. The visible signs of artful leadership are expressed ultimately in its practice."[27] I have observed four consistent and enduring lifestyle practices of skillful pastoral leaders who day in and day out artfully indwell a faithful presence. These indwelled practices aim for longevity; embrace a kingdom mindset; build enduring institutions; and promote truth, goodness, and beauty.

Aim for longevity. When my wife, Liz, and I moved from Dallas to Kansas City to begin Christ Community Church, we embraced a calling, not a career. We were unwavering in our commitment that our local faith community would not be a career steppingstone, rather it would be a long-term commitment. As pioneer church planters, we stepped out in faith not knowing what lay ahead but having a long-term view. We didn't know much, but what we did know was that God was calling us to a particular place for the long haul. While "bigger and better" opportunities would come over the years, our strong calling tethering us to a particular place and people has proved wise and brought to our grateful hearts a sense of deep joy. Aiming for longevity was a guiding perspective and an embodied practice informing all aspects of our life and work. Longevity has allowed us to deepen in our own spiritual formation, to truly know and be deeply known by a faith community, as well as to experience the joy of fruitfulness that comes with time.

James Hunter paints a compelling picture of the goodness of longevity of calling to a people and a place.

> For most, this will mean a preference for stability, locality, and particularity of place and its needs. It is here, through the joys, sufferings, hopes, disappointments, concerns, desires, and worries of people with whom we are in long-term close relation—family, neighbors, coworkers, and community—where we find our authenticity as a body and as believers. It is here where we learn forgiveness and humility, practice kindness, hospitality, and charity, grow in patience and wisdom, and become clothed with compassion, gentleness, and joy. This is the crucible within which Christian holiness is forged. This is the context within which shalom is enacted.[28]

While there are times when God calls us for whatever reason to a short-term work with a congregation, pastors who embrace faithful presence serve with a long-term framework in mind. Practicing longevity, pastors of faithful presence settle into a community and roll up their sleeves, eager to fulfill their calling to a distinctive people in a particular place. Pastors of faithful presence are curious students of their people and community, recognizing the history and forces shaping their present experience. Over an extended period of time, empowered by the Holy Spirit, pastors of faithful presence will gain a greater and more intricate understanding of the congregational locale, its wounded history and complexity. With the longevity of faithful preaching, teaching, and life example, pastors of faithful presence will slowly convert the congregational imagination, cultivate congregational virtue, and expand congregational mission.[29] Pastors who practice longevity refuse to run from hardship, difficulties, and weakness, instead leaning into them as a catalyst for their own leadership growth and a maturing love for their congregation.

It is painfully ironic that as pastors we can be so frustrated with the lack of our congregants' growth and at the same time overlook our own need for growth as leaders. We cannot take a congregation further than we have been ourselves. Yet despite our growth challenges, inadequacies, and weakness, God's grace is operative in our lives and work. The apostle Paul himself, who struggled with his inadequacy as a spiritual leader, was encouraged by Jesus' words, "My grace is sufficient for you, for my power is made perfect in weakness" (2 Cor 12:9). How true these words have been in my life and pastoral leadership. It is often in our weaknesses and failures where God does some of his greatest work in our lives and most transformative work in our congregation. God's work in the midst of our weaknesses protects us from pride and brings him the greatest glory.

For many of us, the most visible, fruitful years of ministry will be evident not in a handful of years but in decades. I remember an earlier mentor saying to me that we overestimate what we can do in a year and underestimate what God can do in a decade. His wise words have been welcome companions to my soul, often reminding me of the goodness of pastoral longevity. Resting in God's sovereign wisdom, calling, and care, aim for pastoral longevity.

Embrace a kingdom mindset. Another practice of pastors of faithful presence is embracing a kingdom mindset. While pastors' primary responsibility is to shepherd their own flock, they must recognize and engage in God's broader kingdom work in the world. After speaking to a group of pastors in our city, Dallas Willard said to me words that I have never forgotten: "Tom, I have often wondered how God would be glorified and his gospel mission advanced in the world if pastors would tithe ten percent of their time to serve other pastors and other ministries in a city." Dallas's words challenged me at a heart level and altered my schedule. I have sought to tithe my time, looking for ways to bless the lives of other pastors, encouraging them in their struggles and rejoicing in their successes.

As I encounter pastors, I am regularly reminded how, beneath our professional pleasantries, we can really only be about "our" church and "our" ministry. The inconvenient truth is that many pastors have a prideful spirit of competition with other pastors and leaders rather than a loving spirit of encouragement for the multifaceted work God is doing in many other places of his already, not-fully-yet kingdom. A spiritual discipline I have incorporated in my life is to pray for God's blessing and favor on my fellow pastors when I drive by the churches they serve. Not only does this keep my heart from a competitive spirit, but it reminds me God is doing much more in my city beyond the small reach of my hands and the congregants I serve.

Pastor Tim Keller has beautifully modeled a faithful presence approach in his many years of pastoral ministry in New York City. He often reminds pastors of the goodness of diversity of many churches in a city. "There is no single way of doing church that employs the right biblical or even cultural model. So the city as a whole needs all kinds of churches."[30] One of my longtime pastor friends serves a congregation in the urban area of Kansas City. Pastor Stan Archie has practiced a lifestyle of longevity with a kingdom mindset. Both of us have had the privilege of serving our congregations for more than thirty years. When we get together, Pastor Stan often speaks about and prays for the advancement of God's kingdom agenda in our city. While we honor our own ecclesial boundaries and specific pastoral responsibilities, over many years we continue to work together for the flourishing of our congregations and our city. Although it has not always been easy, we have sought to mend racial distrust and divides, addressing the deep racial wounds in our city's history. Together with the congregations we shepherd, we seek justice for the exploited and care for the marginalized, and we serve the poorly resourced in our city.

We also work to encourage other pastors to personally mentor a new generation of pastors for the church. In addition to keeping a kingdom agenda in front of us, we have several pastoral and civic networks we maintain. This has helped build trust and is nurturing a gospel ecosystem in our city.[31] We link arms with broad and diverse networks committed to the common good.[32] Having a kingdom mindset means we practice collaborative partnerships. We partner with local, national, and global organizations—many who share our faith commitments, but also others of good will, building bridges of trust across religious, racial, and political divides.

Pastors who practice a kingdom mindset will place a strong emphasis on equipping congregations to live fully into their vocational Monday worlds. The entrepreneurs in the congregation are encouraged to think about ways to empower and bring opportunity to underresourced areas of the community. Of particular importance are not only job creation, but providing access to capital and workplace training as well. Educators who are part of our local church are challenged to think beyond their own schools to the broader educational challenges in our city, where many schools are failing and an emerging generation is at increasing risk. Marketplace leaders are encouraged to embrace a multiple-bottom-line approach to their businesses, which includes providing access and opportunity for minority and vulnerable populations. Public officials who are part of faith communities are encouraged to further public policy that promotes human flourishing. Pastors of faithful presence are committed to equipping their churches for Monday, seeing their congregants called to a kingdom mission in the world. A faithful presence pastor and a kingdom mindset go hand in hand.

Build enduring institutions. Outside my office window is the entrance to our church's preschool. I often pause a moment from my work to watch and marvel at all the children and parents who walk each weekday through the welcoming doors. For more than two decades, thousands of parents and families have entrusted their children to our amazing pre-school staff. Parents from all walks of life and worldviews attend our preschool, knowing that their children will be loved and cherished as they are taught the foundations of the Christian faith and Christian virtue. Our church's preschool—with its gifted leadership, excellent teachers, nurturing culture, quality facility, and abundant management resources provided by our church family—has become an enduring insti-tution of faithful presence in our community. It is not uncommon for me to be shopping at a grocery store or having coffee with a friend when a virtual stranger will walk up to me and offer affirmation to our church and its preschool.

I share the ongoing story of our preschool and its sizable impact in our community not to pat ourselves on the back, but as an example to draw attention to the importance of seeing the church not only as an organic entity, but also an enduring institution. Our preschool's sustaining excellence would not be possible without the structural support of our larger church institution. This is also true of our church's pastoral residency program that trains postseminarians in an immersive two-year leadership development experience. In many of our ministry programs and church initiatives, our ongoing strength and vibrant health as an institution make possible a dynamic long-term impact. The insightful saying rings true: without individuals, nothing ever changes, but without institutions, nothing endures. As shepherding leaders, we want to leave a legacy that outlasts us, but that will mean taking more seriously building enduring institutions.

As pastoral leaders we often recognize the important roles we play of preacher, teacher, or spiritual director, but less often do we grasp the vital role of institutional developer. As pastors we tend to focus on individual transformation and pay less attention to the ongoing health of the institution that provides the context for ongoing change in individual lives and communities over longer periods of time. Buildings, budgets, boards, policies, and organizational structures may not be the most exciting, but they provide a physicality of ongoing presence and continuity of ministry in a community. These are the kinds of important practices the faithful presence pastor embraces in the ongoing task of institutional building. James Hunter reminds us of the institutional aspect of faithful presence. "What I am suggesting again is a new paradigm of being the church in the late modern world. The institutional aspect of faithful presence means that Christians and the church are settling in for the duration."[33] Pastors of faithful presence grasp that both individual transformation and institutional health are important stewardships of pastoral leadership.

As pastoral leaders we may have an anti-institutional bias lurking within us. While the local church is more than an institution, it is not less. Like other institutions, the local church can be healthy and life-giving or be mired in mediocrity or even lose its way. Yet as an institution, the local church ought not be abandoned or neglected; rather, pastors should do the hard, prayerful, and patient work of renewal. Pastors of faithful presence know they are called to shepherd not only people, but also the institution they serve. William James put it this way: "The great use of a life is to spend it for something that outlasts it."[34] Pastors of faithful presence build enduring institutions that will outlast them.

Promote truth, goodness, and beauty. Pastors of faithful presence promote truth, goodness, and beauty in their congregations and communities. Shepherd leaders are not only artists of the soul, but artists of beauty as well. Beauty, whether it is in nature or on a painter's canvas, brings healing and breathes hope in our world. Practicing truth, goodness, and beauty forms us as pastors and allows us to see the goodness of the artist's calling and the unique role artists play in the broader culture. Artist Makoto Fujimura presents a compelling challenge to pastors. "The church has kept the structure of truth, but we have largely lost touch with the Spirit in creating beauty. The church is no longer where the masses come to know the Creator of beauty."[35] How should we respond? Will we shrug our shoulders or roll up our sleeves and address this deficiency?

The local church I serve has sought to promote truth, goodness, and beauty in several ways. One of the most visible ways we highlight truth, goodness, and beauty is by hosting the Four Chapter Gallery in our downtown campus.[36] Pastor Gabe Coyle leads our downtown campus and from its very inception has seen the Four Chapter Gallery as integral to their gospel mission. Hundreds of people who are milling through the arts district of Kansas City on "First Fridays" walk through our downtown campus home. The high-quality, beautiful art displayed exposes the broken human condition and often presents a hopeful redemptive theme. Volunteers from our downtown campus warmly greet visitors, fostering a fun and welcoming atmosphere. The Four Chapter Gallery also structurally frames and visually enhances our downtown campus worship experience on Sundays, reinforcing a liturgical seamlessness of truth, goodness, and beauty.

In addition to the Four Chapter Gallery, our congregation financially supports and promotes artistic organizations and endeavors in our city. We have had a long and supportive relationship with the Culture House, which trains hundreds of young artists in our city.[37] The Culture House is led by two of our church members, Jeremiah and Mona Enna, who for many years have modeled Christian faithfulness for the common good in our city. The Culture House is also home to the Stoerling Dance Theatre that has gained national respectability and notoriety in our city for their outstanding work in advancing greater racial understanding and reconciliation. Pastors of faithful presence affirm the artist vocation, seeking to support the arts individually and institutionally in their communities.[38]

REST IN HIS FAITHFUL PRESENCE

The practices of faithful presence and the skills needed for pastors to navigate the ever-changing currents of culture can at times feel daunting and overwhelming. Yet even amid the sizable burdens that come with leading, we can find joyful rest in our Good Shepherd, who is always there for us and faithfully present to us. Tim Laniak encourages us to remember that at the end of the day, our Good Shepherd is in charge and will accomplish his purposes in our lives and the congregation we serve:

> The only true consolation for the relentless burden of leadership is the reality that God, the ultimate Shepherd of the flock "neither slumbers nor sleeps." God is already committed to ceaseless supervision of our communities, because the people we care for are his. "It is he who has made us, and we are his, we are his people and the sheep of his pasture."[39]

8

CULTIVATING A FLOURISHING CULTURE

*The vast majority of organizations today have more than enough
intelligence, expertise, and knowledge to be successful.
What they lack is organizational health.*

PATRICK LENCIONI, *THE ADVANTAGE*

I had no idea the church I was asked to pastor was so unhealthy."
These were the disillusioning and heartfelt words verbalized to me
by a younger pastor who was now leaving his first local church
assignment. With high hopes and youthful idealism, he and his wife had
moved across the country, bought a house, settled into the community,
and enthusiastically rolled up their sleeves, eager to serve. Sadly, their
pastoral honeymoon ended quickly. For years, congregational members
had experienced high staff turnover and a lack of pastoral care; they were
emotionally guarded, some even distant and unwelcoming. Congregational factions quickly surfaced, having been formed around bitter
feelings from unresolved conflicts in the distant past. Church staff
morale was low. After the last pastor had left, church attendance had
declined, finances were tight, and the staff had experienced reduced
health care benefits. Staff meetings were polite, professional, and guarded.
Entrenched in ministry silos, church staff guarded their turf, mistrusting

each other. Ossified and ineffective church programs were off limits to needed change. The micromanaging church board prided themselves in hands-on involvement in the day-to-day operations of the church. Power pockets on the board led to meeting after meeting, and wealthy historical families overly influenced the church. While the church had a well-crafted mission statement, the actual mission had really become congregational comfort and institutional survival.

Sensing opposition at every turn and seeing the writing on the wall, this young pastor, who had only been at the church two years, resigned. Hearing him share his story, my heart went out to him. Here was a gifted young leader who—after being immersed in a toxic local church culture— was seriously questioning whether he would continue being a pastor. I wish I could say this pastor's heartbreaking story was a rarity, but it is all too common. It is not surprising that for many pastoral leaders, the most important question in considering a pastoral call is not the denominational affiliation, the location, or even the size of the church, but the health of the church. When we peek behind the Sunday corporate worship curtain, what will we find? Will we find a toxic or a flourishing organizational culture?

What may be overlooked is really one of the most essential skills for pastors to master: the preservation and ongoing cultivation of a flourishing organizational culture. The local church—both as a living organism and an enduring institution—thrives when leadership places continual, disciplined attention on cultivating and preserving organizational culture. Jim Collins reminds us that leadership continually requires preserving the core as well as stimulating progress.[1] A large component of preserving the core is giving careful attention to organizational culture. It has often been observed that organizational culture eats organizational strategy for lunch. My years of pastoral experience shouts loudly to this truth—not in any way lessening the importance of good strategy, but rather accentuating the essential importance of healthy church culture. All pastoral leaders must make organizational culture and the organizational health it promotes one of the highest priorities of their leadership calling and stewardship. While having a higher seat in the organization may have more influence, we can create pockets of great culture that infuse into the rest of the organization.

CULTURE MAKERS

What do we mean by culture? Andy Crouch's working definition of culture is helpful. "*Culture is what we make of the world.*" Culture is, first of all, the name for our relentless, restless human effort to take the world as it's given to us and make something else.[2] At the very heart of our human job description is the making of culture. When we look back at the creation account presented to us in Genesis, we discover an integral triune God creating an integral creation. The sparkling crown of God's creation is humankind designed and crafted according to God's very image (Gen 1:27). As his image bearers we are intrinsically relational creatures, and we reflect our Creator in many ways, including fashioning and shaping the environment around us. This is explicitly evident in the Genesis 2 picture of the incompleteness of creation and our integral role as image bearers to continue to complete God's good work. The Genesis writer makes the point of saying, "there was no man to work the ground" (Gen 2:5). In response to man's initial absence, God forms man, plants a garden, and places man in the garden (Gen 2:7-8). Humankind's design—fit within the created order—is then summarized. "The LORD God took the man and put him in the Garden of Eden to work it and keep it" (Gen 2:15). Here we discover the foundational human job description as both cultivating and protecting the world in which humankind is placed. Our English word *cultivate* is tied etymologically to the word *culture* and for good reason.[3] Gardens and cultures have much more in common than we might at first realize. To be healthy and flourish, both gardens and cultures need to be attentively cultivated.

Gardens and greenhouses. Pittsburgh is a beautiful city with its many bridges and rivers, but the city skyline in the dead of winter is often a cold and cloudy gray. I was invited to Pittsburgh for a conference for college students and professionals focused on vocational calling. One cloudy gray afternoon while on a break from the conference, my wife, Liz, and I visited Pittsburgh's famed Phipps Conservatory and Botanical Gardens. Walking in the door, we left the barren, cold, and gray winter world behind and entered the large glass greenhouse with its twenty-three distinct gardens. The warm breath of fresh air flowing from and through the vibrant and fragrant ecosystem of the gardens was simply overwhelming to our senses. The beauty of the multicolored plants and flowers took our breath away. In this lovely paradise of flourishing, joy greeted us at every step.

As I slowly strolled through this greenhouse garden, I was reminded how the botanical garden staff continually cultivated the conditions for a flourishing ecosystem to emerge and grow. With disciplined attentiveness, they had cultivated and preserved the necessary soil nutrients, ongoing water needs, and optimum light conditions for the vibrant flourishing of diverse plant life. Carefully and meticulously, with skillful hands, they had fashioned a flourishing world of interdependent and symbiotic diversity. What a remarkable and beautiful achievement the master gardening staff had accomplished for thousands of visitors like me to enjoy. Yet in a sense that is what each one of us is called to do in the world. Andy Crouch points out the close connection between the vocation of gardening and culture making:

> Cultivation in the world of culture is not so different from cultivation in the world of nature. One who cultivates tries to create the most fertile conditions for good things to survive and thrive. Cultivating also requires weeding—sorting out what does and what does not belong, what will bear fruit and what will choke it out.[4]

Relational primacy. Returning to the first garden, we can't miss the integral next step of the story. The narrative in Genesis 2 exemplifies the thing necessary for cultivating the garden after the man is placed in the garden: Alone, he needed an equal helper. So God created the woman to join him in shaping and fashioning the ground. At the center of culture creation is relational cultivation. Relational creatures, imaging the triune God, create in relationship, which means relational primacy is not only a matter of a pastor's relationship with God, but the primacy of relationship as the soil for healthy culture in the church.

Unfortunately, in the earlier years of my pastoral leadership, I failed to see the primacy of relationships and to prioritize living relationally. It was not that I did not have some close friends or that I didn't believe relationships mattered. Neither did I think nourishing local church community was unimportant. My challenge was that I saw the lens of leadership primarily through mission. As a leader, I was much more concerned about mission drift than I was about relational drift. And even more blinding was that I looked to a biblical example to validate the primacy of mission over relationship. In the book of Acts, we discover one of the early leadership conflicts between Paul and Barnabas. Their colleague John Mark had not performed very well and Paul was adamant that they not take him on their upcoming missionary journey. Barnabas was adamant that they should take him and give John Mark more opportunity. Clearly they were at a leadership impasse. "And there arose such a sharp disagreement, so that they separated from each other" (Acts 15:39). It would seem Paul felt the mission was more important and Barnabas felt the relationship was more important. While both were clearly important, we get a hint later on that Paul now saw the mission and John Mark through a more relational lens. Paul instructs Timothy to "Get Mark and bring him with you, for he is very useful to me for ministry" (2 Tim 4:11). As pastoral leaders we must take our mission seriously, but we must also see relationships as primary in accomplishing that mission.

Attachment love. Cultivating a lasting culture formed by relational primacy requires the relational attachment love at the heart of spiritual formation and organizational cultural health.[5] When we look at the New Testament Epistles, we are often surprised to find so many individual names listed, yet this reminds us of the centrality of attachment love in authentic spiritual community. For example, Paul concludes his masterful letter to the Romans by devoting virtually an entire chapter offering personal affectionate greetings to a host of individual friends and colaborers he loves and cherishes.[6] Relational primacy was at the heart of the first-century church. A flourishing local church culture manifests the fruit of the Spirit, empowering attachment love relationships continually growing both in breadth and depth. Though Max DePree doesn't explicitly mention attachment love, he does describe it when he exhorts leaders to the essential task of fostering relationship cultivation throughout the organization they lead. "Leaders need to foster environments and work processes within which people can develop high quality relationships— relationships with each other, relationships with the group with which we work, relationships with our clients and customers."[7] As shepherd leaders, just as our leadership flows from the primacy of our relationship with our Shepherd, so does cultural health flow from the primacy of relationship deeply rooted in attachment love.

CONDITIONS FOR FLOURISHING CULTURE

That we were created and placed in a garden and then given the job description of a gardener ought to profoundly inform and shape our understanding of pastoral leadership. The contours of skillful pastoral leadership begin not in the New Testament, but in the early chapters of Genesis. When it comes to leadership, a shepherd and a gardener have much in common. With the Holy Spirit's empowerment and guidance, pastoral leaders are called to be skillful cultivators, nurturing an organizational ecosystem. A flourishing local church is a kind of healthy garden, a relationally rich close-knit spiritual community with a vibrant organizational culture. The local church to which we are called is both a living organism and an enduring institution requiring from its leaders the ongoing nurturing of organizational culture and health. The art of shepherd leadership involves the ongoing attentive, disciplined, and skillful work necessary to provide the most optimum environment for sheep to flourish. In many ways, attentive shepherds are like farmers working the fields or horticulturalists tending a garden; cultivating the right conditions matters. What are the necessary conditions pastoral shepherds need to nurture for the sheep to flourish? While there are many conditions of church health needing our prayerful attention, four conditions for a flourishing organizational local church culture are foundational. As established above, the soil for the four conditions is the primacy of relationship. A healthy garden requires relationship. After establishing some ways to cultivate relational primacy in our churches, we will take a closer look at a generous orthodoxy, tribal storytelling, core values, and missional clarity.

Authenticity and vulnerability. We nurture a relationally healthy culture that promotes loving, close-knit relationships at all levels of the organization through modeling authenticity and pursuing vulnerability. I remember as a young boy observing with insatiable curiosity and jaw-dropping wonder when the piano in our home was tuned. The skilled piano tuner used a tuning fork to set the proper pitch for the first note and guide his adjustment of all the keys. The tuning fork proved indispensable to bringing out the best tonal quality of a piano. In many ways, pastoral leaders are like a tuning fork, setting the relational tone to which others around them stay on key. Pastoral leadership sets the relational tonal quality of a faith community. I have often said to young, burgeoning, resident pastors at our church that the congregants they serve will not remember all they say, but will remember that they loved them. As pastors, whether we consciously recognize it, members of our congregation are not only listening to our words but are watching us, and in mysterious ways, modeling their lives after us. Chris Lowney concludes, "No leadership tool is as effective as the example of the Leader's own life: what he or she does, what values his or her actions reflect, and how well the 'walk' matches the 'talk.'"[8] Relational primacy in an organizational culture is powerfully reinforced in ongoing demonstrative example of its leadership. So is vulnerability.

When my daughter Sarah was in elementary school, she gave me some of the best pastoral advice I have ever received. I was heading out of town for a speaking assignment and as I was walking out the door,

Sarah looked at me with her blonde curls, chocolate brown eyes, and wide smile and said, "Dad, don't forget to be yourself, but be your best self, okay?" I have learned that if I am going to be myself—to be my best self, one who is increasingly comfortable in my own skin—pursuing relational vulnerability is essential. My willingness to be vulnerable is remarkably contagious to those around me. Pursuing vulnerability means that I push back on anyone placing me on a pastoral pedestal. Like everyone around me, I regularly remind my congregation that I too am a mixed bag of brokenness, imperfections, failures, pain, and human limitations. Pete Scazzero lays a wise cornerstone of healthy local church culture modeled first by its pastoral leaders. Pete writes, "Everyone is broken, damaged, cracked and imperfect. It is a common thread of all humanity—even for those who deny its reality in their life."[9] For many pastoral leaders, the theology of the pervasiveness of sin within the human condition they so often preach somehow does not permeate their own leadership philosophy. Pastoral leadership requires a delicate balance between sharing both our encouraging strengths and signs of growth in our lives as well as our ongoing struggles. Yet even if we get hurt by others who do not safely steward our vulnerability, as a pastoral leader staying vulnerable is vital for our emotional maturity and also our leadership growth. Emotional maturity is the lid of leadership.[10] Pursuing vulnerability is a big part of the journey to emotional maturity.

Making room for relational connection. Pastoral leaders not only organize their lives around relational primacy, they also seek to provide spaces and pathways where relationships between congregants can grow and deepen. While we must not minimize the goodness of our large corporate worship gatherings, a good deal of our attention and energy should be devoted to encouraging small group formation and vibrancy. Small groups can be formed around Bible study and specific spiritual growth curricula. Small groups may also be organized around various life stages and interests, minimizing friction of entry for newer people to relationally connect to others in the congregation. In the congregation I serve, we often see deepening relational connection through common opportunities to serve our community in building homes, assisting the seniors, and caring for the homeless. People who roll up their sleeves together often experience not only the joy of giving, but also discover deepening friendships and life-giving spiritual community. A flourishing local church culture is infused with relational primacy. This soil is primary in relation to the following four conditions.

A generous orthodoxy. A flourishing local church is built on the essential revealed truths of Holy Scripture. For in the Holy Scriptures, we encounter the written Word of God and the living Word of God, our Lord and Savior Jesus Christ. When it comes to a flourishing local church culture, truth matters. Truth is foundational. When revealed truth is lost, Christian community is lost. Dietrich Bonhoeffer makes the important point that the very basis of authentic local church community is revealed truth. He writes, "Christian community means community through and in Jesus Christ. On this presupposition rests everything that the Scriptures provide in the way of directions and precepts for the communal life of Christians."[11] The apostle Paul exhorts the first-century church at Colossae to be a truth-bathed community. "Let the word of Christ dwell in you richly, teaching and admonishing one another in all wisdom, singing psalms and hymns and spiritual songs, with thankfulness in your hearts to God" (Col 3:16).

The pastoral leader who desires to nurture a healthy local church culture will skillfully and gracefully make the reading, teaching, memorizing, singing, and applying of Holy Scripture a constant and continual focus of congregational life. A healthy local church culture will reveal a congregation that is gospel-centered, filled with the Spirit, growing in apprenticeship with Jesus, sacrificially loving one another, graciously applying the Holy Scriptures to all dimensions of life. Pastors not only shepherd people, they also shepherd the truth revealed in Holy Scripture. Properly understood, authentic Christians are people of the book. The apostle Paul repeatedly emphasizes to pastor Timothy the essential importance of revealed truth and vigilance in guarding sound doctrine. "For the time is coming when people will not endure sound teaching, but having itching ears they will accumulate for themselves teachers to suit their own passions, and will turn away from listening to the truth and wander off into myths" (2 Tim 4:3-4).

In our increasingly secular culture, implausibility as well as implicit and explicit hostility to the teachings of Holy Scripture is rising. The Holy Scriptures, once seen as a repository of virtue and goodness for human salvation and flourishing, are increasingly being viewed as an oppressive and discriminating metanarrative.[12] For pastors, the temptation to minimize doctrine, dismiss, distort, or even neglect scriptural truth that goes against the grain of contemporary culture is both unrelenting and enticing. Pastoral leaders must graciously and courageously teach what the Bible clearly teaches with the words they say and by the way they live their lives.[13]

In contrast, a generous spirit comes from an epistemic humility, humble confidence, and winsome kindness, by which pastoral leaders are called to speak the truth in love with a willingness to suffer the consequences of perceived irrelevance, open ridicule, demeaning accusation, and stinging rejection—from both within the congregation and in the broader world. Yet timeless truth tethers us to reality and provides the authority for pastors to lead as humble servants with gentle wisdom and courageous boldness. Max DePree says it well. "The first responsibility of a leader is to define reality. The last is to say thank you. In between the two, the leader must become a servant and a debtor. That sums up the progress of an artful leader."[14]

Having a spirit of generous orthodoxy toward all Bible-believing apprentices of Jesus as well as honoring the particular doctrinal boundaries of one's specific Christian faith tradition are important for a flourishing local church culture. Doctrinal boundaries should not be seen as barriers, but rather as providing a sense of rootedness and continuity for congregational growth and unity. But what makes generous orthodoxy actually generous is that it looks for common ground, building bridges of mutual love and respect with other Christian traditions, seeking collaborative efforts for advancing the common good. In my particular denominational tradition, we often refer to the humble spirit and timeless wisdom captured well in this culture-creating adage: "In essentials unity, in nonessentials freedom, in all things charity."[15]

Tribal storytelling. Few American writers have captured the art of tribal storytelling better than Wendell Berry. Wendell Berry has spent his distinguished literary career emphasizing the importance of human flourishing and its relationship to rootedness and place. As a novelist, Wendell Berry has brought to life the fictitious small Kentucky town of Port William with its many common yet colorful inhabitants. Perhaps one of the most intriguing members of Port William is Jayber Crow, the small-town barber. From over the shoulder of Jayber Crow, Berry gives a transparent glimpse into the heartaches, longings, joys, eccentricities, dreams, and intertwined common history of a tight-knit community who through thick and thin do life together. Berry's storytelling prowess and remarkable insight shines through Jayber as he reflects on how the story of his past is connected to place. "I don't remember when I did not know Port William, the town and the neighborhood. My relation to that place, my being in it, and my absences from it is the story of my life. That story has surprised me almost every day . . . as if it all happened to somebody I don't quite know."[16]

We are storied creatures. Stories not only shape and define us; they also powerfully connect us together.[17] From the way our brains are wired to our interaction with others, stories matter. Christian psychiatrist Curt Thompson writes, "Humans' ability to tell stories, which distinguishes us from all other living creatures, is a crucial part of how our minds connect us to God and others."[18] As pastoral leaders who are called to nurture healthy local church community, the art of storytelling is essential. Even a cursory glimpse of the New Testament writers tells us that Jesus himself was a brilliant storyteller, affirming the primacy of stories within human community. Effective leadership and storytelling go hand in hand. Healthy local church culture is rich in storytelling.

A primary calling of pastoral leaders is to skillfully tell and retell God's big story given in Holy Scripture. The Bible is not merely a repository of a systematic and logical set of doctrines to believe, but a story we are invited to root our entire lives in. We are new creations in Christ where we dwell moment by moment, nurtured and sustained by the manifest presence of God who is always with us. A flourishing local church culture must not only embrace the goodness of systematic theological categories, but also a robust biblical theology that encompasses the entire sweep of canonical revelation. The biblical "big God-story" is first and foremost a coherent story of a triune God who created the world, that world gone wrong, God rescuing the gone-wrong-world through the sending of his Son, Jesus, and the world one day being made whole again. This is the four-chapter story from above, the *ought, is, can,* and *will* (see chapter two).

I remember meeting with a young couple in my congregation whose marriage was really hurting. They had come to see me seeking my counsel and encouragement. After empathically listening for an extended time, I asked them if they knew God's story of marriage? They were a bit puzzled at the question, but then requested that I tell them. So I did. I told them the biblical story of marriage using the four-chapter *ought, is, can, will* framework. I shared with them God's beautiful and integral design of marriage (the *ought*), and how sin had entered the world and distorted God's design, (the *is*). When I got to this part of the story, the wife looked at me and transparently said, "Tom, the *is* of marriage is pretty ugly isn't it?" I said, "Yes, the *is* is pretty ugly at times, but the good news is that the *is* is not the end of God's story for marriage." I then shared with them passages of Scripture that paint the redemptive picture of what can be in a Christ-centered marriage and that one day in the new heavens and earth we will not be married as we are now, but in a way unimaginable to us within the limited confines of time, we will have a greater sense of relational intimacy than we can ever know now. When this hurting couple left my office, they not only were infused with hope, but they saw themselves in a bigger story where they were now excited to live more fully into the hopeful biblical picture of marriage. Whether the presenting challenge is marriage, singleness, relationships, illness, failure, work, money, or a host of everyday challenges congregants face, helping them see their lives and circumstances through the lens of God's big story and to indwell that story transforms local church life.

As pastoral leaders we also need to be good storytellers of our own lives, our faith tradition, and the unique history of the local church we serve. It has been said that leaders need two things to lead well: a sense of history and a good night's sleep. Telling and retelling the stories that have shaped us as leaders and have marked the history of the congregation provides a sense of authentic connection, rootedness of place and people, and it reminds each one of us of God's goodness, trustworthiness, kindness, and faithfulness. In the local church I serve, during new member orientation and staff orientation we often tell stories of God's past faithfulness in our individual lives and our communal history. We tell stories of how we have come to faith as individuals, but we also tell stories of our early beginnings as a congregation. We share dramatic "Red Sea" and "Jordan River" moments, where God protected and provided for us in undeniable ways that now span more than three decades. It is not that we live in the past, but the past powerfully shapes the present and points us to a hopeful future. Pastoral leaders dare not forget the past but keep the past alive through storytelling.

Pastoral leaders who cultivate healthy local church culture recognize the importance of encouraging and providing intentional smaller group contexts for congregants to transparently and vulnerably tell each other their own stories. The New Testament writers speak a great deal about the importance of local church leaders modeling and fostering transparent, safe, vulnerable, and loving community. We must not miss the vast number of apostolic references to the local church as an interdependent body as well as the many "one another" exhortations.[19] One of the most important aspects of small group community is storytelling. The importance of the healing nature of storytelling is being increasingly validated by neuroscience and interpersonal neural biology. Christian psychiatrist Curt Thompson makes the point that our brains are actually altered in storytelling. "People change not just their experiences, but also their brains—through the process of telling their stories to an empathic listener. When a person tells her story and is truly heard and understood, both she and the listener undergo actual changes in their brain circuitry."[20] If congregations are to flourish, shepherding leaders must realize that everyone has a story to tell and everyone needs someone to whom they can tell their story. Every person who is entrusted to us within the congregation needs to know others and be known by others. Storytelling is a primary way that deep relationships are formed and sustained and that joy is released.

As shepherding pastors, we must grasp the importance of encouraging and equipping our congregational members not only to share their stories with one another, but to share their unique story with others who may not yet know Jesus. Many times the word *evangelism* conjures up a host of negative associations and fearful emotions, and while there is nothing inherently wrong with the word, perhaps a better framework is "storytelling." Shortly before his ascension into heaven, the resurrected Jesus commissioned his followers to be his witnesses. "But you will receive power when the Holy Spirit has come upon you, and you will be my witnesses in Jerusalem and in all Judea and Samaria, and to the end of the earth" (Acts 1:8). Witnesses of Jesus have a story to tell. A big God-story, a story of who Jesus is, why he came to earth, the good news he brings and how Jesus has transformed our lives. John Newton's own story of gospel transformation from slave trader to apprentice of Jesus found its way to the world through one of our most beloved hymns:

> Amazing grace, how sweet the sound
> That saved a wretch like me!
> I once was lost, but now am found,
> Was blind but now I see.[21]

A healthy local church culture is a storytelling culture.

Core values. He was an unlikely leader who would change the world and leave a lasting legacy. Ignatius Loyola was born in Azpeitia, a tiny village near the French border in the remote area of Northern Spain. History tells us he had a skimpy resume and many flaws. As a military officer he stared failure in the face, which cost his career, his sense of confidence, and very nearly his life. Eccentric in many ways yet experiencing a life-altering religious conversion around the age of forty, Ignatius Loyola, with drive, conviction, creativity, and remarkable resilience launched and led the Society of Jesus. What became known as the Jesuit order would alter the course of history, educate much of the Western world, and touch the globe.

In his insightful book *Heroic Leadership*, Chris Lowney describes the remarkable impact and influence of the Jesuits:

> Founded in 1540 by ten men with no capital and no business plan, the Jesuits built, within little more than a generation, the world's most influential company of its kind. As confidants to European Monarchs, China's Ming emperor, the Japanese shogun, and the Mughal emperor in India, they boasted a Rolodex unmatched by that of any commercial, religious, or government entity.[22]

The history and story of Jesuit leadership has profoundly influenced my understanding of pastoral leadership. Many things made the Jesuit model of leadership so enduring and influential over time, but foremost was their paradigm that everyone was a leader. A misconception we can promote is that people are either leaders or followers, but Hunter shares a similar attitude to the Jesuits:

> a simple dichotomous view that divides people into leaders and followers either with influence or without it is ... mostly useless, for it does not describe the reality of the world or our lives in it. Leadership then, is an issue not for the clergy alone, nor for the "rich," the "powerful," or the talented. Everyone is implicated in the obligations of leadership. In varying degrees, and varying ways, all Christians bear this burden.[23]

The Jesuits also placed a primacy on four core values: self-awareness, ingenuity, love, and heroism; and each of these values reinforced each other in an organizational culture of compelling virtue and sacrificial commitment.[24]

Core values animate the way we do things together as an organization. In a sense, core values are like super glue, binding together gifted, diverse people without coercion, manipulation, or strong top-down authoritarian command and control. Core values unleash the motivational energy for obedience to the unenforceable. Core values provide the coherent framework for stakeholders of an organization as to "why we do things the way we do them around here." When embodied throughout the organization, core values inform our daily behavior, reinforce a nurturing culture, and energize missional synergy.

When we encounter an organization for the first time, whether it is a profit or nonprofit entity, it is not hard to discern the cultural values being embodied by its members. One of my regular habits as a pastoral leader is to be observant of the organizational values I encounter at various local businesses, especially those my parishioners work in, manage, or own. If the business entity is a restaurant or a supermarket, an auto repair shop or a corporate office, I pay particular attention to how I am treated as a customer. What are the attitudes of the employees, the quality of work being done, and the design of the built environment? I often take a few notes and then, when given the opportunity, I provide feedback from my experience. What organizational cultural values did I experience? Did my experience line up with the stated values of the organization? Many times it is an opportunity to cheer on the good work of my congregants, but sometimes I am able to provide input that helps them better close the gap between the stated values of the organization and its actual values lived out.

I also seek out direct feedback from first-time visitors to the local church I serve. What was their experience? What values did they perceive as they encountered our staff? What did they sense mattered most to us as a church family? I also take the initiative to thank the many suppliers, contractors, landscape workers, and delivery persons who serve our church. In addition to expressing my appreciation for their good work, I often ask them what their experience with our church and church staff has been and how they think we might improve. This kind of helpful feedback allows us as a church leadership team to continue to evaluate how we are doing to better communicate and embody our core values. Our staff reviews address not only matters of performance, but also matters of core-value alignment and the daily embodiment of those values in the work environment. This commitment to our core values also applies to our many volunteers both in how we orient them as well as how we provide ongoing training and coaching in embodying the values we cherish as a local church family. For our entire organization, we continually anchor our core values in the clear teaching of Holy Scripture, emphasizing our dependence on the Holy Spirit to incarnate these values for the ultimate purpose of glorifying God in all that we think, say, and do.

When a local church culture is not flourishing, one of the first places to examine carefully is core values. Core values need to be clearly defined, regularly communicated, modeled by leadership, incarnated by all, and enthusiastically celebrated.[25] Patrick Lencioni emphasizes the vital importance of core values in creating a flourishing organizational culture. "Core values are not a matter of convenience. They cannot be extracted from his or her person. As a result, they should guide every aspect of the organization, from hiring and firing to strategy and performance management."[26] A flourishing local church culture makes its core values a high priority.

Missional clarity. A healthy organizational culture must also maintain a sharp focus on missional clarity. Mission drift is an ever-present danger shepherding pastoral leaders must closely watch with attentive eyes and prayerful discernment.[27] At the heart of mission is a clear and compelling purpose. Simon Sinek reminds us that the most important question leaders must continually ask are not the "what" or the "how," but the "why": why our organization exists.[28] In one sense this seems so obvious, but seasoned leaders know how easy the big "why" gets lost in the many incessant activities, diverse opinions, continual distractions, and political realities of a complex organization. Embedded in our ultimate "why" is our organizational mission. The apostle Paul seems to reinforce missional clarity by expressing what might be best described as a mission statement in his letter to the church in Colossae. "Him we proclaim, warning everyone and teaching everyone with all wisdom, that we may present everyone mature in Christ. For this I toil, struggling with all his energy that he powerfully works within me" (Col 1:28-29). The apostle Paul's focus here is the local church's mission to proclaim the good news of Jesus and form followers into maturing apprentices of Christ.

From the inception of the local church I serve, we have had a mission statement that has inspired and guided us. Let me share that with you, not because it needs to be yours, but that you might get a glimpse into how we have sought to maintain missional clarity over the span of three decades. Our mission statement reads, "To be a caring family of multiplying disciples influencing our community and world for Jesus Christ." Each word of our mission statement has been carefully crafted to reflect deep theological foundations and convictions. Our mission statement is often verbalized and, for many of our congregants, memorized. Our mission statement guides and informs our strategic planning and budgetary priorities. This allows us to have an organizational culture influenced not by the whims of changing personalities, faddish trends, or the latest church growth strategy, but the methodical and steady outworking of disciplined thought and action over time. Like people, organizations can be busy, but undisciplined, doing a lot, but accomplishing little. It is often said that if we aim at nothing, we will hit it every time. We must know clearly what we are called to be and do, and not lose sight of where we are aiming.

As shepherd leaders of our local church, we have pressed into our mission statement, gaining greater clarity around the very core of our mission. Jim Collins describes this core as an organizational "hedgehog." Jim Collins describes the hedgehog as "a basic principle or concept that unifies and guides everything."[29] Our church's particular hedgehog nuances our unique and sovereign positioning, resourcing, and gifting within our broader mission statement. It is our mission's innermost ring. Our hedgehog is "equipping integral and influential apprentices of Jesus." Jim Collins describes what happens when an organization gains missional clarity by getting their hedgehog right. "When you get your hedgehog concept right, it has the quiet ping of truth, like a single, clear, perfectly struck note hanging in the air in the hushed silence of a full auditorium at the end of a quiet movement of a Mozart piano concerto. There is no need to say much of anything, the quiet truth speaks for itself."[30] The prayerful and diligent work required to clarify your hedgehog is worth the effort for it will bring greater missional clarity and make your organizational culture more fertile and flourishing.

Gaining and maintaining missional clarity is one of the most important stewardships of a pastoral leader. Missional clarity helps define reality and allows all the stakeholders of an organization to remain energized; stay hopeful; and persevere against hardships, setbacks, and discouragement.

THE BEST PLACE TO WORK IN KANSAS CITY

Pastors are not supposed to be proud, but my proudest moment as pastor was when our church was nominated as one of the best places to work in Kansas City. As senior pastor, I was invited to a luncheon in celebration of the nominees from all categories ranging from large corporations to small businesses. During the luncheon, when our nomination was announced from the platform, the business executive sitting next to me leaned over to me and with a stunned look on his face, smiled and said, "I have never heard of a church being nominated before—that is impressive. Tell me about your church." Hearing his words, I was both encouraged and saddened: encouraged, that the church I serve was viewed in the larger community as a place of excellence and goodness for those who worked there; saddened, to think that so many leaders in our city do not think of a local church as an organization of excellence and human flourishing. How I want that perception to change, for I believe the local church can and should be setting the pace for healthy organizational culture. Shepherding pastoral leaders cultivate healthy local church culture. They also prioritize whole-life discipleship, connecting Sunday to Monday, which is where we focus our attention next.

9

CONNECTING SUNDAY TO MONDAY

If discipleship is for the world, then the primary place of discipleship
is at work, because that's where we spend most of our time, and this
is where the need is greatest. When you look at all the difficulties we
face in our world . . . ask yourself, What would it be like if those places
were inhabited by disciples of Jesus who were doing their work to the
glory of God and the power of his name?

DALLAS WILLARD

Confession may be good for the soul, but it's hard for pastors. Yet somehow I managed to muster up the courage and make a heartfelt confession to my congregation. I blurted out what my heart had been holding back for way too long. Amid pin-drop silence, I confessed. My confession was not for sexual impropriety or financial misconduct, but for another serious failure. I had been committing pastoral malpractice. I confessed that I had been spending the minority of my time equipping the congregation for what God had called them to be and to do the majority of the week. Transparently, my primary pastoral focus had been how well I did on Sunday rather than how well our congregation lived on Monday. I was not seriously equipping my congregation for their Monday worlds, particularly their places of work. Because of an impoverished theology and a deficient pastoral paradigm, I had been perpetuating a Sunday-to-Monday gap in my preaching, discipleship, and pastoral care.

Not only had individual parishioners been spiritually malformed, our collective church mission had also suffered. I had failed to see—from Genesis to Revelation—the high importance of vocation broadly, but particularly the central thread of human work and the vital connections between faith, economic wisdom, and human flourishing. Somehow I had missed how the gospel speaks into every aspect of life, connecting Sunday worship with Monday work in a seamless fabric of Holy Spirit–empowered faithfulness and fruitfulness. I also had failed to see that a primary work of the church was the church at work. On the day I stood before my congregation, I did more than confess my failure. I promised that by the grace of God, I was going to change, our language was going to change, pastoral practices and priorities were going to change, our Sunday worship was going to change, and much of our discipleship would be revamped. We would now be committed to narrow the Sunday-to-Monday gap, equipping the congregation in whole-life discipleship that focused not on the slim minority of their lives, but rather the majority of their lives, where God had called them throughout the week. God-honoring shepherd leadership meant we were not merely a church for Sunday, but a church for Monday. We would shepherd the flock with Monday in mind.[1]

PASTORAL MALPRACTICE

Pastoral malpractice may seem a rather severe self-assessment, but I cannot find a more accurate description for my vocational failure. The inconvenient truth was I had given little sustained thought about what my parishioners spent so much time doing throughout the week. I did believe my congregation's work mattered, especially at offering time on Sunday or during a capital campaign, but actually what really mattered most was my work and the numerical growth of the gathered church on Sunday. I may not have verbalized it explicitly, but I lived as if my vocational calling as a pastor was far more important than my parish-ioner's vocational callings. My pastoral malpractice can best be summed up as a professionally accepted yet blinding vocational failure. Without malice and with good intention, my pastoral vocational paradigm had been deformed by a theological deficiency. With the best of intentions but with far-reaching ramifications, I had been perpetuating a large Sunday-to-Monday gap.

The Sunday-to-Monday gap. I wish I could say my pastoral mal-practice was an isolated problem, but tragically it is not. For many pastors and Christian leaders, a large Sunday-to-Monday gap exists between how we understand the integral relationship between worship on Sunday and work on Monday. Many sincere and well-intentioned pastors spend the majority of their time equipping their congregations for what they do the minority of their time, virtually ignoring the importance of everyday work and the workplaces inhabited so many hours of the week. The negative consequences of this all-too-common form of pastoral mal-practice are both striking and sobering.

Researcher John Knapp interviewed Christians nationwide on how they experience work and church. He concludes,

> Our study yielded two striking conclusions. First, Christians across a broad spectrum of occupations had little difficulty recalling ethical challenges encountered in their work lives. Second, an over-whelming majority reported that the church has done little or nothing to equip them for faithful living at work. They mostly perceived the church and its clergy as preoccupied with the private sphere of life—family, health, and individual relationships with God—and disinterested in the spiritual and ethical stresses of weekday work.[2]

Researchers Denise Daniels, Elaine Howard Ecklund, and Rachel C. Schneider also conducted a national representative survey of over thirteen thousand people regarding faith and work. Congregants who heard their faith leaders talk directly about the workplace and workplace issues were relatively rare. Only sixteen percent of practicing Christians said their faith leader often or very often discussed how congregants should behave at work.[3] The research ought to be a wake-up call for shepherd leaders. Many congregants need much more encouragement and support for their work as well as guidance for how to integrate their faith in their workplaces. Clearly the prevalent Sunday-to-Monday gap is a big problem.

What is really at stake? I remember a preaching professor in seminary saying, "If there is a mist in the pulpit, there is a fog in the pew." While my professor was driving home the importance of sermon clarity, his wise words also speak to the influence of pastoral leadership flowing from the pastoral pulpit. While a mist of confusion in the pulpit is far-reaching, what I didn't hear my professor talk about were the perilous consequences when there is not merely a mist in the pulpit, but instead a thick, blinding, and mind-numbing fog. What does it mean for a congregation when a pastoral leader is foggy in his or her theological thinking on the integral nature of faith, work, and economic wisdom, and its direct correlation with whole-life discipleship? A pastor who has embraced an impoverished theological and vocational paradigm will inevitably fall short of faithful local church leadership.

The full and far-reaching impact of a pastor failing to connect Sunday to Monday with an integral whole-life discipleship mission is hard to fully grasp; it is fair and reasonable to conclude, however, that a thick pastoral fog cannot be a good recipe for congregational flourishing and cultural influence. I have become increasingly convinced from my own personal experience, a wide range of sociological research, and my conversations with many pastoral colleagues that the Sunday-to-Monday gap is much wider and more prominent than we care to admit. What is at stake is the rightful worship of God, the spiritual formation of congregants, gospel plausibility, gospel proclamation, and the furtherance of the common good.

Rightful worship of God and spiritual formation. If congregational members see Sunday morning as the primary time they worship God and do not see what they do on Monday morning as prime-time worship, then our good and great triune God who is worthy of worship 24/7 receives puny and impoverished worship from his new covenant people. In original creation, God designed us to work and worship in a seamless way. There was no Sunday-to-Monday gap. While we are not to worship our work (for that is idolatry), we are to see the work we do—though presently marred by sin and now redeemed by the gospel—as an act of worship done unto God and for the good of others (Col 3:23). In the saving grace of Christ and through the indwelling power of the Holy Spirit, apprentices of Jesus are called to live and work before an audience of One in a seamless life of worship.[4] Grasping this truth with heart, mind, and body transforms not only each individual, but the entirety of a local church faith community.

If we perpetuate a Sunday-to-Monday gap, the spiritual formation of followers of Jesus into increasing Christlikeness is also impoverished. If congregants see their spiritual formation as primarily something that occurs on Sunday or is reserved for a spiritual discipline they do during the week and not a vital aspect of the work they do every day, then their spiritual growth will be greatly hindered. The work we are called to do every day is one of the primary means the Holy Spirit uses to conform us to greater Christlikeness. We shape our work, and our work shapes us and infuses a sense of experiential meaning in our daily lives. It was the Swiss psychiatrist and holocaust survivor Viktor Frankl whose remarkable insight into human nature concluded that humans find a sense of meaning not only in the relationships we forge, but also in and through the work we do.[5] Yet many followers of Jesus who grace the Sunday morning pews feel like second-class citizens where their everyday work is implicitly and sometimes even explicitly diminished both in its intrinsic meaning and importance. One of the greatest heartaches I have experienced as a pastor is encountering so many followers of Jesus who have confided in me that in their local church community, because they are not a pastor or missionary, they feel like second-class Christians. This suffocating deception not only burdens my heart but truly breaks the

heart of Christ, who delights in them and in where he has called them
to serve him in their workplaces throughout the week.

Gospel plausibility and proclamation. If local church congregations are
not equipped to connect Sunday to Monday, then our gospel witness is
less persuasive and convincing to an increasingly secularized culture.
Both the great dissolution of faith as well as the profound differences of
the myriad faiths in a pluralistic world foster greater implausibility for
the uniqueness, truth, importance, and believability of Christian faith.[6]
The gospel we cherish not only needs winsome and persuasive proclamation in our late modern cultural context, it also needs daily incarnation of what a gospel-centered life looks like lived out in and through
the messy, broken workplaces God's people inhabit each and every day.

In and through daily work, fellow employees and colleagues who are
not yet Christ-followers have the opportunity to see the gospel's transforming reality lived out both in the quality of work Christians do as
well as the attitudinal way in which Christians approach their work.
Jesus reminds us that we are to be influential salt and light in the world—
not just in what we say to others, but by what others see in us. Our good
works speak truth to others, pointing them to the good God we love and
serve (Mt 5:13-16). Good works are not merely reserved for religious acts
of piety but encompass the good work we do every day. Dorothy Sayers
speaks with compelling clarity when she asserts, "The only Christian
work is good work well done."[7] Our vocational faithfulness can expand
coworkers' plausibility structures, adding to the beautiful fragrance of
common grace the wooing attraction of saving grace.

If our congregations are not equipped to connect Sunday to Monday,
the proclamation of the gospel to a lost and dying world is muted. Since
many of our congregants spend a great deal of time each week in their
workplaces, gospel witness both in deed and in word finds great opportunity and transformational impact there. Never before in human history
has the world been more closely connected as a result of the internet, jet
travel, and a global economy. Through their daily work, our congregants
are now able to touch the globe and have the unprecedented opportunity

to share the gospel with their neighbors near and far. While many people will not darken the church door on Sunday, God has sovereignly placed our congregants to work with them on Monday. Are we encouraging and equipping our congregants to share their Christian faith with their coworkers? The greatest and most effective evangelism opportunity today is the Monday workplace. Bill Peel points out with prophetic clarity, "God calls every Christian to be a witness for Him. So for most of us, our mission field is where we spend the bulk of our time: the workplace."[8] To not intentionally equip the flock for that Monday mission is a most egregious shepherding oversight.

The common good. If we don't seek to better connect Sunday to Monday, then the common good of all peoples is diminished, human culture is impoverished, and the local church's mission is hindered. John Knapp insightfully points out:

> In failing to bridge faith and work, the church has failed itself and society with far-reaching consequences, for the challenges facing business, government, and other sectors in the twenty-first century raise profound questions about the purposes of our institutions, the value of human beings, and the criteria for good work. These are ethical questions having to do with how we ought to live, collectively and individually. Yet the moral terrain of our work lives is mostly defined by law and economics rather than theology, leaving us with an uninspired ethical pragmatism lacking in wisdom and heart.[9]

The gospel compels us to actively seek and continually further the well-being of all image bearers of God regardless of whether they have yet to put their faith in Christ. As seen earlier, Jeremiah admonishes God's covenant people in exile to seek the common good. "But seek the welfare of the city where I have sent you into exile, and pray to the LORD on its behalf, for in its welfare you will find your welfare" (Jer 29:7). What does seeking the welfare of a city entail? Jeremiah helps us with this important question when he encourages God's covenant people not to form an isolated cultural ghetto, but to get married, have children, work hard, and robustly engage in the economic life of the city of Babylon. It is not insignificant that the city of Babylon was a very pagan city with a plethora of idol worship, gross sin, and untethered evil. Yet even despite such a godless context, God's covenant people are called to live holy lives in the midst of a very unholy place—all the while seeking the flourishing of their neighbors. Few individuals modeled common grace for the common good better than Daniel, the Jewish exile who faithfully served in the Babylonian government.

All followers of Jesus are called and empowered by the Holy Spirit to bloom where they are planted. Living fruitful lives in our Monday vocations and stewarding well our work in the Babylonian marketplaces of our time, not only are we recipients of God's blessings, those around us also flourish as they enjoy the very tangible blessings of common grace. The writer of Proverbs puts it this way: "When the righteous prosper, the city rejoices" (Prov 11:10 NIV). Amy Sherman points to the three essential commitments—affirmation, education, and support—that pastors wisely embody as they seek to encourage congregants to bloom where God has planted them on Monday.[10] Indwelling common grace for the common good, our congregants not only embody the generous and kind love of God, but also become inviting signposts to the saving grace of Christ.[11]

Shepherding with Monday in mind. Pastors know that Sundays matter. Guiding and serving the gathered church is an essential stewardship of shepherding leadership. As pastors we need to do Sunday well, planning and implementing Spirit-anointed corporate worship experiences as well as offering a consistent and balanced diet of expository preaching and teaching of the Holy Scriptures. What we all too often miss is that our calling to equip congregants involves preparing them as apprentices of Jesus for their Monday worlds. Writing to followers of Jesus in Ephesus, the apostle Paul points out that God has given gifts of leadership to the local church. Paul goes on to describe the purpose of these leadership gifts. Paul writes, "to equip his people for the works of service, so that the body of Christ may be built up until we all reach unity in the faith and in the knowledge of the Son of God and become mature, attaining to the whole measure of the fullness of Christ" (Eph 4:12-13 NIV). Pastoral leaders are called to equip followers of Jesus living out their faith in local church community with the goal of both individual and collective spiritual maturity, manifesting the character of Christ. While equipping Christians to use their gifts and to serve within the local church body is important, Paul goes on in the rest of his epistle to focus on life outside the walls of local church community. In his leadership role, Paul equips the Ephesian Christians in their marriage and family relationships as well as in work and economic life.

Faithful shepherding leadership seeks to equip followers of Jesus to serve others not only within the walls of local church community, but also in their messy Monday worlds of relationships, family life, work, and economic realities. A primary responsibility of shepherding leadership is encouraging and equipping apprentices of Jesus for their Monday worlds, those majority places where God has called them to be his kingdom ambassadors. Of particular importance for the shepherd leader is to equip congregants to recognize the manifest presence of Christ and to employ spiritual practices in their places of work. Denise Daniels and Shannon Vanderwarker write, "By using spiritual practices in the workplace, we begin to be attentive to the ways in which God is already present—speaking and acting. . . . By incorporating spiritual practices into your daily work rhythms, you too can be shaped by God's transforming hand."[12] What a difference it would make if congregants understood the transforming presence and power of walking in the power of the Holy Spirit when they entered their Monday workplace.

In addition to equipping for spiritual formation in the workplace, shepherds also need to help parishioners navigate the complex ethical challenges in a global marketplace. A vital aspect of spiritual formation is ethical formation. I remember speaking at a conference in New Mexico where a sizable contingent present were engineers working at Los Alamos labs, where nuclear weapons are developed. After I had finished speaking and connecting faith with work, several engineers who are devoted followers of Jesus spoke of the ethical challenges they faced in producing weapons that insured the freedom of the nation they loved, but also produced mass destruction. They wondered, at what point do weapons become immoral, and at what point does the follower of Jesus cross that line? I did not have simple answers for them, but I was reminded of the ethical complexity they faced in their Monday worlds of work. Are we as pastors taking our equipping responsibility seriously—with prayerful intentionality—or is there a large Sunday-to-Monday gap lingering in our thinking, planning, and practice?

Leading organizational change. Shepherding leadership with Monday in mind means first addressing the Sunday-to-Monday gap in your thinking as a pastor or Christian leader, but it does not end there. For sustained transformation of a church culture, the broader leadership community of professional staff and congregational leaders must also recognize the peril of the Sunday-to-Monday gap and become catalysts for systemic and organizational cultural change. This will take concerted prayer, gentle patience, and a long obedience in the same direction, but both pastoral faithfulness and faithful gospel mission are on the line. We must be patient yet determined Holy Spirit–empowered change agents; for the local church, which God designed and Jesus' loves, is the hope of the world.

One of the most important considerations in bringing needed change is for pastors to realize how much language matters. Language is one of the most foundational artifacts of culture. Pastoring my local congregation through disruptive change, our elders and staff members were deputized to become language police. Don't get me wrong, this was not some oppressive totalitarian endeavor, rather all of us serving our local church tuned our ears attentively to hear the written and spoken words we were using. We then evaluated whether this language rein-forced a Sunday-to-Monday gap. When we encountered any language that was working against our goal of shepherding with Monday in mind, we graciously made the needed correction. Over the months, we discovered just how deeply embedded dichotomous language was in our staff and congregational culture. We were often using language that was undermining our robust theology and whole-life-discipleship mission.

Become aware of dichotomous language you may use, such as words like *sacred* and *secular*. While these terms may be descriptive, they tend to connote to the hearer an inappropriate elevation of the importance of what is often deemed "sacred," like church activities, over Monday work activities. Parishioners will often say to me, I have a secular job or I go to a secular school. While I know they are trying to be descriptive, the sacred-secular dichotomy is not only theologically problematic, it also reinforces a Sunday-to-Monday gap in many people's thinking. Take note of any language you may use both in public speaking as well as personal conversation that suggest a hierarchy of vocational callings. We should also avoid language describing pastors, missionaries, or para-church staff as "full-time Christian workers." Such verbiage tends to project an undue elevation of certain vocational callings and diminish other vocational callings. We do not lessen the goodness and importance of these callings in any way; rather, we raise the importance of the priesthood of all believers and affirm their callings in the world.

If you are going to narrow the Sunday-to-Monday gap, another matter of language will require careful navigation. Both the words *worship* and *work* need to be addressed. The word *worship* often connotes a gathered experience of what we do at church, particularly singing. While not minimizing the high importance of our liturgical engagement as a gathered faith community, we need to help congregants understand that all of life is to be an act of worship (Col 3:23). In our local church context, we describe our Sunday morning gathered experience as corporate worship. Adding the modifier *corporate* does not in any way diminish the high importance of our Sunday liturgy, but it does implicitly reinforce there are other important aspects of worship that are not contained within the boundary of the gathered church experience.

The word *work* also needs to be clarified for congregants. In our culture, the word *work* is almost exclusively tied to the things we do that are economically monetized, namely, our job. For example, when after a season of unemployment, we might say, "I went back to work last week." Or in entering a season of retirement, "I stopped working." Yet *work* needs to be redefined for our congregants as "making a contribution" and not merely "acquiring compensation." In our church context, we refer to work in two categories, paid work and nonpaid work. I often hear from stay-at-home spouses, students, and retirees who are highly encouraged when their work, though not monetized with a paycheck, is enthusiastically affirmed by their pastor.

Congregants' Monday worlds. If we are going to be faithful to our pastoral vocation, we must embrace pastoral priorities and practices that truly applaud our congregants' work. With the many demands the pastoral vocation brings, we must prayerfully seek to make a more coherent connection between equipping people for whole-life discipleship and reshaping our pastoral priorities and practices. I believe it is imperative as pastors that we assume a humble posture of curiosity both in expanding the breadth of our reading to include learning about the various vocations of our parishioners, but also carving out the time to visit our congregants in their workplace settings.

A congregational member I visited at work told me that in nearly forty years of church attendance, no pastor had ever been to his workplace. What a tragic commentary on an impoverished pastoral vocation. While some workplaces will not be open to our presence, all congregant work is open to our curiosity and learning. A regular reading diet of helpful guides such as the *Wall Street Journal*, *The Atlantic*, and *The Economist* will assist pastors to be conversant in the arena of our business and marketplace parishioners. In addition, we can peruse specialized journals in other vocations to gain greater understanding of the challenges facing other congregants. If we are dedicated to offering pastoral care and equipping well our congregants for all of life, then we will commit to the practice of regular workplace visits with the same intentionality and sensitivity as hospital visits. Building regular workplace visits into my schedule has been one of the most transforming and powerful pastoral practices I have ever embraced. Today it is as common in my local church context for pastoral staff to visit a parishioner's place of work as it is to visit them in the hospital when they are sick.

BECOMING A CHURCH FOR MONDAY

If we are going to become a church focused on the Monday world of our parishioners, then we need to attune our ears to what so many of our congregants are feeling. The heart cry of so many parishioners I hear is, "Pastor, does my work matter? I know your work matters, but does what I do every day matter to God and matter in the world?" When missionaries and pastors are celebrated for their callings, many congregants feel like their vocational callings are unimportant. Many feel like second-class citizens in the church because they have not been taught the robust theology of vocation and work that the Bible clearly and compellingly presents. After a long, exhausting day at the office or on the way home from the tiring clamor of the workshop, many congregants face melancholy moments of reflection. Whether they have achieved the pinnacle of career success or have experienced the deep valleys of job failure, a sense of emptiness often haunts them. Is there more to life than this? How does my gospel faith speak into what I do each and every day? Unable to answer these musings of the soul adequately, it is easy for many to settle for a conveniently compartmentalized life where Sunday faith and Monday work remain worlds apart. Yet this dualistic approach is not the path to human flourishing. The good news is that the Bible speaks about a flourishing integral existence, not an impoverished, bifurcated, or compartmentalized life. Seeing this integral reality lived out by our congregants in their Monday world will require intentionality in our discipleship efforts. We will need to communicate to our congregants by our own life and words that being a yoked apprentice of Jesus is lived out in a vast and beautiful diversity of expressions in the world. The spiritual life properly understood does not necessarily require us to change our vocational pursuits. What apprenticeship with Jesus in our Monday worlds does mean is that we now eagerly become who Jesus would be in thought, word, and deed if he walked in our shoes.

Pathways for whole-life discipleship. Equipping our congregants for their Monday worlds will not occur accidentally. We will need to become much more intentional on preparing our congregants for the workplace. Formal and informal surveys can be very helpful to get a better sense of the work needs and challenges of our congregants. One crucial aspect of a survey will gather invaluable information as to what jobs our congregants have and where they are working throughout the week. This data can be used for job networking within the faith community as well as asset mapping our congregation. Asset mapping around congregational workplaces allows us to know what work callings are most represented in our faith community and what needs and opportunities for mission emerge. Asset mapping of the workplaces of our congregation also assists us in developing discipleship efforts geared with greater vocational specificity. Pastoral staff can facilitate the forming of small groups around common jobs, professions, similar careers, or industries. I have seen in my congregation vibrant small groups of lawyers, physicians, architects, educators, or small business owners get to know each other and become a source of mutual encouragement to one another. Not only do congregants receive mutual encouragement, but they inevitably know God more fully in the abundance and diversity of their specific vocational callings as they encounter the surprising, creative, and beautiful evidences of God's grace-filled presence in their Monday worlds. With hearts and minds focused on Jesus in their daily vocational spaces, the endless worries of work fade and become a rich, creative pursuit of making Jesus known to others in our workplaces.

Whatever our present discipleship structures and initiatives, they will need to be evaluated both on a relational and a curricular level. How are we preparing our people—children to students to senior adults—to be growing apprentices of Jesus in their Monday worlds? Amy Sherman highlights four discipleship pathways that have proven effective and transformative for churches. These include blooming where congregants are planted, donating vocational skills, launching social enterprises, and participation in church-targeted initiatives.[13]

Bringing Monday into Sunday. Shepherd leaders who connect Sunday to Monday also bring Monday back into Sunday. Regardless of our liturgical and ecclesial traditions, when a pastor or Christian leader embraces a more robust theology of vocation, it will seamlessly seep into corporate worship planning and execution. Teaching a robust theology of vocation and cultivating a liturgical regularity that reinforces the importance of our congregants' Monday worlds is vitally important. Matthew Kaemingh and Cory Willson describe well the common disconnect many parishioners feel as they gather for corporate worship:

> Walking into a sanctuary, many workers feel like they are visiting another world, a world quite detached from their world of work. Sitting in the pews, workers feel as if an increasingly wide chasm has opened up between the rituals they are being asked to perform in the liturgy and the rituals they perform in their daily work.[14]

How we arrange our gathered worship experience, what we talk about and celebrate communicates to our congregation what we value. Narrowing the Sunday-to-Monday gap will mean evaluation and changes in our gathered church experience.

Our sermon preparation will gain a heightened awareness of the strong thread of work woven throughout the biblical canon. Many pastors will choose to preach a focused series on faith and work. Another sermon series worthy of consideration is one on economics and the common good.[15] In addition to a sermon series, the topic of work and vocational stewardship should regularly find its way into sermon preparation. The *Theology of Work Bible Commentary* is a very helpful sermon preparation tool for the expositor of Holy Scripture.[16] In our sermons, we will not only take note of the work themes of the biblical text, we will also bear in mind the various work contexts of members of the congregation. Our sermon illustrations will feature workplace settings as well as the challenges and opportunities they bring along with how the gospel speaks into Monday life. Sermon applications should also take seriously not only how biblical truth shapes family life and relationships, but also how it informs Monday work. Sermons will also avoid dichotomous language such as "the sacred and the secular" or other language that suggests a hierarchy of vocational callings.

We not only express a robust theology of vocation not only through our preaching, but we also celebrate it in congregational singing. Those charged with planning corporate worship services will give greater attentiveness to song lyrics and intentionality in song selections. Pastors are wise to notice some well-established hymnody of the church that reinforces a dualistic Sunday-to-Monday gap, and instead affirm a more integral understanding of gospel faith. For example, the song "Turn Your Eyes Upon Jesus" has many good lyrics, but it also has lyrics such as, "the things of earth will grow strangely dim in the light of his glory and grace." These lyrics may subtly diminish the importance of the created world, reinforcing an unbiblical dualism as well as distance gospel faith from Monday morning work duties and responsibilities. On the other hand, the hymn, "This Is My Father's World," while recognizing the present brokenness of the created world, integrally emphasizes the goodness of creation and the blessings of common grace.

Personal testimonies of gospel transformation offered up during a corporate worship service should include stories from congregants regarding their vocational stewardship and workplace mission. Testimonies should include those paid for their work but also stay-at-home spouses, volunteers, and retirees whose vocational callings are not financially compensated.

In my particular ecclesial context, we embrace a variety of both video and live testimonies under the brand banner of "This Time Tomorrow." Testimonies take an interview format in which a pastor asks a congregant two or three brief questions followed by a pastoral prayer. The workplace testimony questions may include questions such as: Where has God called you to serve him this time tomorrow? As a follower of Jesus what do you find most fulfilling in your work? What do you find most challenging? How can we pray for you in your work? Few things are more encouraging and hope-inspiring to a congregation than hearing from other followers of Jesus in their faith community who are called to similar vocations.

Cultivating a more liturgical regularity that brings our congregants' Monday worlds into our Sunday experience will influence pastoral prayers, pastoral commissioning, and benedictions. Pastoral prayers will not only address the brokenness of our world and the physical and emotional needs of congregants, but also the needs faced in the workplace. Pastoral prayers will reflect in both tone and content a growing pastoral sensitivity to the relational difficulties, the stressful economic challenges of a global economy and the very complex ethical realities congregants face in their jobs. Pastoral prayers will speak into economic realities such as unemployment and underemployment, economic injustice, workplace harassment, and discrimination. Pastoral prayers come before God asking divine assistance in workplace endurance, wisdom, strength, and opportunity for gospel witness in our congregants' Monday worlds.[17]

While we must continue to celebrate commissioning of missionaries and church workers, we can celebrate other vocational callings, too. Often corporate worship liturgies will include congregational commissioning of various vocational sectors. With the beginning of a new school year, we may highlight the vocational calling of teaching, affirming and commissioning all teachers within the congregation. Other times throughout the year, health care workers, government workers, blue-collar workers, other white-collar professionals, business owners, and students are featured during the corporate worship gathering.

Pastoral benedictions will take on a new importance as the local church leadership reminds members of the church that as they leave to become the scattered church, their vocational faithfulness is highly important to their discipleship and to advancing God's mission in the world. A pastoral benediction from Psalms might include,

Let your work be shown to your servants,
    and your glorious power to their children.
Let the favor of the Lord our God be upon us,
    and establish the work of our hands upon us;
    yes, establish the work of our hands! (Ps 90:16-17)

THANK GOD IT'S MONDAY

For many years since my confession of pastoral malpractice, the professional staff and congregant leaders whom I serve with have been working diligently to narrow the Sunday-to-Monday gap in our local church.[18] Our Sunday worship services increasingly reflect the reality that the gospel speaks to and transforms all of life including our work. As a local church community, we continue to press into how the gospel speaks to our Monday work, neighborly love, social justice, wealth creation, wise financial management, and economic flourishing. We are still unlearning and learning as we go, doing our best to navigate what it means to embrace an integral, gospel-centered faith and to narrow the Sunday-to-Monday gap.

The true test of congregational transformation is when congregants feel a joyful gratitude for where God has called them to serve him and their neighbor on Monday. They are not working just to get a paycheck or living for the weekend but embracing the richness of being both the gathered and scattered church, loving Sunday and Monday. My heart is increasingly encouraged when I receive an email from a CEO or a stay-at-home mom or a student or a retiree in our congregation who now see their Monday lives through the transforming lens of a biblical theology of vocation and an integral faith. As a pastor I find increasing joy for my congregants who now embrace their paid and nonpaid work as an offering to God, an opportunity for gospel witness as well as a contribution to the common good. Many of my parishioners have a bigger bounce in their step and a new shout in their souls. And they are seeing some work colleagues come to faith in Christ. The gospel has become not only amazingly coherent, but also incredibly compelling, not only for their own lives, but also in sharing it with others in various vocational settings and spheres of influence throughout the week.

Our congregants' work matters more than we often realize.[19] The work they are called to do is a primary means of their worship and a large contributor to their spiritual formation. Faithfulness in vocational stewardship also prepares our congregants for the good work they will one day do in the future new heavens and new earth. In his parable of the talents, Jesus strongly affirms the very earthly money managers who were faithful in their work. Jesus says, "Well done, good and faithful servant. You have been faithful over a little; I will set you over much. Enter into the joy of your master" (Mt 25:23). The work our parishioners do now is a seedbed of preparation for their fruitful work in the future. Every Monday morning they arrive at a job, it is infused with profound eternal significance. Let us help our congregants to grasp just how much God cares about their work. Let us equip those entrusted to our care to see their work as God sees it. Let us help them withstand the sinful gravitational tug toward work idolatry and work slothfulness. Let us come alongside our church members and help them discover what faithful vocational stewardship looks like. Let us show our congregants that their work and workplace are primary places for their spiritual formation and gospel mission.

Looking back I can't imagine how I had served for so long with such an impoverished pastoral paradigm. Shepherd leadership tends to all the spheres of our congregants' lives, especially the spheres they spend most of their time. Narrowing the Sunday-to-Monday gap, my own vocational fulfillment is much higher, and the congregation I serve now is more beautiful in its expression and more effective in its disciple-making mission. I have the joy of greater job satisfaction knowing I am being a more faithful and fruitful pastor, constantly drawing attention to Christ's presence moment by moment. Confession of pastoral malpractice is good for the soul and it may very well be good for you and your congregation.

10

A NEW SCORECARD

The goal of thinking hard about leadership is not to produce great, or charismatic or well-known leaders. The measure of leadership is not the quality of the head, but the tone of the body. The signs of outstanding leadership appear primarily among the followers. Are the followers reaching their potential? Are they learning? Serving? Do they achieve the required results? Do they change with grace? Manage conflict?

Max DePree, *Leadership Is an Art*

One of the things I enjoy most during warm summer evenings in Kansas City is going to a Royals baseball game. There is something about the beautifully manicured field and the flowing fountains of Kaufmann stadium that present an inviting and relaxing backdrop to the captivating game of professional baseball. While I am a dyed-in-the-wool Royals fan, a friend of mine is a more informed fan, bringing his scorecard, filling it out carefully as the game unfolds. I tend to focus more on the outcome of the game, the wins and losses, the possibility of a playoff berth. My friend watches carefully a host of other observable indicators that speak to the skill and effectiveness of each player—all pointing to the likelihood of the team's future failure or success.

In baseball, every player's performance is broken down into demonstrated skill in every facet of the game, continually monitored through the lens of statistical analysis. What I have learned is that informed and highly knowledgeable fans of baseball keep their eyes on the scorecard. Scorecards are a way to evaluate both personal and team performance and measure progress over time. Scorecards help us to answer important questions like these: How are we doing? What progress are we making? Are we experiencing success or failure? Are we furthering our mission?

What is common in the game of baseball is also a reality in pastoral leadership. Whether it is explicitly stated or implicitly assumed, we have measures of assessment that assist us in answering questions of how well we as shepherding leaders are doing in our work. What we deem important we measure, and what we measure reveals what we believe is important. What we value on our scorecard we tend to celebrate in our community of faith. But what if our pastoral leadership scorecard needs a sizable revision?

WHAT SCORECARD ARE WE USING?

A common scorecard for pastors is often referred to as the three B's: bodies, budgets, and buildings. Increasingly in our information age, the fourth B, brand, is often added on to the scorecard. Pastoral success or failure is regularly framed in the expectation of pastoral leadership performance that points to ever-increasing attendance at the gathered worship services, an incrementally growing financial budget, and demonstrable evidence of increased buildings capacity that continue to fuel a larger and larger gathered local church footprint. With the exponential growth of the online presence of many churches, virtual engagement as well as brand recognition is now also being measured and evaluated with greater scrutiny and celebration. While these assessment measures are often helpful and not inconsequential, they are often overvalued and overshadow other evaluative measures that in many cases are more revealing as to the effectiveness or noneffectiveness of pastoral leadership in any given context. Pastoral performance is often myopic in its short-time horizon, centered more on a pastor's ability to quickly draw a crowd. Elder boards, other church leadership, and pastors themselves focus little value and evaluation on whether they are moving a gathered crowd from mere passive spectatorship to a tight-knit spiritual community of committed apprentices of Jesus. When it comes to a pastoral scorecard, it is not just widening our reach that is important, so is deepening our congregation.

Over the years I have talked with many pastors who serve under an explicit or implicit evaluative scorecard that values first and foremost increased gathered worship attendance growth. Pastors will often confide in me the suffocating internal pressure they feel to "perform" on Sundays as well as the subtle pressures to preach in nonprophetic and non-offensive ways that draw and keep a comfortable crowd of religious consumers. Pastors will also speak of the heavy burden of board expectation to keep adding creative and innovative ministry programs and the constant comparisons to superstar pastors or a fast-growing church in their community. I am not saying a proper and prayerful expectation of growth and increased skill in pastoral preaching is unimportant. Pastoral leaders must take seriously the high stewardship of the preaching calling. Yet the ongoing pressure many pastors feel creates a very isolating, toxic inner world and all too often leads to some very bad outcomes not only for the pastor, but also for his or her family and the church.

But our pastoral scorecard must seek to evaluate more than bodies, budgets, buildings, and brand. Instead, we look for demonstrable evidence of a growing movement of multiplying disciples of Jesus who love their neighbors well and influence their Monday worlds for Christ and his kingdom. Can we seek to ascertain whether the gospel is transforming lives, whether a local church congregation is becoming more virtuous and spiritually formed, more effective in their mission and more beautiful in their expression as salt and light in the world? It is not that evaluating quantitative metrics like attendance, giving trends, or baptisms don't matter, but other more qualitative measures need to also be assessed and increase in their importance. This will mean asking different evaluation questions regarding leadership effectiveness, looking to anecdotal and narrative indicators as important components of our pastoral scorecard.

A shepherding scorecard. As shepherding leaders, we are called to nurture our parishioners' souls and to equip them for their callings and contributions in the world. We should also care deeply about their physical, emotional, relational, and economic well-being. As pastoral leaders we must become more attentive to the well-being of our communities, the flourishing of the most vulnerable, and stewarding well the natural environment. Shepherding leader, let me ask you a penetrating question: "If Jesus were to give your annual review, what would he say?" What would Jesus say about who you are becoming, the proper ordering of your loves, and how you are leading? What would Jesus say about the spiritual health and vitality of the local church you serve? Quiet listening to his brilliant, gentle voice, which can so easily be drowned out in noisy living, has been one of the most helpful evaluative reflections in my life, shaping my thinking about what should be included on a pastoral performance scorecard.

In the upper room the night before his crucifixion, Jesus said to his disciples, "By this—my Father is glorified, that you bear much fruit and so prove to be my disciples" (Jn 15:8). Jesus inextricably links the authenticity of our followership with the evidence of our fruitfulness—fruitfulness manifested in our intimacy with him, our character transformation in becoming like him, and our diligent labor for him. Jesus calls us, shepherding leaders, to a faithful fruitfulness in all that we are becoming and all we are doing. An important foundation of faithful fruitfulness, as King David reminds us, is effective shepherding leadership that reflects growing integrity of heart and increasingly skillful hands (Ps 78:70-72). The ways we often define and assess ministry "success" or "failure" need prayerful reevaluation, courageous recalibration, and in many cases, heartfelt repentance. Our truest task in our work is to experience Christ's presence with us and as we do, to bear much fruit. Our confidence as faithful shepherds is in a God who will reveal to us our clever rationalizations that justify numbers or external successes over faithful obedience in the intimacy of the ordinary.

Repentance regarding my own distorted scorecard came gradually for me as I began to realize how I had overemphasized quantitative indicators such as congregational attendance numbers and budgetary growth at the expense of other more qualitative measures of whole-life-discipleship growth in my congregation. My first step of repentance was to be honest with myself and with God. Transparently, one of my most anxious times of the month was when the attendance numbers were presented in our leadership meetings. On a heart and emotional level, I knew I was basing my sense of worth and degree of joy on how the congregation was numerically growing or not. I confessed to God that attendance numbers had turned into heart idols. My second step of repentance was to admit to my church leadership of my idolatrous struggle with numerical growth and to have them pray for me. This hard-fought honesty opened the door to have a needed conversation about the role of quantitative numbers in our leadership evaluation and planning. As a leadership team, we do evaluate numerical data, but we also look at evidence of qualitative transformation. While I continue to work and pray toward numerical church growth, my heart and emotional state is not tethered to its measurement. My scorecard repentance and reframing has freed me up to lead as a shepherd much more joyfully and effectively. For many of us, I believe it is time we rethink and reframe our pastoral scorecard.

FIVE MARKS OF SKILLFUL SHEPHERDING

Max DePree wisely pointed out, "We do not grow by knowing all the answers, but rather by living with the questions."[1] What are the questions we should be asking as it relates to faithful, fruitful shepherding leadership? Let me suggest several that I believe are vitally important:

- Are our congregants being loved well?
- Are the vulnerable being cared for well?

- Are congregants being equipped for all of life?
- Are a growing number of leaders being multiplied? Is there increasing institutional strength and health?

Addressing these important questions, I believe our pastoral scorecard should include at least five distinguishing marks that point to effective pastoral leadership of fruitful faithfulness. Skillful shepherding leadership will be evidenced in loving people well, caring for the vulnerable, equipping congregants for Monday, building leadership depth, and fostering institutional health.

Loving people well. While many of even the best sermons pastors preach are often forgotten, the tangible expressions of pastoral love a congregant experiences are seldom forgotten. I was reminded of this truth when a single mom named Rita became part of our congregation. When Rita entered our faith community, she had just recently lost her husband to death. She and her young children were facing many new challenges, and Rita experienced the warm welcome of our congregation and many tangible expressions of care and support. Rita and her children were a delightful part of our congregation for several years, and during that time she heard many sermons that I believe were encouraging and nurturing to her soul. Yet when a job transfer relocated her to another part of the country, she pulled me aside in a tearful farewell moment and thanked me not for my sermons, but rather for a small moment of pastoral care that frankly I had forgotten. During Rita's time of working through grief and facing so much uncertainty in her future, I had given her a call simply to check in on her and pray with her. With tears in her eyes, she expressed how encouraging my small act of pastoral care had meant to her on that particular day.

I share this story not to pat myself on the back, but rather to remind pastoral leaders that our tender love and demonstrations of care for congregants are the enduring foundation of leadership effectiveness over the long haul. Our preaching can be faithful exegetically to the biblical text, even homiletically impressive, but without a heartfelt pastoral love for our people, the words we say will have little lasting impact and will fail to move our mission forward. The apostle Paul reminds us with vivid and discordant imagery that without love, we are merely noisy gongs and clanging cymbals (1 Cor 13:1). At the heart of loving well is listening well. Bonhoeffer writes discerningly:

> The first service that one owes to others in the fellowship consists in listening to them. Just as love to God begins with listening to His Word, so the beginning of love for the brethren is learning to listen to them. It is God's love for us that He not only gives us His Word but also lends us His ear. . . . Christians, especially ministers, so often think they must always contribute something when they are in the company of others, that this is the one service they have to render. They forget that listening can be a greater service than speaking."[2]

When it comes to whether our congregation is becoming a truly loving community, our own love for congregants is the first thing we ought to honestly examine. When we peek behind the pastoral curtain, a most tragic and painful truth is revealed. Far too many pastors truly do not wholeheartedly love their congregants sacrificially. Is it any wonder then that many local faith communities often fail to love one another well when their leaders do not love them well? Yet Jesus reminds us our love for one another is the authenticating mark and the ultimate apologetic that we are his disciples. Jesus said, "By this all people will know that you are my disciples, if you have love for one another" (Jn 13:35). We must highly value the question "Are our congregants being loved well and loving well?" in the ongoing assessment of our pastoral leadership. While we may not be able to define love completely, or assess it quantitatively, we can observe its presence when lived out in a community of faith. Often our pastoral love is seen most as we walk with our congregants in the very real and raw depths of their heartaches and suffering.

The love the Bible speaks of is not merely something we feel, it is also something we do, a secure attachment love we incarnate in our relationships with others. Truly knowing others and being truly known by others makes it possible to better love others in tangible ways. The skill of loving others well grows with time. In marriage, for example, learning to love a spouse takes time fueled by a deepening understanding of the other and increasing self-sacrifice of our own preferences and desires. In a similar way within the local church community, loving well takes time, is continually nurtured with intention, and is empowered by the Holy Spirit. Paul encourages believers to love each other well, saying, "Let all you do be done in love" (1 Cor 16:14). All too often lurking behind the glittery curtain of celebrity image, brand, and quantified metrics of success, there is a beaten-down flock, followers of Jesus feeling used, manipulated, and malnourished.

Lisa Slayton is a valued friend and gifted leader who served for several years as CEO of the Pittsburgh Leadership Foundation. Lisa has taught me about shepherd leadership and its tangible manifestations in nurturing an organization where people flourish and the mission is advanced. Lisa regularly reminds pastoral leaders as she coaches them that people are not a means to an end, they are an end to themselves. As a shepherd leader, Lisa begins her day with a consistent liturgy of prayer. "Lord, who would you have me be with today and how would you have me be with them?" Lisa makes the point that this centering liturgy informs her leadership calling, placing before her a love-focused orientation to her colleagues and other stakeholders of the organization she serves.[3]

To speak of love as foundational to the pastoral scorecard is not to suggest some kind of dreamy, mushy, sentimental love, but rather to incarnate a hands-on kind of love that is not only attentive and affirming, but willing to have the hard conversations that are required by leaders who steward not only individuals, but the overall well-being of the organization. A shepherd leader's scorecard should reflect the tenderness of caring as well as the tough and courageous decisions that love for the individual and for the organization require. Some of my most difficult, as well as most loving, pastoral decisions have been in relationship to church staff or employees who need to find a new place of employment and service. While this love in action can be painful, shepherd leaders do everything they can to not make it harmful for the individual or the organization. Over time, both the tender love as well as the tough love of a shepherd leader are observable, informing the leadership effectiveness scorecard.

Over the years, I have been inspired by the love-driven leadership of Truett Cathy, whose Christian faith so profoundly informed his entrepreneurial energy and buttressed his success. In the early years of Chick-fil-A, founder Truett Cathy made the important point to his management team that the focus of their restaurants would not be getting bigger but becoming better. Truett believed that he was first in the people business and that if their organization would increasingly provide a better product and more satisfying customer experience, then quantitative growth would follow. At the heart of the remarkable success of Chick-fil-A is an organization irrevocably committed to loving others well. Truett was well-known for making the case that if the president of the United States came into one of their restaurants, the president would be treated with the greatest respect and careful attentiveness. That same posture of love and care was to be the way every customer was to be treated.[4] There is much pastoral leaders can learn from this remarkable business leader. How true this loving attentiveness ought to be for a local church faith community. Made in the very image of God, every person we encounter is of immeasurable value and dignity and ought to be treated as such.

With impassioned intentionality, our church's mission statement begins with the phrase "being a caring family." Loving well is at the very heart of all that we seek to be and to do. Jesus' model of the basin and towel both motivates us and permeates our programming and church activities. When I visit with those newer to our faith community, I asked them what their experience has been. I hope that the sermon and corporate worship services have been meaningful and challenging to their faith. Yet I mostly want to know if they have been warmly welcomed and loved attentively by our staff and volunteers. Loving people well may be harder to measure than the number of people attending a corporate worship service, but it may be a more important measure of assessment and the two may be correlative. Loving people well often leads to a warm and inviting culture for new people to become part of our local church family.

Caring for the vulnerable. After my father died when I was young, I grew up in a single-parent home. My mom worked in herculean ways to keep a roof over our heads and food on our table. One of the most painful realities of my childhood was how uninvolved our local church community was in caring for my mom in tangible ways. Our local church family gathered faithfully every Sunday to hear the transforming teachings of Holy Scripture, yet somehow the very down-to-earth mani-festation of love to care for the vulnerable both within the church and the community was often absent.

Caring for those on the margins—those physically, emotionally, and economically vulnerable—is one of the highest priorities and steward-ships of pastoral leadership. Jesus' strong words of sober judgment are directed at those who neglect the economically poor, the sick, the imprisoned, and the stranger. Jesus describes them as "the least of these," saying, "Truly I say to you, as you did it to one of the least of these my brothers, you did it to me" (Mt 25:40). The New Testament writer James frames the authenticity of our Christian faith as caring for widows and orphans (Jas 1:27). In his farewell address to the local church leaders at Ephesus, the apostle Paul reminds them of the imperative to generously help the weak (Acts 20:35). Dietrich Bonhoeffer writes, "The exclusion of the weak and insignificant, the seemingly useless people, from a Christian community may actually mean the exclusion of Christ; in the poor brother Christ is knocking at the door."[5]

As shepherding leaders, we not only develop leaders, we nurture a caring culture and create systems and structures to wisely and compas-sionately come alongside the vulnerable in our churches and broader community. In the local church I serve we have a very active benevolence program designed to meet immediate needs such as food, rent, medical care, and other necessities. We also provide resources for mental health counseling. One of our main priorities is to come alongside those who face unemployment and underemployment by providing networking throughout our city.

As a local church, we partner with other skilled organizations focused on the vulnerable in our city. Organizations such as The Salvation Army and City Union Mission are valuable partners in caring for the poorest of the poor. Many of our congregants sign up for Care Portal that connects them with specific needs social workers in our community have uncovered in their working with the poor and vulnerable. Individual congregants can then respond to a specific need, whether that is a financial gift or a specific tangible gift of an urgent item. We also partner with organizations that are furthering the common good, addressing economic and racial injustice and furthering economic and educational opportunity. How the most vulnerable among us and in our communities are being cared for, defended against oppression, and given opportunities to flourish is an important indicator of the effectiveness of pastoral leadership.

Equipping congregants for Monday. After a workplace visit, a pastor on our staff sent me a heartfelt email. He had just come back to his office and debriefed the experience with a younger pastoral resident that had accompanied him to the offices of an international corporation located near his campus. My pastoral colleague described in his email the joy of interacting with his congregants in their workplace, how their eyes lit up when he entered their Monday worlds. He penned these words:

> It said to them loud and clear: My pastor and my church care about me and they care about my work. They believe what I do matters, and they believe it enough to make the effort. And for me? I know how to love them better, preach to them more effectively and pray for them more accurately. I can picture Ryan in his desk, Josh before his huge aviation monitor, Michael in his cube, Mark in his office. And that makes me a better pastor.

Maybe—just maybe—I need to spend less time in my office, less time worrying about how many people show up to visit me at my place of work, and more time loving them in theirs, encouraging them to serve Jesus right where they are. What would that do for our people? What would that do for our communities? What would that do for our world.[6]

A pastoral leader who is focused on equipping congregants for the callings God has for them in their Monday world aligns his or her prayers, priorities, and practices in light of the scattered church's gospel, disciple-making mission. Pastors often speak of their commitment to whole-life discipleship but all too often are not discipling congregants for their whole life, for where they spend the majority of their time. Pastoral responsibilities do include compassionate pastoral care and leading well the gathered church in its corporate worship services. However, the scorecard of pastoral leadership must be expanded to include assessment regarding the effectiveness or noneffectiveness of equipping congregants for the entirety of their lives throughout the week. This will include equipping in the areas of sound biblical doctrine, sexuality, marriage, parenting, family life, multigenerational stewardships, wealth management, and finances. But we must not forget the high importance of equipping our congregants for their paid and nonpaid work life.

Bringing a greater Monday focus to the local church, our scorecard needs to look for evidence of sermons regularly addressing work, vocation, and economic flourishing. Sunday worship gatherings will reflect a liturgical regularity reflecting a robust theology of vocation and a vocational missiological emphasis. Pastors will also need to demonstrate that the discipleship pathways of the church have a strong faith, work, and economic wisdom component in curriculums.[7] Effective pastoral leadership will encourage not only asset mapping of a community, but also asset mapping of individual congregants. In the church I serve, we have hosted half-day seminars and one-day conferences around the integration of faith and work, as well as matters of economic and racial injustice. We are committed to do justice as we seek the common good of our communities and our city. These concentrated conversations and collective initiatives have helped members of our congregation continue to be equipped for their Monday callings.

The pastoral scorecard must take seriously how God's people are being encouraged and equipped to be the scattered church on mission. Pastors are like coaches cheering on congregants who are becoming more intimate apprentices of Jesus and serving Christ in their vocations and appointments throughout the week in the transforming power of the Holy Spirit. Rather than putting our primary leadership focus on how well we are doing on Sunday, we reorient to care for how well our people are doing on Monday.

Building leadership depth. One of the greatest evidences of effective pastoral leadership is the quality and number of integral and skillful leaders being developed within the organizations we lead. High on our pastoral scorecard must be evidence of our developing other leaders deeper in their Christlikeness, soaring to new heights of effectiveness. John the Baptist said it well, but in my opinion, he didn't say enough. John the Baptist declared, "[Jesus] must increase, but I must decrease" (Jn 3:30). That Jesus must continually increase and we must decrease is a vital reality of growing spiritual formation and leadership maturity. However, when it comes to faithful and fruitful shepherding leadership, it is not only that Jesus must continually increase and we must decrease, it is also true that others must continually increase around us. At the very heart of effective pastoral leadership are the integral well-being, effectiveness, and flourishing of the other leaders we are encouraging and nurturing in becoming increasingly integral and skillful—a growing number of Christlike shepherding leaders being multiplied for the church and for the world.

At a leadership gathering in South Carolina, I had the joy of meeting a seasoned surgeon whose life work has been focused on training a new generation of surgeons. In our conversation, I asked him some questions regarding the greatest insights he has gained in developing others in his field. He pointed out the most intensive and transformative learning space is the scrub sink. The scrub sink is where the surgery team gathers before a surgery to make sure they are as germfree as possible. But the scrub sink is also that place where the seasoned surgeon and the rest of the team members, many early in their career, gather and talk about what the surgery they are about to do entails. When they are done at the scrub sink, together they go and perform the surgery. When the surgery is completed, they gather at the scrub sink not only to clean up, but also to debrief on what they have together experienced: observations made, lessons learned, and relationships deepened. The surgeon, who over the span of his distinguished career has trained hundreds of surgeons, said to me that the scrub sink is the key to leadership development.

His insightful words reinforced in my mind and heart the vital importance of the apprenticeship model of life-on-life leadership development not only in the health care profession, but also within the church. By its very nature, leaders with integrity of heart and skillful hands emerge out of a rich tacit knowledge environment that best takes place not in the classroom but in the dynamic incarnational laboratory of organizational life. Scrub-sink spaces not only matter in hospitals, but in churches as well. I truly believe that God designed the family and the local church to be the most dynamic leadership development enterprise in the world. For the church to be transformative, we must wholeheartedly embrace what Jesus taught and modeled about leadership.

One of the most glaring inadequacies of pastoral leadership development in our time is the lack of scrub-sink apprenticeship opportunities in a healthy, empowering local church where young pastors learn from more mature pastors how to live and lead well. While the theological classroom is important, equally important is life-on-life, day-to-day apprenticeship in a local church. Local churches need to establish pastoral residencies, becoming like "teaching hospitals" for the apprenticeship training of a new generation of pastors.[8]

Jesus was the most brilliant leader to ever grace our sin-ravaged planet. Not only is Jesus our Savior and Lord, he is also our ultimate leadership coach. As apprentices of the Good Shepherd, pastoral leaders are invited into the Jesus school of leadership to learn to live and lead like Jesus (Mt 11:28-30). Jesus turned the leadership model of his day upside down, teaching his disciples that leading was not about coercive power or positional authority, but personal servanthood (Mk 10:42-45). Jesus taught and lived a highly relational, tacit-rich apprenticeship model of leadership. While Jesus preached the gospel of the kingdom to crowds and healed many, his primary mission was investing his time and energy in a small band of disciples to whom he imparted his life and wisdom. The gospel writers seem to suggest that of the twelve disciples, three were invited into a closer inner circle of apprenticeship.

Both Jesus' leadership model and multiplication method ought to inform our pastoral priorities and practices but also be reflected on the pastoral scorecard. The apostle Paul reminds pastor Timothy of the high priority of developing leaders who will develop others. "And what you have heard from me in the presence of many witnesses, entrust to faithful men, who be able to teach others also" (2 Tim 2:2).

Faithful and fruitful pastoral leadership ought to be able to point to ongoing evidence of how shepherding leaders are being mentored and multiplied. In the church I serve, we have a leadership development pathway for congregants prominent on our scorecard.[9] We also have a pastoral residency where, following classroom preparation in seminary, young pastors join our staff team in a two-year immersive mentoring experience. Our pastoral residency not only is transformational for the young pastors involved, it also provides a leadership pipeline for future expansion and succession. As a local church, our goal is to continue to build greater and greater leadership depth, to never have to rebuild, but simply reload. We realize the breadth of our missional impact is dependent on the depth of our effectiveness in leadership development. As shepherding leaders, may we heed the wise words of the psalmist: "So even to old age and gray hairs, O God, do not forsake me, until I proclaim your might to another generation, your power to all those to come" (Ps 71:18). As a pastoral leader my high stewardship is to invest my life in the people and institutions that will surely outlast me.

Fostering institutional health. Shepherding leaders recognize the local church is not only a dynamic organism; it is also an enduring institution. We can overspiritualize and forget that the church is an institution: the people, policies, values, finances, and programs that nurture local church health from cradle to grave. The church is a physical presence, a signpost of eternity. The institutional nature and day-to-day realities of local church faithful presence within a community create the consistent context where individual transformation can take place for congregants throughout their lives. Shepherding leaders embrace a longtime horizon that makes institutional health and strength a high priority. We must grasp that both individuals and the institutions that nurture them matter. Recalling the wise adage also shared in chapter seven: Without individuals nothing ever changes, but without institutions nothing endures.

Prominent on the pastoral leadership scorecard ought to be indicators that point to a healthy and flourishing institution. Is the local church's institutional strength increasing and its health continuing? Regardless of size and complexity of a local church, its institutional health and strength can and should be regularly assessed.

Assessing the ongoing institutional health of a local church will include several areas. An evaluation of financial strength and integrity looks to giving trends and includes management audits, transparency, and regular communication with the congregation. Church staff health, morale, and longevity need monitoring. Low staff morale and a high staff turnover may well indicate a lack of effective pastoral leadership and floundering institutional health. Another area of assessment includes the expansion and maintenance of church buildings and technology infrastructure. Looking for areas of growing diversity, innovation, and creativity also provide additional evidence of institutional health.

As with building equity in a house over time, being founder and senior pastor of an organization brings an equity I can utilize to foster needed change, including reframing the success scorecard. But what if you are serving in a pastoral role and do not have the organizational equity or influence to change the scorecard? What do you do? While I don't have easy answers, I would encourage you to first reframe the success scorecard for your particular area of service in the church. Wherever we are serving, whatever our job description within the organization, we can prayerfully and diligently create a pocket of health and effectiveness. Any example of flourishing can serve as a credibility bridge to the higher levels of organizational leadership. Needed change can come from the top down, but also the bottom up. In some cases, serving in an organization with a faulty scorecard will mean change is simply not possible. Faulty scorecards can lead to very toxic work cultures. When this is the case, you may need to leave the organization—not only to preserve unity, but also to take seriously the stewardship of your self-care and to nourish your spiritual formation.

THE SCORECARD THAT MATTERS MOST

While we should take regular assessment of our leadership effectiveness, at the end of the day, the scorecard that matters most is the one Jesus will have for us when we meet him face to face.[10] Using a parabolic story of three money managers, Jesus reminded his disciples that they would be held accountable for their lives and in particular their vocational callings. While each apprentice of Jesus receives different abilities, gifts of grace, and opportunities, each one of them without exception is evaluated on what they did with what they had been given. The one money manager whose evaluation revealed a woeful lack of stewardship received a severe reprimand along with sobering consequences. The other two money managers whose evaluation revealed vocational diligence and good stewardship received high commendation along with greater opportunities to serve in the future. "Well done, good and faithful servant. You have been faithful over a little, I will set you over much" (Mt 25:21). Yet the greatest reward for vocational faithfulness was not merely the commendation by Jesus, but the grace-filled invitation and expectation to experience the deep and intimate relational joy of Jesus. As shepherd leaders we so often overlook this invitation, extended for those who adoringly follow Jesus with holy intentionality and humble service. The closing words of Jesus' praiseful commendation is the ultimate reward we await. It is the words from Jesus our Savior, our Lord, and our brilliant leader, "Enter into the joy of your master" (Mt 25:21).

11

FINISHING WELL

*When all the pieces come together, not only does your work move
toward greatness, but so does your life. For, in the end, it is impossible
to have a great life unless it is a meaningful life. And it is very
difficult to have a meaningful life without meaningful work. Perhaps,
then you might gain the rare tranquility that comes from knowing
that you've had a hand in creating something of intrinsic excellence
that makes a contribution. Indeed, you might even gain that deepest
of all satisfactions: knowing that your short time on earth has been
well spent, and that it mattered.*

JIM COLLINS, *GOOD TO GREAT*

Growing up, I was passionate about wrestling. I absolutely loved
everything about the sport: the adrenaline-filled challenge of
facing an opponent, unleashing all the intensity I could muster,
pinning my opponent's shoulders to the mat. The thrill of victory enraptured me with pure joy. I was rewarded with a good deal of success, but
I would not have enjoyed that level of achievement without the wisdom
of my coach. My coach often reminded me that wrestlers who win train
well for the third period. Desiring to be a champion wrestler required

training throughout the year. In the fall, I ran cross-country not because it was my sport, or even because I liked it, but because the endurance it built in my mind and body prepared me when I found myself on the mat in the third period.

In the sport of wrestling, a champion-level wrestler will defeat an average opponent in the first period, a good opponent, in the second period. But it will be in the third period where a great opponent is defeated. Champion wrestlers continually train not for the first period, or even the second, but for the third period, for in the third period they face the greatest challenges and require the most endurance. What I learned as a wrestler early on in my life taught me a crucial leadership lesson. Shepherd leaders must train well for the third period, for the third period determines whether we will finish well or fall woefully short of the stewardships we have been given.

Stephen Covey rightly reminds us that we must begin with the end in mind.[1] Yet no matter where we find ourselves in life's adventurous journey, we are wise to live every day with the end in mind. Observing our current cultural moment and reading the pages of history painfully reminds us of how few leaders truly finish well. Some leaders suddenly flame out and some slowly rust out, yet regardless of the contours of a poor finish, the sad and sometime dire consequences leave lasting ramifications for the organizations they lead and the generations to follow. It is not uncommon to start well, what is uncommon is to finish well.[2] How we finish will greatly shape the leadership legacy we leave behind.

THREATS TO OUR LEADERSHIP LEGACY

We are especially reminded of leadership legacies in the Old Testament books of 1 and 2 Kings and 1 and 2 Chronicles. While these inspired Old Testament books do capture a good deal of the up-and-down history of God's covenant people, they also provide timeless reminders of how few leaders actually finish well. King Solomon walked with God and was known for his extraordinary wisdom. Yet as he grew older, he found his heart for God divided because he held fast in love to wives who were devoted to other gods, "For when Solomon was old his wives turned away his heart after other gods, and his heart was not wholly true to the LORD his God, as was the heart of David his father" (1 Kings 11:4). Even Solomon's great wisdom wasn't enough for him to finish well. King Asa was one of the brightest leadership lights of Judah, for his heart was fully committed to the Lord. However, in his old age he refused to listen to wise advice and foolishly entered into unwise military and political alliances (see 2 Chron 16). The book of Ecclesiastes speaks to the folly of aging leaders like Asa, "Better was a poor and wise youth than an old and foolish king who no longer knew how to take advice" (Eccl 4:13). Asa, now a foolish king, is also an angry old man. In anger Asa threw his wise adviser into prison and unleashed oppression on some of his nation (see 2 Chron 16:7-11). When illness struck Asa in his old age, he refused to seek the Lord (2 Chron 16:12). King Uzziah in his earlier years sought the Lord and led with courage and commitment, yet as he experienced the favor of the Lord, personal pride became his downfall. The biblical writer summarizes it bluntly, "But when he was strong, he grew proud to his destruction" (2 Chron 26:16).

The leadership legacies of kings like Solomon, Asa, and Uzziah are sobering reminders that finishing well is not easy. Like these leaders of old, we too can be tripped up along the way—especially in the latter years of our lives—by disordered loves, divided loyalties, unwillingness to heed advice, and personal pride. In the third period, many shepherd leaders fade in the stretch. In addition to these perils, some leaders stop growing, some are mired in resentment and bitterness, some hold on to power, some do not prepare the next generation, some are disqualified, some become indulgent, and some simply coast. Steven Covey describes well an ongoing struggle of the third period of our lives, "The older we become, the more we are in the crosscurrents between the need for more self-discipline and temperance and the desire to let down and relax and indulge. We feel we've paid our dues and are therefore entitled to let go."[3] While it is quite common to speak of the foolishness and sins of youth, it is all too uncommon to speak of the foolishness and sins of mature adults. Regardless of what period of life we now inhabit, there are no guarantees we will finish well. Shepherd leaders of all ages are wise to keep their eyes peeled on three consequential challenges. These three challenges are restless rooftops, rogue waves, and black swans.

Restless rooftops. The psalmist looks to King David's life as our model of shepherding leadership. David leads with integrity of heart and guides with skillful hands (Ps 78:72). The biblical writers also describe the unvarnished truth regarding David's adulterous sin with Bathsheba and cover-up murder of Bathsheba's husband Uriah, one of his most trusted military leaders. King David, who in his youth had courageously slain Goliath the giant, later in life is slain by the giant of sexual lust. So what happened to King David? How could someone, a person after God's own heart, do something so horribly wrong?

We are given a couple of possible clues as to the contributing factors that led to David's actions. First, David became undisciplined in his leadership role. While David's previous pattern was to go out to battle with his troops, David remains in his palace in Jerusalem (2 Sam 11:1). Second, David's indiscipline led to a restless indulgence. The biblical writer describes it this way: "It happened, late one afternoon, when David arose from his couch and was walking on the roof of the king's house, that he saw from the roof a woman bathing; and the woman was very beautiful" (2 Sam 11:2). The picture presented to us is David chilling out on his couch in the middle of the day. He gets up and heads to his rooftop where he is pacing back and forth. Then his eye catches Bathsheba. Temptation suddenly greets a restless indiscipline and temptation tragically wins. The indiscriminate shrapnel of pain unleashed by David's foolishness and disobedience simply cannot be adequately described. David's adultery, murder, abuse of power, and cover-up dishonor God and bring lasting consequences to himself, his family, and the nation he was called to serve.

What can we learn from David's experience? As shepherd leaders we must pay close attention to what we are paying attention to. We keep in touch with what is going on inside us at a soul level. Our rooftops of vulnerability are often less exposed in difficult leadership times, but more exposed in times when we are experiencing the fruits of leadership success. Up to this point in David's life, just about everything he touched turned to gold. Surrounded by the accoutrements of God's favor, David forgets that the greatest battles of his life are not against external foes, but the internal foe of his fallen heart.

For shepherd leaders, rooftops of vulnerability can be clinging to positions of power; looking to money, wealth, and comfort for our security and joy; entertaining lustful thoughts, using pornography, or secretly cultivating an emotional connection with someone who isn't our spouse. We can also be seduced to restless rooftops by life's disappointments, shattered dreams, and unresolved issues of our childhood. We need a close friend or personal counselor to whom we can be transparent. A wise life coach can also help us see what we often cannot or refuse to see in our own lives. Paying close attention to matters of the heart is important at every stage of our journey, but perhaps it is most important when we find ourselves in the third period of our lives with both its perils and possibilities. Ruthlessly do whatever is necessary in your life to avoid temptations that corrode your ability to resist sins and alluring webs. Pray diligently for the Lord's protection on your life and for God's gracious and merciful deliverance from the secret ways you may attempt to justify sin.

Let's remember that when David is confronted by the prophet Nathan regarding his grave sin, David repents, finds forgiveness, embraces deepening intimacy with God, and grows in wisdom (see Ps 51). God's amazing and generous grace carries David to the finish line. It would seem that David's repentance for his sin with Bathsheba altered his behavior. A young beautiful woman by the name of Abishag is brought to King David to care for him in his elder years. David honors God and Abishag, maintaining a sexually pure relationship.[4] Our restless rooftops can find healing and hope in humble repentance, and this can open the door to a deeper intimacy with God.[5]

Rogue waves. The Pacific Ocean with all its grandeur, the rugged coastline, and the sunsets with all their brilliant colors make Mendocino one of the most beautiful places in the United States. The quaint town of Mendocino, California, is a favorite vacation getaway. In Mendocino, walking along the rugged coastline, I first encountered a warning sign that said, "Watch out for deadly sneaker waves." Growing up far away from the ocean, I had no idea what sneaker waves were or why they were so dangerous. With a little research, I learned that sneaker waves are rogue waves that seemingly come out of nowhere. These rogue waves are at least twice the average of the normal surf heights, crashing the shoreline with massive power and force. Sneaker waves can occur during the daytime, but they also occur under the cover of darkness. The residents of Mendocino and those experienced with the Pacific Ocean in this particular region of California live with a daily truth. It is not wise to turn your back on the ocean. On the other hand, tourists like me are simply not aware of the danger these unpredictable sneaker rogue waves present. We need warning signs from those more experienced to help us pay attention to what we may not know is there and cannot see.

Writing to his younger protégé, the apostle Paul warns pastor Timothy to watch his back for a sneaker rogue wave. This rogue wave had the name of Alexander. "Alexander the coppersmith did me great harm; the LORD will repay him according to his deeds. Beware of him yourself, for he strongly opposed our message" (2 Tim 4:14-15). We do not know what specifically Paul has in mind when he warns Timothy about Alexander. We can only speculate that perhaps Paul's imprisonment was in large part due to Alexander's words and actions. Paul's strong warning to Timothy to keep his eye out for Alexander speaks of a grave peril lurking in the shadows of local church leadership. Paul does not want Timothy to be naive about the surprising and sudden dangers that come with pastoral leadership.

Shepherd leaders cultivate a high level of trust in those around them, but they also keep their discerning eyes open. The rogue wave of an obstructive board member can wreak havoc on the unity and synergy of church leadership as well as the entire church. Rogue waves may come in the form of a disloyal staff colleague or a false accusation toward you as a leader. They may also seemingly come out of the blue when compelling evidence presents itself as to a staff member's compromise of moral integrity or financial malfeasance. A sudden financial setback or a sizable, unexpected expense in the church budget can also take a pastoral leader by surprise. Sudden and surprising rogue waves will be part of a shepherd leader's journey. Stay on your knees, keep your eyes open, watch your back, and continue to trust God to guide you and give you courage to confront these very difficult challenges of leadership. Hold the prophet Isaiah's hopeful and comforting words close to your heart, "Fear not, for I am with you; be not dismayed, for I am your God; I will strengthen you, I will help you, surely I will uphold you with my righteous right hand" (Is 41:10).

Black swans. The term "Black Swan" was developed by Nassim Nicholas Taleb to describe nonpredictable high-impact events.[6] Black swans are surprising and strong outliers that leaders may encounter, events way outside the normative expectations they have about the future. In addition to their surprising nature, black swans bring with them a great deal of disruption and high levels of uncertainty, often significantly rearranging the very terrain of the organization's environment. Like a one-hundred-year flood, black swans are virtually impossible to predict, bringing with them both new perils as well as new possibilities. While it can be argued that the global coronavirus pandemic that began in 2020 may not perfectly capture Taleb's precise definition of a black swan, it is the closest experience I have ever had of leading in the context of a free fall of uncertainty as well as massive disruption of everyday life.

How do shepherd leaders lead well in black swan-type environments, times that are highly uncertain and massively disruptive—when leading feels like flying a plane upside down in dense fog with no reliable instruments? If you find yourself in a black swan environment—in uncharted territory, where planning is extremely difficult and constantly fluid—let me encourage you to keep four reminders close to your heart: lean into wisdom, remain relational, build endurance, and stay on mission.

When you are in a black swan environment, lean into wisdom. Remember that which is most timely is what is timeless. In highly uncertain times, leaders tend to continually seek more and more information, yet what happens is that much of the information will be fast changing, ambiguous, and often contradictory. Focus less on gathering more information and more on gaining wisdom. Look to the biblical text for wisdom. Pursue older generations, who have more life experience, both for getting needed encouragement and gaining a longer perspective. Focus more on what you do know with confidence than on what you don't know at the moment. Spend less time reflecting on what-ifs and more on what is next. In some cases, a black swan environment can be a watershed moment of increasing clarity. A pastor shared his reflections on leading through a global pandemic. "Many of the props had been taken away in my life. I realized how much I have been depending on the wrong things."[7] This provides a renewal opportunity to seek the Lord's intimate presence and wisdom in prayer. Cling to the promise that when we ask for wisdom, our Good Shepherd will give it to us generously.[8]

In times of great uncertainty and disruption, a common tendency is to get busier, work harder, and put in longer hours. As leaders we tell ourselves if we simply do more and plan more, then things will work out better. It has been said that humans are the only species on the planet that when lost, simply go faster. Speed means you are working harder but not necessarily moving forward. Black swan events are not about speeding up but about slowing down: slowing down to pursue spiritual formation, personal well-being, and deeper relationships with others. When you don't really know what to do, be honest with yourself. Be willing to say to others around you, "I don't know." When decisions are painfully difficult and choices are limited, you can still love others well no matter what. Reach out to family members, close friends, and work colleagues. Regular touch points are life-giving. Take the time to check in on others, listen well to what their hearts are saying. Empathy matters. Without hurry, take the initiative to affirm your love and commitment to others around you. Deepen your relationships, don't let them erode out of busyness or be dissolved by neglect. Black swan events call for a greater commitment to remain relational and love others well. The apostle Paul reminds the Corinthians, "Let all that you do be done in love" (1 Cor 16:14). Shepherd leaders who remain relational also reach out to other pastoral leaders during times of disruption and uncertainty. Sharing transparently, praying together, and encouraging one another will put wind in your leadership sails.

Black swan environments are highly disorienting, very taxing, and bring a ton of stress with them. Because it is impossible to discern the duration of a black swan event or all that it will mean for the present and the future, emotionally prepare yourself and those you lead to take a long view. Building greater endurance and staying buoyant with hope are inextricably linked. When endurance wanes, hope fades. When hope fades, endurance wanes. Flourishing in black swan times will require building greater endurance in your life, deepening your leadership ballast with regular infusions of life-giving hope. Anchoring his words in the glorious truths of gospel grace, the apostle Paul brilliantly connects suffering, hope, and endurance:

> Through him we have also obtained access by faith into this grace in which we stand, and we rejoice in hope of the glory of God. Not only that, but we rejoice in our sufferings, knowing that suffering produces endurance, and endurance produces character, and character produces hope, and hope does not put us to shame, because God's love has been poured into our hearts through the Holy Spirit who has been given to us. (Rom 5:2-5)

Paul's inspired words are a leadership lifeline when leading in highly disruptive, painfully turbulent, and uncertain times. God is faithful, so stay faithful.

Seasons of major disruption and uncertainty can lead us down the perilous path of mission drift. While a lot changes in black swan events, the shepherd leader's disciple-making mission does not. In time of great uncertainty and disruption, the main thing of leadership is to keep the main thing the main thing. Pivoting around strategy will be needed, but it is essential to stay firmly tethered to our organizational mission. Strategy changes, mission does not. Paul encourages pastor Timothy to stay on mission, "And what you have heard from me in the presence of many witnesses entrust to faithful men, who be able to teach others also" (2 Tim 2:2).

The coronavirus pandemic and its massive disruption of in-person gatherings forced churches and a myriad of organizations to make a sharp pivot to virtual gatherings. The implications of this pivot have been profound in shifting priorities, deploying financial and human resources around online presence and small group gatherings. One of the good things that can emerge in a black swan environment is the unleashing of innovation, creativity, and collaboration. Serious and sudden disruption of the status quo provides a window of innovative opportunity for shepherd leaders. Many changes that would have been resisted more vociferously in more tranquil times are now more readily embraced in turbulent times. Needed change in the leader's life as well as the organization he or she leads may prove to be one of the greatest grace gifts of a black swan event.

THREE REMINDERS FOR FINISHING WELL

In his inspired second letter to pastor Timothy, the apostle Paul nears the end. Paul's last recorded words are chock-full of wisdom and encouragement tailor-made to Timothy's shepherding leadership calling. In the grace of his crucified and resurrected Lord, Paul is finishing well and is looking forward to what lies ahead. Paul encourages Timothy to do the same. "For I am already being poured out as a drink offering, and the time of my departure has come. I have fought the good fight, I have finished the race, I have kept the faith" (2 Tim 4:6-7). Embedded in Paul's encouraging words are three metaphors of shepherding leadership that have guided and sustained him to the end. Paul employs a military metaphor, an athletic metaphor, and a monetary metaphor revealing three truths that shepherding leadership is a battleground, a marathon, and a sacred trust.

Shepherding leadership is a battleground. Paul declares, "I have fought the good fight." Paul's words picture for us a contest, a battle between opposing foes. Shepherding leaders who finish well recognize they live and lead each and every day in the context of a raging, invisible war between the forces of darkness and light. Writing to the Ephesians, Paul reminds the church of the invisible war, this clash of two opposing kingdoms:

> Finally, be strong in the Lord and in the strength of his might. Put on the whole armor of God, that you may be able to stand against the schemes of the devil. For we do not wrestle against flesh and blood, but against the rulers, against the authorities, against the cosmic powers over this present darkness, against the spiritual forces of evil in the heavenly places. (Eph 6:10-12)

In what might well be his most brilliant writing, C. S. Lewis paints for us a picture of the invisible war from the perspective of the demonic realm. In his masterpiece *The Screwtape Letters*, the seasoned demon Uncle Screwtape writes words of guidance to Wormwood, his younger apprentice:

> Our policy for the moment is to conceal ourselves. Of course this has not always been so. We are really faced with a cruel dilemma. When the humans disbelieve in our existence we lose all the pleasing results of direct terrorism and we make no magicians. On the other hand, when they believe in us, we cannot make them materialists and sceptics.[9]

Lewis strikes a proper balance of how we as shepherd leaders must pay attention to the unseen realm; yet not overfixate on it.

We must keep in mind that two intelligent and powerful opposing kingdoms are vying for the hearts and affections of the image bearers of God. This pervasive invisible war influences people, families, institutions, and governments. A powerful and perverse trinity of world, flesh, and devil bring hell's fury to our hearts and minds and to this entire fallen world. Satan hates the bride of Christ, the church, and all shepherd leaders who serve the church have a big target on their back. Satan knows if he can discourage, distract, deceive, or disqualify a shepherd leader, Christ is dishonored, the good news of the gospel is discredited, and the sheep are more vulnerable. While the crucified and resurrected Jesus has defeated Satan and his fellow conspirators, the battle continues to rage until that day when the evil one will be thrown into the lake of fire (Rev 20:10).

Shepherding leadership is not a playground; it is a battlefield. Writing to pastor Timothy, Paul will employ the imagery of a highly disciplined and singularly focused soldier who faces difficulty and suffering (2 Tim 2:3-4). While our enemy is formidable and we are soldiers in that sense, we have been given supernatural power, unconditional love, transformational truth, spiritual community, and radiating beauty to resist Satan and confront evil. Paul writes words of great encouragement:

> For though we walk in the flesh, we are not waging war according to the flesh. For the weapons of our warfare are not of the flesh but have divine power to destroy strongholds. We destroy arguments and every lofty opinion raised against the knowledge of God, and take every thought captive to obey Christ. (2 Cor 10:3-5)

Our primary focus must be on staying yoked to Jesus, prayerfully walking in the supernatural power of the Holy Spirit. God's Word reminds us, "he who is in you is greater than he who is in the world" (1 Jn 4:4). If we are going to lead well and finish well, Jesus' hopeful words need to be tucked deeply within our hearts. Shepherding leadership is a battleground. Will we be a battlefield casualty or a spiritual catalyst?

Shepherding leadership is a marathon. Paul declares to pastor Timothy, "I have finished the race" (2 Tim 4:7). Paul's word picture frames in our minds an athletic contest, particularly a long race. One of Paul's frequent metaphors of the spiritual life and leadership is an athletic race (see 1 Cor 9:24-25; Gal 2:2; 5:7; Phil 2:16; 2 Tim 4:7). In Paul's mind is not a short sprint but something more like a long marathon.

I am not a marathon runner, but I do run regularly to keep in shape as well as to nurture my mental, physical, and emotional well-being. I have friends who run marathons and they always undergo months of rigorous training before running the race. Marathoners don't just decide on a whim one day to go run twenty-six miles. No matter how much desire or willpower they might have, it will not be enough to move a body that has not been well-trained to meet the rigorous challenges of going the distance of a marathon. My friends also tell me that marathons do not run alone. The camaraderie of running with others helps them keep going, especially when they hit the wall where their bodies tell them it is impossible to go one step further.

Shepherd leaders who run the race well don't run alone, nor do they finish well alone. They form close friendships and run with a band of brothers or sisters who vulnerably encourage each other not to throw in the towel when things get rough, but to keep their eyes on Jesus and finish the race. Shepherd leaders know it is not just about trying harder, but training better. Shepherd leaders never outgrow the need to embrace the spiritual practices that bring the strength, joy, and endurance required for a lifetime of faithful and fruitful leadership. We never outgrow the fundamentals, the basics of the spiritual life. Paul reminds pastor Timothy of the primacy of maintaining sound doctrine and self-discipline, describing a connection of physical discipline with spiritual discipline:

> If you put these things before the brothers, you will be a good
> servant of Christ Jesus, being trained in the words of the faith and
> of the good doctrine that you have followed. Have nothing to do
> with irreverent, silly myths. Rather train yourself for godliness; for
> while bodily training is of some value, godliness is of value in every
> way, as it holds promise for the present life and also for the life to
> come. (1 Tim 4:6-8)

Skillful artists such as cellists know the consequence of skipping practice. If they miss practice one day, they know it. If they stop practicing for a week, their fellow cellists know it. If they don't practice for a month, the world knows it. Shepherd leaders, you know it and others around you see it. Are you continuing to grow in greater intimacy, to stay curious, to stay disciplined in your walk with Jesus? Those who finish well stay disciplined. They know it's about practice, not perfection. Shepherd leader, train for the long and arduous leadership road ahead, so that rather than fading in the stretch, you break the tape of pastoral faithfulness.

Shepherding leadership is a sacred trust. Reflecting a sense of exhilaration, Paul says to pastor Timothy, "I have kept the faith" (2 Tim 4:7). Paul frames his finishing well around a word picture of being a faithful fiduciary of someone else's wealth or property. Paul's words hint of Jesus' parable of the faithful money managers who were required to give an account to the owner for their investment and the rate of return they earned.[10] Throughout Holy Scripture we are reminded that we are not autonomous owners, but ultimately accountable stewards. The psalmist declares, "The earth is the LORD's and everything in it" (Ps 24:1 NIV).

As a shepherd leader, King David is entrusted by God "to shepherd Jacob his people, Israel his inheritance" (Ps 78:71). Paul speaks to the church leaders at Ephesus, reminding them of the sacred trust they have been given. "Pay careful attention to yourselves and the flock, in which the Holy Spirit has made you overseers, to care for the church of God, which he obtained with his own blood" (Acts 20:28). The apostle Peter instructs local church leaders to shepherd the flock well and then points to the reward that someday awaits them when the chief Shepherd appears (1 Pet 5:4).

As a violinmaker, Martin Schleske has learned much about the spiritual life and leadership as he carefully crafts violins with his skillful hands. He beautifully articulates the calling of the musician that in many ways I believe parallel the sacred trust extended to shepherd leaders:

The pressure on your shoulders can be removed only when you understand your calling: you comfort hearts, you touch hearts, you bless hearts. In your music you make heaven's language audible so that we can bear this world and love it despite all of its adversities. It lifts our hearts. As a musician, you must understand the meaning of your calling. You are not a performer of your abilities, but a servant with permission to bless people.... You are not led onto the stage to show what you can do but because God wants to speak through the voice of your sound. God knows the needs and circumstances of the people listening to you and knows how to bless them. And so you are called to be an instrument.[11]

As shepherd leaders we are instruments in our Lord's hands. Our lives and leadership callings are a sacred trust; they are not ours to squander. Will we hear, "Well done, good and faithful servant, enter into the eternal joy that awaits us?"

ETERNITY IN OUR HEARTS

We were created with eternity in mind. The writer of Ecclesiastes tells us what we deeply feel: God has put eternity in our hearts (Eccles 3:11). In this short parenthesis we call *time*, along with fallen creation we too groan for all to be made new (Rom 8:19-25). As shepherd leaders we hear the hopeful words of the apostle John as he is given a glimpse of the Lamb who was slain for us, who will be our eternal shepherd. "For the Lamb in the midst of the throne will be their shepherd, and he will guide them to springs of living water, and God will wipe away every tear from their eyes" (Rev 7:17).

Dallas Willard—who touched so many lives, including my own, in such profound and transformational ways—would often pray for those who were with him, that we would live a radiant life and experience a radiant death. As an apprentice of Jesus, Dallas lived and died what he believed and what he prayed. Gary Moon, who was with Dallas as he took his last breath, describes the moment:

In a voice clearer than [Gary] had heard in days, he leaned his head back slightly and with his eyes closed said, "Thank you." Gary did not feel that Dallas was talking to him, but to another presence that Dallas seemed to sense in the room. And those were the last words of Dallas Willard. "Thank you," he said to a very present and now finally visible to him God.[12]

The greatest lover of his soul—the one who had put eternity in his heart, rescued him, carried him, loved him, and taught him—welcomed Dallas into his presence and his heavenly home.

Shepherd leader, may you hold closely eternity in your heart, live a radiant life, and experience a radiant death. May you finish your race well with a joy-filled hope and a grateful heart. Crossing the finish line, may the words penned by Andraé Crouch be your tribute to the Lord Jesus Christ:

All that I am and ever hope to be I owe it all to Thee.[13]

ACKNOWLEDGMENTS

Many years ago, I remember being told that the books we read, the people we rub shoulders with, and the choices we make each day tell the true story of our lives. In many ways the words on the pages of this book reflect other authors who have been my teachers as well as amazing people who I have had the privilege of rubbing shoulders with in my life and work. I simply cannot name each and every person who has been such a gift of grace to me. Even if I do not have room to mention your name, you know who you are and I hope you know how very much I am grateful for you.

This writing project would not have been undertaken or completed without the continual encouragement of my wife, Liz. Liz not only believed in the importance of this book being written but also worked diligently and sacrificially to carve out the necessary time in our schedules for it to happen. Liz provided wise input to the manuscript and her beautiful heart and insightful reflections find their way in each chapter.

My younger pastoral colleague, Joseph Luigs, has been with me every step of the way. Joseph's encouraging heart, brilliant mind, and tireless assistance in shaping and reshaping the manuscript cannot be overstated or overappreciated. Joseph, thanks for your insightful generational perspective, diligent work ethic, and our growing friendship that is a true treasure. Steve Harvey is a cherished longtime friend who faithfully serves as my administrative colleague. Steve has done yeoman's work coordinating my schedule and managing so many details. Steve, I could not do what God has called me to do or flourish without you.

I am grateful for Chris Armstrong, Jeff Wright, and Andrew Jones who were willing to be early manuscript readers. Your helpful critique, gracious encouragement, and guiding wisdom were priceless. Let me say a special thanks to Chris Brooks for his encouraging friendship, believing so strongly in this project and being eager to write the foreword.

Partnering with InterVarsity Press has once again been a true delight for me. I truly love the InterVarsity Press culture of excellence and its God-glorifying mission. From beginning to end, Cindy Bunch has been a cheerleader for this book and with her skillful hands has shaped beautifully its development from conception to completion. Rachel Hastings has been an amazing project editor, making this book much better each step of the way! Cindy and Rachel, I would climb any manuscript mountain with you at my side.

I want to thank my esteemed Made to Flourish colleagues Matt Rusten and Kevin Harlan as well as all our national staff and city network coordinators. Thanks for the privilege of serving with you in a most important mission to equip pastors and their churches to integrate faith, work, and economic wisdom for the flourishing of their communities. I am most grateful for Made to Flourish board members, Rod Brenneman, Lisa Slayton, Kyle Bode, Jeff Wright, Chris Brooks, Bill Wells, and Scott Gulledge, who have been supportive of this writing project and serve so faithfully with such rare wisdom and tireless devotion.

One of the treasured grace gifts of my life and work is the encouraging friendship and generous support of the Kern family, the Kern Family Foundation staff, and the Kern Family Foundation board. I am so thankful that in God's good and mysterious sovereignty our paths crossed, and our hearts have been knitted together in a worthy mission. Keep up the great work you are doing in promoting and furthering the common good. You are writing a wonderful story and forging a long-lasting legacy.

I am deeply grateful for the high privilege of serving the Christ Community Church family now for more than three decades. My eyes fill with joyful tears when I realize I have had a front row seat in the development, growth, and influence of such a remarkable local church congregation. It has been quite an exhilarating journey. Each one of you who call Christ Community home continue to teach me what it means to be a shepherd leader and an apprentice of Jesus, flourishing with joy in the rugged terrain of bold faith. I want to especially thank the Christ Community elder board for their faithful leadership as well as encouraging support for this book. I also want to express my deep gratitude for my Christ Community pastoral colleagues and staff who continue to be encouraging colaborers and wise teachers in my life. A special thanks to Nathan Miller, Mark Askins, Andrew Jones, Reid Kapple, Bill Gorman, Gabe Coyle, and Tim Spanburg. May you always shepherd the flock with integrity of heart and skillful hands.

In this season of nourishing a healthier life, a deeper intimacy with Christ, and stewarding greater generativity in my life and work, God has given me a treasured gift in the friendship and coaching of Bill Hendricks. What a joy it has been, Bill, to reconnect with you after many years. I am so grateful for your depth of experience, remarkable wisdom, and impeccable character. On several occasions, you have exhorted me to steward and share what I have been given to a new and rising generation. I trust that this book is a tangible response to your exhortation. Thank you for that exhortation and may your heart be warmed as you read it.

Lastly, I want to thank every pastor for your service to the bride of Christ. You matter and your calling matters. Whatever ministry context God has placed you in and whatever circumstances you are facing, my prayer is that you would sense the tender, unmistakable presence of the Good Shepherd in your life who delights in you and chose you. May you know in the deepest depths of your heart that Jesus the Good Shepherd delights in you. May you shepherd with integrity of heart and skillful hands, keeping the good news of the gospel close to your heart. May you live each day with eternity on your heart leaning into that hopeful expectation of hearing, "Well done, good and faithful servant, enter into the joy of your Master."

Soli Deo Gloria

DISCUSSION GUIDE

Introduction and Chapter 1:
A Calling in Crisis

REFLECT

1. When a pastor flourishes, what other entities does Nelson say flourish as a result?

2. According to the author, what external forces and internal realities make pastoral leadership "a calling in crisis"?

3. What three paths highlighted in this book do some pastors follow to become "lost shepherds"?

4. How do disordered loves contribute to each of the broken leadership paradigms surveyed in chapter one?

5. What factors contribute to the rise of a celebrity pastor?

RELATE

1. Nelson writes that young pastors see "way too few examples of pastors who continue to flourish over the long haul of pastoral leadership." What flourishing—or floundering—pastoral leaders have influenced you?

2. Nelson indicates that "classic spiritual disciplines, interpersonal neurobiology, and attachment theory" comprise part of his pastoral formation skills. What practices and disciplines have most affected your own pastoral formation?

3. Dietrich Bonhoeffer said, "The man who fashions a visionary ideal of community demands that it be realized by God, by others, and by himself," and that when the ideal does not come to pass, "he becomes, first an accuser of his brethren, then an accuser of God, and finally the despairing accuser of himself." When have you seen this pattern in yourself or others?

4. What model of pastoral effectiveness has been held up as the ideal in your church, your denomination, or your own mind? How do these compare to the "perilous paths" Nelson lays out?

APPLY

1. What in your own life convinced you that God was calling you to the pastoral vocation?

2. When have you, like the author's new acquaintance Dave, been in a season of ministry where you were "smiling on the outside, but dying on the inside"?

3. Which of the "lost shepherd" pastors are you most in danger of becoming? What heart idols does this suggest?

4. What relationships do you need to rekindle or seek out to increase life-giving authentic connection and avoid pastoral isolation?

SESSION TWO

Chapter 2: Finding Our Way Home
and Chapter 3: The Lord Is My Shepherd

REFLECT

1. What does Nelson refer to as "our true north"? How would you express this in your own words?

2. Why is it so important for pastors to embrace the truth that "the gospel is about a person"?

3. What are Nelson's "five navigational guideposts" for the journey as a pastoral leader?

4. A shepherd's call to leadership "is to provide, protect, and guide." Whom (and what) do pastors provide for, protect, and guide?

5. What does Nelson mean when he says, "Pastors who lead well are well led"?

RELATE

1. A. W. Tozer said, "What comes into our minds when we think about God is the most important thing about us." What comes to your mind?

2. How do you see yourself in and embody the good-news story of "original creation, fall, redemption, and new creation"?

3. What challenges the ability of pastoral leaders to see and embrace that "obscurity is a good place to be"?

4. How are you working on building your leadership competency? How can you communicate within your local church the importance of growing in this area?

5. How would we, and other pastors, flourish better by truly knowing that our shepherd will never abandon us?

APPLY

1. Practice retelling the "four-chapter story" to yourself, your pastoral colleagues, or a mentor. How does this good-news story animate your heart, soul, body, thoughts, and words? How does this story apply to the pastoral vocation?

2. Galatians 4:9 says, "But now . . . you have come to know God, or rather to be known by God." Do you think of yourself as known by God? Do you feel known by God? Is there something within you that resists being known by God?

3. What time horizon have you been focusing on in your ministry? How could this relate to the successes or struggles you are facing?

4. Read Psalm 23 aloud, thinking about experiencing God's shepherding leadership of you specifically in your pastoral calling.

5. What great need, overwhelming challenge, broken relationship, or other circumstance do you need to place in God's loving, caring, and capable hands? Take time right now to do so.

SESSION THREE

Chapter 4: The Integral Life,
Chapter 5: Apprenticeship with Jesus,
and Chapter 6: Pursuing Wholeness

REFLECT

1. What does it mean to say that "integrity is an ontological reality"?

2. Nelson says that living before an audience of One is "not only the ongoing cultivation of intimacy with God, but also the daily realization of our accountability to God." How are these ways of living connected, and how are they distinct?

3. Without Jesus' Great Invitation, "the Great Commandment becomes the Great Setup" and "the Great Commission becomes the Great Omission." Explain what Nelson means by this.

4. What are some common themes of proper self-care for a pastor?

RELATE

1. How does understanding the integral life to which God calls us redefine what an influential life looks like? Who in your life has shown this kind of influence with you?

2. Like the friend who suggested that Nelson's egocentric language might reflect a heart desire to look good in front of others, have

you ever had someone probe the heart motivations of your word choices in teaching and preaching? How did you react?

3. How does the image of being yoked to Jesus differ from other models of pastoral leadership?

4. What is the closest thing to an apprenticeship relationship that you have experienced in your life? What "tacit" knowledge or skills did you gain from that person?

5. How are you "breathing in beauty" in your home environment and in your life overall? Give some concrete examples of steps you have taken or can take.

APPLY

1. In what ways does your heart reveal a fragmented disintegration? Is there any area of your life that is presently off limits to the guidance, encouragement, comfort, and transformation of Jesus' presence? Seek out a spiritual director or a safe pastoral colleague to help you uncover any areas of willful disobedience in your life. Trust that healing confession and life-changing, heart-level repentance will be invaluable both to you and to the people you serve as a pastoral leader.

2. Read Matthew 11:28-30, envisioning Jesus speaking these words directly to you in the context of your pastoral leadership vocation. How have you responded to Jesus' Great Invitation?

3. In what practical ways are you pursuing comprehensive wholeness—that is, practicing virtue, living relationally, seeing seamlessly, and walking wisely? Which of these is a weak area for you?

4. What priority does stewarding your physicality—particularly, your physical health—currently take in your life? How are you embracing the sabbatical principle in your life? How are you ruthlessly eliminating hurry?

5. How has your family of origin shaped and misshaped you? What are your biggest stressors and anxiety triggers? How does stress negatively influences you with illness, irritability, forgetfulness, and relational depletion? Consider seeking out a professional counselor to help you grow in emotional well-being and personal maturity.

SESSION FOUR

Chapter 7: A Faithful Presence
and Chapter 8: Cultivating a Flourishing Culture

REFLECT

1. How does Nelson define "skillful hands"?

2. In what ways do pastors have the "vital role of institutional developer" within their churches?

3. List the four foundational conditions for a flourishing organizational culture in a local church.

4. What is the difference between a mission statement and a "hedgehog"?

RELATE

1. Nelson says, "Discerning our particular times will require us to read historically and widely, listen attentively, and observe carefully shapers of the broader culture such as education, economics, media, movies, technology, art, and politics." What resources help you do this? What areas are a weak point for you?

2. How does Nelson's description of "faithful presence" correspond to or contrast with your local church's current role in your community?

3. Nelson writes about the Four Chapter Gallery at their downtown campus. What other church initiatives that you know of successfully collaborate with artists, share the beauty of nature, or otherwise promote truth, goodness, and beauty?

4. In what ways do your experiences with church leadership bear out or challenge the idea that as pastors, we "must take our mission seriously, but we must also see relationships as primary in accomplishing that mission"?

5. In what ways have you as a pastor kept "the past alive through storytelling"? What particular type of storytelling is most needed in your church right now?

APPLY

1. Examine your heart for a spirit of competitiveness with other pastors or other organizations in your community. Determine, instead, to embrace a kingdom mindset. How could you better serve and support other pastors in your community? What collaborative partnerships for the common good could your church support better?

2. Pastors create the relational "tone" for a church, cultivating a soil of close, loving relationships within the church. What opportunities are you providing for congregants to connect deeply with each other in a small group context? How are the sheep you shepherd knowing others and being known by others?

3. How have you experienced the "temptation to minimize doctrine, dismiss, distort, or even neglect scriptural truth that goes against the grain of contemporary culture"? How have you responded to that temptation?

4. What are the clearly defined core values of your local church? How do you as a pastoral leader communicate those core values? How does your church orient new members of your staff and congregation to your core values? What core values need greater attention?

5. How are you evaluating the level of present embodiment of your church's core values in your staff and stakeholders? Consider how you can gain feedback from others about their perception of the core values at your church.

Chapter 9: Connecting Sunday to Monday,
Chapter 10: A New Scorecard,
and Chapter 11: Finishing Well

REFLECT

1. Explain Nelson's use of the term "pastoral malpractice" for failing to equip his congregation for their Monday worlds.

2. What does Nelson mean by "plausibility structures," and how are these altered by Christians doing excellent work with Christlike attitude?

3. What "five marks of skillful shepherding" does Nelson say should be prominent on the pastoral ministry "scorecard"?

4. How does Nelson label and define four major threats to finishing well as a pastor?

5. What are "black swan" events, and how do pastors weather them faithfully?

RELATE

1. What professions are represented in your church? How can you learn more about how congregants spend the majority of their time?

2. What are some ways you have affirmed the mission field of "work" during a Sunday worship services? What other practices would

you consider incorporating? (See the section "Bringing Monday into Sunday.")

3. What is the same about your external pastoral ministry "scorecard" (such as a performance review) and your internal pastoral ministry "scorecard"? What is different?

4. In what ways have you seen other pastoral leaders invest their lives in the people and institutions that will outlast them?

5. Read 2 Timothy 4:6-7. How do the military, athletic, and monetary metaphors of this passage relate to other Scriptures addressing long-term faithfulness?

APPLY

1. Ask God to search your heart for an elevation of the pastoral vocation that subtly considers those not employed in vocational ministry as "second-class citizens" or as merely providing the necessary funding for the "real" work of the church. Pay attention to the words you use over the next week and reflect on how they reveal your heart attitude.

2. Begin to think and pray about the best way to influence your church culture toward closer connections with congregants in their workplaces.

3. If Jesus were to give your annual review, what would he say about who you are becoming, the proper ordering of your loves, and how you are leading?

4. How are you intentionally investing your life and wisdom into a smaller group of leaders?

5. How will you continue to grow in greater intimacy, to stay curious, to stay disciplined in your walk with Jesus? How will you embrace discipline and practice while keeping relational intimacy with Jesus at the center?

NOTES

INTRODUCTION

[1]Though the terms *vocation* and *calling* have historically been used synonymously, we are using the phrase *vocational calling* as a contemporary nuance to mean the work God calls us to.

[2]See the following books and articles using various methodologies to analyze the state of pastors in ministry: Barna Group, *The State of Pastors: How Today's Faith Leaders Are Navigating Life and Leadership in an Age of Complexity* (Ventura, CA: Barna Group, 2017); Matt Bloom and The Flourishing in Ministry Project, "Flourishing in Ministry: Emerging Research Insights on the Well-Being of Pastors" (Notre Dame, IN: Mendoza College of Business, 2013), https://wellbeing.nd.edu/assets/198819/emerging _insights_2_1_.pdf; M. Chaves and A. Eagle, "Following Wave III: Religious Congregations in 21st Century America" (Durham, NC: Department of Sociology, Duke University, 2015), https://sites.duke.edu/ncsweb/files/2019/02/NCSIII_report_final.pdf; Holly G. Miller, "Sustaining Pastoral Excellence: A Progress Report on a Lilly Endowment Initiative" (Durham, NC: Leadership Education at Duke Divinity, 2011); R. J. Proeschold-Bell and J. Byassee, *Faithful and Fractured: Responding to the Clergy Health Crisis* (Grand Rapids, MI: Baker Academic, 2018).

1 A CALLING IN CRISIS

[1]See the full report in Matt Bloom, *Flourishing in Ministry: How to Cultivate Clergy Wellbeing* (Lanham, MD: Rowman & Littlefield, 2019). Bloom provides a helpful summary:

> It appears that more pastors today are finding their work too tough and demanding. We find that a significant portion of pastors experience high work demands and high levels of work-related stress. Our data also show that a considerable number of pastors report low levels of work-life balance. Perhaps most alarming, we find that over one-third of pastors are experiencing high to severe levels of burnout.

These data are clear indicators that some pastors—too many in our view—are overburdened. . . . The potential for overinvestments in ministry work are high because it can be difficult for pastors to find the tipping point between positive engagement and over sacrificing, between fatigue due to a ministry job well done and exhaustion due to overinvesting.

[2]Bloom, *Flourishing in Ministry*, 6.

[3]Henri J. M. Nouwen, *In the Name of Jesus: Reflections on Christian Leadership* (New York: Crossroad Publishing, 1989), 20.

[4]"The immanent frame" is a term penned by philosopher Charles Taylor to describe the loss of the plausibility of a transcendent reality in the secular West. A larger explanation can be found later in chapter seven. See Charles Taylor, *A Secular Age* (Cambridge, MA: Harvard University Press, 2007).

[5]Note the broader explanation framed in Ralph H. Alexander, *Ezekiel*, TEBC (Grand Rapids, MI: Zondervan, 1986), 911:

> Israel's leaders had thought only of themselves and material gain. They had not cared for the "flock" (v. 3). Instead of feeding the flock, they fed on the flock, taking for themselves instead of providing for the people. They had failed to provide for the needy—those weak and sick. They had not sought for sheep that had been lost. They did not care what happened to the people as long as the leaders had all their own personal needs met. They were harsh and brutal in their rule (v. 4). God makes it clear that a leader has a primary responsibility to care for those he leads, even at the sacrifice of his own desires. . . . Lack of leadership always leads to the disintegration of God's people and personal and corporate heartache and injury. Leadership carries an awesome responsibility.

[6]Ezekiel's message is not only hard-hitting in Ezekiel 34, it becomes hopeful. Ezekiel establishes that God himself will take on the role of shepherd (Ezek 34:11-12) and then will appoint a shepherd in the line of David (Ezek 34:23-24). Here God points in these two persons—God and the Davidic king—to the incarnate Son: the perfect shepherd whom the people of God have desperately longed for (cf. John 10:11).

[7]For Saint Augustine, the proper ordering of love makes virtue, and loving things out of order results in vice. In a real sense, the heart of disordered love is idolatry. Yet having our loves in the right order allows us to love all things properly, with the result that we ourselves take on the right form, since according to the African saint, we are what we love. Thus, it is not the things themselves that are wrong; it is the way these things are loved. "This is true of everything created; though it is good, it can be loved in the right way or in the wrong way—in the right way, that is, when the proper order is kept, in the wrong way, when that order is upset." See Saint Augustine, *City of God*, XV.22.

[8]David French, "The Crisis of Christian Celebrity," *The French Press*, accessed December 14, 2020, https://frenchpress.thedispatch.com/p/the-crisis-of-christian-celebrity. Similarly,

see Ben Sixsmith's article on Hillsong's Carl Lentz in "The Sad Irony of Celebrity Pastors," *The Spectator*, December 6, 2020, https://spectator.us/life/sad-irony-celebrity -pastors-carl-lentz-hillsong/.

[9]French, "Crisis of Christian Celebrity."

[10]i.e., the effects of "liquid courage."

[11]Whereas his actual words are, "[Christ] must increase, but I must decrease" (Jn 3:30).

[12]Proverbs 29:18 Various translations have contributed to reinforcing the idea of vision. "Where there is no vision the people are unrestrained, but happy is he who keeps the Law" (NASB); "Where there is no vision, the people perish: but he that keepeth the law, happy is he" (KJV).

[13]The NIV translates Proverbs 29:18, "Where there is no revelation, the people cast off restraint; but blessed is the one who heeds wisdom's instruction." The ESV translates Proverbs 29:18, "Where there is no prophetic vision the people cast off restraint, but blessed is he who keeps the law." The Hebrew word under question is *ḥāzôn*. According to Warren Baker and Eugene Carpenter, *The Complete Word Study Dictionary: Old Testament* (Chattanooga, TN: AMG Publishers, 2003), 325, *ḥāzôn* is best understood as meaning "revelation by means of a vision ... [in which] the primary essence of this word is not so much the vision or dream itself as the message conveyed. It signifies the direct, specific communication between God and people through the prophetic office." Notice how *revelation* better captures this idea, since *vision* tends to prototype seeing into the future or looking into insightfully, ultimately foregrounding the seer, whereas *revelation* brings to mind the fact of God communicating with people. Following this semantic prototype, John Goldingay prefers the term *revelation* and accepts the translation "where there is no revelation" to mean "where God's revelation is ignored"; see John Goldingay, *Proverbs of Solomon*, NBC (Downers Grove, IL: InterVarsity Press, 1994), 604. In other words, the author of Proverbs appeals to the readers to heed the revealed word of God in prophetic oracles just as they would the law. This is apparent in the negative-positive parallelism of "no revelation leads to no restraint" (negative) and "keeping the law leads to blessing" (positive). Revelation parallels the law in a loose ABAB pattern in the Hebrew. Clearly then, this is not referring to "vision" as used in present pastoral parlance.

[14]Note the word translated "law" is the Hebrew word *Torah* that here refers specifically to the first five books of the Old Testament.

[15]Dietrich Bonhoeffer, *Life Together* (New York: HarperCollins Publishers, 1954), 15.

[16]Jim Bakker, *I Was Wrong* (Nashville: Thomas Nelson Publishers, 1996), 471.

[17]See Lynsey M. Barron and William P. Eiselstein, "Report of Independent Investigation into Sexual Misconduct of Ravi Zacharias," report released by Miller and Martin, PLLC, February 9, 2021, https://s3-us-west-2.amazonaws.com/rzimmedia.rzim.org/assets /downloads/Report-of-Investigation.pdf.

[18]I have felt the personal heartbreak as well as the painful encounter with refugees from abusive, toxic visionary environments. Three very visible examples of this have been, for

me, International House of Prayer, Willow Creek Community Church, and Harvest Bible Chapel.

[19]See Jim Collins, *Good to Great* (New York: Harper Business, 2001). Collins identifies the characteristics that differentiate great organizations from good ones, which includes an abandonment of a leadership model that centralizes one figure: "In contrast to [great] companies, which built deep and strong executive teams, many of the [good] companies followed a 'genius with a thousand helpers' model. In this model, the company is a platform for the talents of an extraordinary individual" (45-46). This contrasts with a leader of a great organization, "who blends extreme personal humility with intense professional will" (21).

[20]Bloom, *Flourishing in Ministry*, 81.

[21]Rae Jean Proeschold-Bell and Jason Byassee, *Faithful and Fractured* (Grand Rapids, MI: Baker Academic, 2018), 74.

[22]Bob Burns, Tasha D. Chapman, and Donald Guthrie, *Resilient Ministry* (Downers Grove, IL: InterVarsity Press, 2013), 20.

[23]Barna Group, *The 2017 State of Pastors* research presentation, www.barna.com /watchpastors2017/.

[24]Johanna Flashman, "Alex Honnold Completes First Free Solo of El Capitan," *Climbing*, June 6, 2017, www.climbing.com/news/alex-honnold-completes-first-free-solo-of -el-capitan/.

[25]*Free Solo*, directed by Jimmy Chin and Elizabeth Chai Vasarhelyi, featuring Alex Honnold (National Geographic, 2018), streaming (Disney+, 2021).

[26]Nouwen, *In the Name of Jesus*, 40-41.

2 FINDING OUR WAY HOME

[1]Philosopher Immanuel Kant's words featured at the Adler Planetarian in Chicago resonate deeply with my wonderment, "Two things astound me: the sky above me and the moral law within me." This is an adaptation of the fuller quote: "Two things fill the mind with ever new and increasing admiration and awe, the oftener and the more steadily we reflect on them: the starry heavens above and the moral law within." Immanuel Kant, "Conclusion," in *Critique of Practical Reason*, www.gutenberg .org/files/5683/5683-h/5683-h.htm#link2H_CONC.

[2]A.W. Tozer, *The Knowledge of the Holy* (New York: Harper & Brothers, 1961), 9.

[3]The typical categories ascribed to these dual realities are general and special revelation. Article 2 of the Belgic Confession speaks of the "elegant book" before our eyes, the created world around us, which makes known to us something of God. Paul reflects this in Romans 1:20 and the psalmist in Psalm 19:1-6. Yet the second book provides the special and final revelation of God in Jesus Christ. Only the contents of this book are the inspired word of God, necessary and sufficient for our salvation. See 2 Timothy 3:16-17; 1 Corinthians 2:13; 1 Peter 1:10-11; Romans 10:10-15.

[4]I want to thank my friend Mike Metzger, who spoke into our faith community and helped translate this into the *ought, is, can,* and *will.*

[5]Simon Sinek, *Start with Why* (New York: Penguin Group, 2009), 39.

[6]Westminster Shorter Catechism's first question is, What is the purpose of human life? The answer: "Man's chief end is to glorify God and to enjoy him forever." www .opc.org/sc.html.

[7]The biblical story of David includes the deepest valleys of human brokenness and also the highest mountains of intimacy. Even in this tension, the biblical authors present the whole of David's story as an example to follow.

[8]See Timothy S. Laniak, *Shepherds After My Own Heart* (Downers Grove, IL: Inter-Varsity Press, 2006). Also see his website, www.ShepherdLeader.com.

[9]Timothy S. Laniak, *While Shepherds Watch Their Flocks* (Franklin, TN: Carpenter's Son Publishing, 2012), 17.

[10]A pastor friend of mine John Yates puts it this way: "If you don't love people, you are in the wrong business."

[11]Larry Osborne, *Lead Like a Shepherd* (Nashville: Thomas Nelson, 2018), 41.

[12]Laniak, *While Shepherds Watch Their Flocks,* 24.

[13]Chapter four will provide a robust definition of integrity and the Hebrew word translated throughout the Old Testament. For now, what is important to note is the semantic range that includes wholeness, uprightness, and integrity. It describes a way of living that is rooted in a transcendent connection with an immanent God.

[14]Originally written by Robert Lowry.

[15]I'm grateful for my friend Stephen Garber for the great phrase, "fabric of faithfulness."

[16]Bob Burns, Tasha D. Chapman, and Donald Guthrie, *Resilient Ministry* (Downers Grove, IL: InterVarsity Press, 2013), 26.

3 THE LORD IS MY SHEPHERD

[1]Larry Osborne, *Lead Like a Shepherd* (Nashville: Thomas Nelson, 2018), 21.

[2]Martin Luther, trans. Frederick H. Hedge, "A Mighty Fortress Is Our God," composed between 1527–29.

[3]Eugene H. Peterson, *Working the Angles: The Shape of Pastoral Integrity* (Grand Rapids, MI: Eerdmans, 1989), 166.

[4]Peterson, *Working the Angles,* 57.

[5]Dallas Willard, *Life Without Lack* (Nashville: Thomas Nelson Publishers, 2018), 1.

[6]For a further discussion of the background of Psalm 23 see Frank E. Gaebelein, *The Expositors Bible* (Grand Rapids, MI: Zondervan Publishing, 1991), 5:214. "Its original setting or situation in life is difficult to determine. S. Gelinder concludes that the psalmist was a king who in his trouble was confident in Yahweh's ability to deliver him.... Jack R. Lundblom suggests that the psalm is set in the wilderness at the time of David's flight from Absalom."

[7] Henri J. M. Nouwen, *Show Me the Way* (New York: The Crossroad Publishing Company, 1992), 106.

[8] See the excellent work of Timothy S. Laniak, *While Shepherds Watch Their Flocks* (Franklin, TN: Carpenter's Son Publishing, 2012). Laniak provides both cultural and exegetical clarity around the all-encompassing nature of the shepherd leading. "Three key Hebrew verbs are used for leading a flock. *Nahal* means leading with tenderness and can refer to bringing a flock to a place of rest and refreshment. *Nakhah* [*nāḥâ*] is a straightforward guidance verb. *Nahag* suggests the kind of directive herding accomplished best from the back of the flock, when the will of the shepherd has to be imposed" (196-97).

[9] The world of crisis described by Volatility, Uncertainty, Complexity, and Ambiguity (VUCA) permeates the training expectations for military leadership. It now is well-known and applied to many different fields. See, e.g., David Slocum, "Six Creative Leadership Lessons from the Military in an Era of VUCA and COIN," *Forbes*, October 8, 2013, www.forbes.com/sites/berlinschoolofcreativeleadership/2013/10/08/six-creative-leadership-lessons-from-the-military-in-an-era-of-vuca-and-coin/#414aacf72a5b.

[10] Civilla D. Martin, "God Will Take Care of You," 1904.

[11] Dallas Willard, *Life Without Lack*, xvii.

4 THE INTEGRAL LIFE

[1] Francis Schaeffer echoes my own deep crisis of faith around the lack of spiritual transformation in his own life and those he led in the church. Francis Schaeffer writes transparently to his wife, Edith, about his struggle. "Edith, I feel really torn to pieces by the lack of reality, the lack of seeing the results the Bible talks about, which should be seen in the Lord's people. I'm not talking only about people I'm working with in 'The Movement,' but I'm not satisfied with myself. It seems that the only honest thing to do is to rethink, reexamine the whole matter of Christianity." See Francis Schaeffer, *True Spirituality* (Wheaton, IL: Tyndale House Publishers, 2001), xvi.

[2] Henry David Thoreau poignantly says, "The mass of men lead lives of quiet desperation" in *Walden* (Weymouth, MA: Great Pond Press, 2020), 11.

[3] Os Guinness, *The Call* (Nashville: Thomas Nelson, 2003), 4.

[4] James Davison Hunter, *To Change the World* (New York: Oxford University Press, 2010), 224.

[5] "Heart" (*lēb*) in the Old Testament has no English equivalent. It is used 853 times in the Old Testament; the body's functions (1 Sam 25:37-38), intellect (Prov 24:2), will (Ex 14:5), and spiritual functions (Prov 3:5) are attributed to the heart. Harris, Archer, and Waltke note, "in its abstract meanings, 'heart' becomes the richest biblical term for the totality of man's inner or immaterial nature. In biblical literature it is the most frequently used term for man's immaterial personality functions as well as the most inclusive term for them since, in the Bible, virtually every immaterial function of man is attributed to the 'heart.'"

See Laird Harris, Gleason Archer, and Bruce Waltke, *Theological Workbook of the Old Testament* (Chicago: Moody Press, 1980), 466. Waltke expands, "Paradoxically, the eyes and ears are gates to those factors that shape the heart (Prov 2:2; 4:21-27), and the heart in turn decides what they see and hear." Bruce K. Waltke, *An Old Testament Theology* (Grand Rapids, MI: Zondervan, 2007), 226. For a further biblical theological description of "heart" see Waltke's whole section on *lēḇ*, 225-27.

[6]Dallas Willard, *Revolution of Character* (Colorado Springs: NavPress, 2005), 23.

[7]Curt Thompson, *Anatomy of the Soul* (Wheaton, IL: Tyndale House Publishers, 2010), 169.

[8]Ethics seeks to understand moral duty, what truly moral people ought to do (deontology). In this case, integrity would refer to actions that an integral person should make like telling the truth. Ontology, on the other hand, discusses the very nature of being or existence. Tibor Machan in his *Introduction to Philosophical Inquiries* (Boston: Allan and Bacon, 1977), 343, defines ontology as "The branch of metaphysics that studies the types of being there are or could be. Also the study of the basic kinds of items in reality." For integrity to be an ontological reality means that it does not merely prescribe personal actions, it prescribes personhood, a way of being—who someone is at the core of his or her being. Someone's very nature of being is integral.

[9]The word group for *tōm / tamim* includes both noun and adjectival forms: *tōm* as the noun form and *tom* and *tāmîm* as the adjectival forms. Francis Brown, S. R. Driver, and Charles A. Briggs, *A Hebrew and English Lexicon of the Old Testament* (New York: Oxford University Press, 1952) translates the noun form (*tōm*) with a range of possibilities: completeness, integrity, fullness, innocence, and simplicity (1070). The adjectival forms (*tam / tamim*) follow suit: complete, perfect, sound wholesome, and morally innocent (1071). Ideas of moral action and ethics, then, naturally flow from the idea of completeness. However, the idea is not that of self-righteousness or perfectionism, which is warned against in R. Laird Harris, Gleason L. Archer, Jr., and Bruce K. Waltke, *Theological Wordbook of the Old Testament* (Chicago: Moody Publishers, 2003), 974.

[10]As far as its connection to wise living, Proverbs is littered with the word group usage throughout its entirety (Prov 1:12; 2:7, 21; 10:9, 29; 11:3, 5, 20; 13:6; 19:1; 20:7; 28:6, 10, 18; 29:10). In suffering, the book of Job also demonstrates that faithful suffering requires integrity (see Job 1:1, 8; 2:3, 9; 4:6; 8:20; 9:20, 21, 22; 12:4; 21:23; 27:5; 31:6; 36:4; 37:16).

[11]What is translated "walk before me" is literally "walk in my face." The Hebrew word *pānîm*—which means face—with the imperative "to walk" communicates an intimate walk that is ever before and in the presence of God. The closeness is more akin to walking hand in hand with a spouse than before a distant observer.

[12]Brother Lawrence, *Practicing the Presence of God* (Springdale, PA: Whitaker House, 1982), 59.

[13]Thompson, *Anatomy of the Soul*, 169.

[14]See Jesus' parable of the talents in Matthew 25:14-30.

[15]In the moment of temptation when desire takes over a person, Bonhoeffer says, "At this moment God is quite unreal to us. He loses all reality, and only desire for the creature is real. The only reality is the devil. Satan does not here fill us with hatred of God, but with forgetfulness of God." Dietrich Bonhoeffer, *Temptation*, in "Temptation and Forgetfulness of God: Dietrich Bonhoeffer," *The Sovereign* (blog), June 2, 2014, https://thesovereign .wordpress.com/2014/06/02/temptation-and-forgetfulness-of-god-dietrich-bonhoeffer.

[16]C. S. Lewis, *The Lion, the Witch, and the Wardrobe* (New York: Macmillan Publishing Company, 1970), 75-76.

[17]Again, we have the appearance of the word *tōm*, but it is preceded by the imperatival form of "to be." God the Almighty commands Abraham to walk a life that is not only before him, but is integral. The two commands go hand in hand. An intimate life before God is a life of integrity.

[18]See Genesis 17:5-8.

[19]Charles H. Spurgeon, "All for Jesus," in *The Metropolitan Tabernacle Pulpit, Vol. 20 (Year 1874)* (Pilgrim Publications, 1971).

[20]Steven Garber, *The Seamless Life* (Downers Grove, IL: InterVarsity Press, 2020), 2.

[21]*Tōm* appears sixteen times in the book of Job (Job 1:1, 8; 2:3, 9; 4:6; 8:20; 9:20, 21, 22; 12:4; 21:23; 27:5; 31:6; 36:4; 37:16).

[22]Job 1:8, "The LORD said to Satan, 'Have you considered My servant Job? For there is no one like him on the earth, a blameless [*tōm*] and upright man, fearing God and turning way from evil'" (NASB; cf. Job 2:3).

[23]The verb to "walk" (*hālak*) appears with "integrity" elsewhere: Psalm 101:2b, "I will walk within my house in the integrity of my heart" (NASB). In Proverbs 2:7 and the rest of the book, integrity involves living a distinct way of life. The wisdom of Proverbs suggests that integrity is a lifestyle lived out in the holy fear of God.

[24]See Viktor Frankl, *Man's Search for Meaning* (Boston: Beacon Press, 2006). Frankl made the point that we find meaning in the relationships we have, the work we do, and the suffering we encounter in life.

5 APPRENTICESHIP WITH JESUS

[1]Dietrich Bonhoeffer, *The Cost of Discipleship* (New York: Touchstone, 1995), 89.

[2]Henri J. M. Nouwen, *In the Name of Jesus: Reflections on Christian Leadership* (New York: Crossroad Publishing, 1989), 62.

[3]Francis Schaeffer, *True Spirituality* (Wheaton, IL: Tyndale House Publishers, 2001), 26.

[4]See Matthew 22:34-40.

[5]See Matthew 28:18-20.

[6]Dallas Willard uses this term to describe our impoverished discipleship in the church; *The Great Omission* (New York: HarperCollins, 2006).

[7]A. W. Tozer quotes Samuel Taylor Coleridge's *Aids to Reflection* in *God's Pursuit of Man* (Chicago: Moody Publishers, 2015), 18.

[8] Dane Ortlund captures the "who" well in his elegant and pastoral explanation of the heart of Christ from Matthew 11:28-30 in his book *Gentle and Lowly* (Wheaton, IL: Crossway, 2020). This book is a gift to any pastor seeking to learn and share the heart of Christ.

[9] Bonhoeffer, *The Cost of Discipleship*, 59.

[10] The apostle Paul's sobering words describe the peril of ministerial works done out of wrong motives and for human glory as wood, hay, and stubble, one day tested by fire. "Each one's work will become manifest, for the Day will disclose it, because it will be revealed by fire, and the fire will test what sort of work each one has done" (1 Cor 3:13).

[11] Nouwen, *In the Name of Jesus*, 17.

[12] Elizabeth Akers, Jeff Capps, and Michael Bleeker, "Come to Me," Blecker Publishing, 2011.

[13] Bonhoeffer, *The Cost of Discipleship*, 93.

[14] Gerhard Kittel, *Theological Dictionary of the New Testament*, trans. Geoffrey W. Bromiley (Grand Rapids, MI: Eerdmans, 1964), 2:898-901, says that Jesus' words to come under his "yoke" ("my yoke;" *ton zugon mou*) stands in contrast to the "yoke of the law" (*Torah 'al*) and the yoke of wisdom (Sir 51:17) that rabbis opposing Jesus took apprentices under. Jesus' yoke is personal, marked by a gentle and lowly heart, where under the rabbis the yoke is the heavy law. Likewise, R. T. France indicates that the rabbis, in applying the "yoke of the law," could create a heavy burden for their apprentices, *Matthew*, NBC (Downers Grove, IL: InterVarsity Press, 1994), 918.

[15] Michael Polanyi, *Personal Knowledge* (Chicago: University of Chicago Press, 2015), 53.

[16] Dallas Willard, *The Spirit of the Disciplines* (New York: HarperCollins, 1999), 9.

[17] The exact phrasing in the Greek is *gymnaze de seauton*, but we want to focus on *gymnazō*. The noun form of the word refers to being naked in the ancient world and the verb is literally to exercise naked, which refers to the athletic arena in the ancient world; See Gerhard Kittel, *Theological Dictionary of the New Testament*, (Grand Rapids, MI: Eerdmans, 1977), 1:773-76. Thus, the metaphorical extension that Paul envisions is one of intense training and exercise in the arena of godliness.

[18] Klaus Issler, *Living into the Life of Jesus* (Downers Grove, IL: InterVarsity Press, 2012), 108, advances, "Unless today's believers engage the empowering resource of the Holy Spirit—who is the divine agent of sanctification (Rom. 8:13, 2 Thess, 2:13, Titus 3:5, 1 Peter 1:2)—it is impossible to be formed into the image of Jesus Christ."

[19] Curt Thompson, *The Anatomy of the Soul* (Wheaton, IL: Tyndale House Publishers, 2010), 180.

[20] For a much greater explanation of these spiritual practices, see my book, *The Five Smooth Stones* (Grand Island, NE: Cross Training Publishing, 2001). Also, I would highly recommend Dallas Willard's excellent book *The Spirit of the Disciplines*.

[21] Bonhoeffer, *The Cost of Discipleship*, 45, 54.

[22] See Hebrews 4, which connects God's rest in the garden with Jesus' atoning work on the cross that makes true rest possible when we enter that rest in faith.

6 PURSUING WHOLENESS

[1]Darrin Patrick is quoted in Ed Stetzer, "A Pastor's Restoration Process: Journey to Healing Through the Eyes of Those Closest, Part 1: Darrin," *Christianity Today*, March 16, 2019, www.christianitytoday.com/edstetzer/2019/may/pastors-restoration -process-journey-to-healing-through-eyes.html.

[2]Read about the tragic death in Ed Stetzer, "Darrin Patrick's Death, His Love for Pastors, and How We Need One Another," *Christianity Today*, May 9, 2020, www.christianity-today.com/edstetzer/2020/may/remembering-darrin-pastors-mental-health.html.

[3]Anthony Hoekema, *Created in God's Image* (Grand Rapids, MI: Eerdmans, 1994), 203.

[4]Doug Webster, *The Easy Yoke* (Colorado Springs: NavPress, 1995), 84.

[5]Henri Nouwen, *The Wounded Healer* (New York: Doubleday, 1979), 72.

[6]The phrase "wounded healer" comes from Henri Nouwen's idiolect. For an example, see Nouwen, *The Wounded Healer*.

[7]One of the major reasons we struggle to grasp the importance of spiritual formation with virtue formation directly connects to how we understand the relationship between the body and the soul. Instead, Aristotelian virtue, which is recovered in Thomism, helps us understand the human as a psychosomatic whole, where body and soul form each other. Recovery of a theological psychology shows the need for virtuous embodied action in spiritual formation. Matthew A. LaPine, *Logic of the Body* (Bellingham, WA: Lexham Press, 2020) offers a retrieval theology that revives the theology of Thomas Aquinas's thinking that body and soul are connected in forming the other, in which LaPine calls it a dualistic holism. Likewise, James K. A. Smith, *You Are What You Love* (Grand Rapids, MI: Brazos Press, 2016) unpacks the formational impact of the physical world on the worship of our souls.

[8]Rebecca Konyndyk DeYoung, *Glittering Vices* (Grand Rapids, MI: Brazos Press, 2009), 17. I would highly recommend a careful reading of her excellent book both as a guide to pastoral leadership formation as well as congregational spiritual formation. I would also highly recommend Mark McCloskey and Jim Louwsma, *The Art of Virtue-Based Transformational Leadership* (Bloomington, MN: The Wordsmith, 2016).

[9]It seems that this is another way pastors have become chameleons in culture. David Brooks, in *The Road to Character* (New York: Random House, 2015), captures anemic virtue formation in Western contemporary culture. We are a culture obsessed with what he calls "résumé virtues"—things we put on a job application like skills and external success—and have lost sight of "eulogy virtues," which have preeminence since they are what people remember about us when we are gone. Today, classical virtues like prudence, justice, temperance, and courage subordinate to career building. Aquinas defends these virtues as cardinal virtues since they result from a pursuit and comprehensive understanding of truth and reality. Practical wisdom proceeds from truth-seeking into the cardinal virtue prudence; justice results from reason-guided ordering of the operations of the world; temperance from the ordering of passions. Courage is needed "to be strengthened for that which reason dictates, lest he turn back," *A Shorter Summa* ed. Peter Kreeft (San Francisco: Ignatius Press, 1993), 153-54.

Yet of course, there are the theological virtues of *faith, hope,* and *love* for what Aquinas calls "supernatural happiness." Paul concludes his words on love, "So now faith, hope, and love abide, these three; but the greatest of these is love" (1 Cor 13:13). These are the character-building virtues that should color a pastor, allowing the chameleon-scales of "résumé virtues" to fall off.

[10]The *tōm* root is found twice in Psalm 101:2 and once in Psalm 101:6. For more details on the word group, see chapter four.

[11]See Jim Wilder, *Renovated* (Colorado Springs: NavPress, 2020), on the framing of *ḥesed* in terms of attachment love.

[12]Marcus Warner and Jim Wilder, *Rare Leadership* (Chicago: Moody Publishers, 2016), 134.

[13]Other sources for help in marriage include Mike Mason, *The Mystery of Marriage* (Colorado Springs: Multnomah, 2005); Archibald Hart and Sharon Hart May, *Safe Haven* (Nashville: W Publishing Group, 2003); Tim Keller with Kathy Keller, *The Meaning of Marriage* (New York: Penguin Books, 2011); Tim Clinton and Gary Sibcy, *Why You Do the Things You Do* (Nashville: Thomas Nelson, 2006).

[14]See Wesley Hill, *Spiritual Friendship* (Grand Rapids, MI: Brazos Press, 2015); Sam Allberry, *7 Myths About Singleness* (Wheaton, IL: Crossway, 2019); Barry Danylak, *Redeeming Singleness: How the Storyline of Scripture Affirms the Single Life* (Wheaton, IL: Crossway, 2010).

[15]See chapter seven of Warner and Wilder, *Rare Leadership*, 123-40.

[16]The entirety of Psalm 101 is built around the theme of *tōm*, i.e., integral life.

[17]Martin Luther, trans. Frederick H. Hedge, "A Mighty Fortress Is Our God," ca. 1527–29.

[18]Maltbie D. Babcock, "This Is My Father's World," 1901.

[19]Steven Garber, *The Seamless Life* (Downers Grove, IL: InterVarsity Press, 2020), 47.

[20]Regarding seasons, see Psalm 1 for a season of fruitfulness; for a season for everything see, Ecclesiastes 3:1-8. On soil, see Jesus' parable of the four types of soil in Luke 8.

[21]See the bestselling book by Bessel van der Kolk, *The Body Keeps Score* (New York: Penguin Books, 2015), which shows the reshaping effects of trauma on the body and the use of physical activity as recovery and treatment.

[22]Warner and Wilder, *Rare Leadership*, 42.

[23]Curt Thompson, *The Soul of Shame* (Downers Grove, IL: InterVarsity Press, 2015), 14. I highly recommend Dr. Thompson's book that so powerfully communicates both the pervasive impact shame has on all of us as well as the way forward in healing shame.

[24]John Ortberg, *The Life You've Always Wanted* (Grand Rapids, MI: Zondervan, 2002), 76. John Mark Comer expands on this message he received from Ortberg in *The Ruthless Elimination of Hurry* (Colorado Springs: WaterBrook, 2019).

[25]I am grateful for my phone interview with John as he shared about his faithful life work in ministry.

7 A FAITHFUL PRESENCE

[1]Pastors have experienced intense congregational discord in the global coronavirus pandemic. Corporate gatherings, mask-wearing, and vaccinations couched in a tumultuous election and divisions on racism have wreaked havoc on the emotional life of pastors. Shepherd leaders need resiliency and cultural discernment as never before.

[2]John P. Kotter, *What Leaders Really Do* (Boston: Harvard Business School Press, 1999), 1.

[3]Psalm 78:72, "So he shepherded them according to the integrity of his heart, and guided them with his *skillful hands*" (emphasis added).

[4]The phrase "with skillful hands" is unique in the Old Testament, combining nowhere else the Hebrew word translated "skillful" (*tᵉbûnâ*) with any of the different Hebrew words for hand (*here*). The prototype gloss for *tᵉbûnâ* is "understanding," which includes in its semantic range something similar to wisdom, yet in several locations has the contextual meaning of some skill in the arts. For example, in Exodus 35:31, workers are filled with the Spirit in order to have the skill and "intelligence" (*tabunh*) to make artistic work (cf. Ex 31:3; 36:1). Similarly, workers are given the "understanding" (*tabunah*) to work in bronze (1 Kings 7:14). God himself made the heavens by "understanding" (Ps 136:5). Thus, the semantic range includes the meaning of abilities required for skilled or creative work. It's with this coloring that Psalm 78:72 seems to be using the word.

[5]Max DePree, *Leadership Is an Art* (Lansing: Michigan State University Press, 1987), 3.

[6]Charles Taylor, *A Secular Age* (Cambridge, MA: Harvard University Press, 2007), 2007.

[7]Two books help take the complex ideas of Charles Taylor and appropriate them to the pastoral context. See James K. A. Smith, *How (Not) to Be Secular* (Grand Rapids, MI: Eerdmans, 2014) and Andrew Root, *The Pastor in a Secular Age* (Grand Rapids, MI: Baker Academic, 2019).

[8]In Ephesians 6:12, Paul says, "For we do not wrestle against flesh and blood, but against the rulers, against the authorities, against the cosmic powers over this present darkness, against the spiritual forces of evil in the heavenly places." See also 2 Corinthians 10:3-5.

[9]Chris R. Armstrong, *Medieval Wisdom for Modern Christians* (Grand Rapids, MI: Brazos Press, 2016), 65.

[10]For his excellent summary of Peter Berger's work on the loss of plausibility structures in our late modern world, see James Davison Hunter, *To Change the World* (New York: Oxford University Press, 2010), 202.

[11]Peter L. Berger, *The Many Altars of Modernity* (Boston: Walter de Gruyter, 2014), 32.

[12]See Hunter, *To Change the World*, 200-212, for insightful discussion on difference and dissolution. What has come under question in our contemporary world is whether we can actually articulate something true about the realities of the world. The result of poststructuralism—the work of deconstructionists—is a shattering of any belief we have in the ability to write, talk, or even think of the world as it is; instead, we are confined to systems of construction (history, culture, time, gender, race) in which our words say more about us and our interpretive communities than any truth or reality.

For a robust theological, linguistic, and philosophical treatment of this issue, see Kevin J. Vanhoozer, *Is There a Meaning in This Text?* (Grand Rapids, MI: Zondervan, 1998).

[13]Carl R. Trueman, *The Rise and Triumph of the Modern Self* (Wheaton, IL: Crossway, 2020), 20. Carl Trueman provides a very helpful insight into the shapers and shaping influences that have brought us to the point as a culture to radically redefine self.

[14]John Inazu offers glimmers of hope for a confident pluralism offering continued engagement in the public square, respectful civility, and bridging relational distance even when ideological distance simply cannot be bridged, *Confident Pluralism* (Chicago: University of Chicago Press, 2016), 124.

[15]Luke Goodrich, *Free to Believe* (Colorado Springs: Multnomah, 2019), 180.

[16]Several studies have been conducted on loneliness, the increase in younger generations, the effects on health, and a positive correlation with media. See Katie Hafner, "Researcher Confront an Epidemic of Loneliness," *New York Times,* September 5, 2016, www.nytimes.com/2016/09/06/health/lonliness-aging-health-effects.html; Matthew Pittman and Brandon Reich, "Social Media and Loneliness: Why an Instagram Picture May Be Worth More than a Thousand Twitter Words," *Computers in Human Behavior,* 62 (September 2016): 155-67, https://doi.org/10.1016/j.chb.2016.03.084; Barna Group, "Who Are the Lonely in America?" *Barna,* May 15, 2017, www.barna.com/research /who-are-the-lonely-in-america/.

[17]H. Richard Niebuhr, *Christ and Culture* (New York: Harper Torchbooks, 1951).

[18]See the excellent work D. A. Carson, *Christ and Culture Revisited* (Grand Rapids, MI: Eerdmans, 2008).

[19]See the author's book, highlighting the importance of neighborly love as it relates to economic flourishing. Tom Nelson, *The Economics of Neighborly Love* (Downers Grove, IL: InterVarsity Press, 2007).

[20]Hunter, *To Change the World,* 280.

[21]Paul Williams, *Exiles on Mission* (Grand Rapids, MI: Brazos Press, 2020), 34.

[22]Although James Hunter's work has been critiqued on several levels, I believe his ground-breaking book *To Change the World* continues to make a strong case for a faithful presence approach. For critiques see, Rod Dreher, "The Benedict Option and 'Faithful Presence Within,'" *The American Conservative* October 31, 2016, www.theamericanconservative .com/dreher/straight-talk-benedict-option-faithful-presence-within/; Matthew Lee Anderson, "Expecting to Change the World: A Reply to James Davison Hunter," *Mere Orthodoxy,* July 22, 2010, https://mereorthodoxy.com/expecting-to-change-the-world -a-reply-to-james-davison-hunter/.

[23]Hunter, *To Change the World,* 276. See also James Davison Hunter, Carl Desportes Bowman, and Kyle Puetz, *Democracy in Dark Times* (Charlottesville, VA: Finstock & Tew, 2020), https://s3.amazonaws.com/iasc-prod/uploads/pdf/sapch.pdf, which develops these ideas more in recent research with large amount of data. Hunter does a podcast about this research, "James Davison Hunter and Pete Wehner: Democracy in

Dark Times," *Faith Angle,* January 13, 2021, https://faithangle.podbean.com/e/james
-davison-hunter-and-pete-wehner-democracy-in-dark-times/.

[24]Hunter, *To Change the World*, 253.

[25]Williams, *Exiles on Mission*, 132.

[26]For greater elaboration of a workplace missional focus, see Tom Nelson, *Work Matters* (Wheaton, IL: Crossway, 2011), 187-201.

[27]DePree, *Leadership Is an Art*, 142.

[28]Hunter, *To Change the World*, 253.

[29]For a more expansive reflection of pastors of faithful presence, I recommend Gregory Thompson, "The Church in Our Time: Nurturing Congregations of Faithful Presence," *The Flourish Collective,* October 2011, www.flourishcollective.org/academy/wp-content/uploads/The-Church-In-Our-Time-A-New-City-Commons-White-Paper_4.pdf.

[30]Timothy Keller, *Center Church* (Grand Rapids, MI: Zondervan, 2012), 369.

[31]See Tim Keller's insightful work on Gospel ecosystems; Keller, *Center Church*, 368-77.

[32]Our kingdom agenda with overlapping networks embraces James Hunter's view on cultural change, "Against this great-man view of history and culture, I would argue (along with many others) that the key actor in history is not individual genius but rather the network and the new institutions that are created out of those networks . . . this is where the stuff of culture and cultural change is produced." Hunter, *To Change the World*, 38.

[33]Hunter, *To Change the World*, 270.

[34]Ralph Barton Perry, *The Thought and Character of William James* (1935; Nashville: Vanderbilt University Press, 1996), 237.

[35]Makoto Fujimura, *Culture Care* (New York: Fujimura Institute and International Arts Movement, 2014), 59.

[36]Four Chapters Gallery, https://christcommunitykc.org/fourchapter-gallery/; see also Amy L. Sherman, *Agents of Flourishing: Pursuing Shalom in Every Corner of Society* (Downers Grove, IL: InterVarsity Press, forthcoming; 2022).

[37]Culture House, www.culturehouse.com/.

[38]Amy Sherman features the Four Chapter Gallery far more extensively in *Agents of Flourishing*.

[39]Timothy S. Laniak, *While Shepherds Watch Their Flocks* (Franklin, TN: Carpenter's Son Publishing, 2012), 185.

8 CULTIVATING A FLOURISHING CULTURE

[1]Jim Collins writes, "Enduring great companies preserve their core values and purpose while their business strategies and operating practices endlessly adapt their business strategies and operating practices endlessly adapt to a changing world. This is the magical combination of preserve the core and stimulate progress" in *Good to Great* (New York: Harper Business, 2001), 195.

[2]Andy Crouch, *Culture Making: Recovering Our Creative Calling* (Downers Grove, IL: InterVarsity Press, 2008), 23, italics original.

[3]In Steven Garber, *The Seamless Life* (Downers Grove, IL: InterVarsity Press, 2020), 28-29, Garber insightfully describes the etymological as well as philosophical interconnections of the words, *cult*, *culture*, and *cultivation*. Steve writes,

> Given that I have long believed that for everyone everywhere the first human vocation was to cultivate the created order, to see what is possible to be done on the face of the earth, I began to ponder what cult and culture mean in relationship to cultivation.... And so from our cultic commitments we live and move and have our being, cultivating life and the world.

[4]Crouch, *Culture Making*, 75.

[5]Jim Wilder in *Renovated* makes a persuasive case for the centrality of relational attachment love in Scripture as well as in the process of spiritual formation and healthy local church life. See particularly chapter seven, "Transformed by Loving Attachment," in Jim Wilder, *Renovated* (Colorado Springs: NavPress, 2020), 107-27.

[6]See Romans 15 highlighting the many names.

[7]Max DePree, *Leadership Is an Art* (Lansing: Michigan State University Press, 1987), 25.

[8]Chris Lowney, *Heroic Leadership* (Chicago: Loyola Press, 2003), 285.

[9]Peter Scazzero, *The Emotionally Healthy Church* (Grand Rapids, MI: Zondervan, 2003), 114.

[10]Marcus Warner and Jim Wilder, *Rare Leadership* (Chicago: Moody Publishers, 2016), 42.

[11]Dietrich Bonhoeffer, *The Cost of Discipleship* (New York: Touchstone, 1995), 10-11.

[12]Barna conducted a study on Gen Z (born 1999–2015) and learned that at least one-quarter of Gen Z strongly agrees that morality changes over time and culture. Congruently, a minority of Gen Z respondents select "strongly disagree" in response to the statements "it is wrong to challenge someone's beliefs" and "if your beliefs offend or hurt someone's feelings then your beliefs are wrong." See article "Gen Z and Morality: What Teens Believe (So Far)," *Barna*, October 9, 2018, www.barna.com/research/gen-z-morality/.

[13]Andy Crouch points to the importance of sound doctrine in historian Rodney Stark's *In the Rise of Christianity*, "Stark believes, the church's doctrines were 'the ultimate factor in the rise of Christianity.'... Central doctrines of Christianity prompted and sustained attractive, liberating, and effective social relations and organizations." Crouch, *Culture Making*, 159.

[14]DePree, *Leadership Is an Art*, 11.

[15]The phrase comes from a German theologian in the seventeenth century named Rupertus Meldenius. Professor Mark Ross says it gained much traction with the notable Puritan pastor Richard Baxter. See more on the significance of the phrase by an article by Mark Ross, "In Essentials Unity, In Non-Essentials Liberty, In All Things

Charity," *Ligonier Ministries*, September 1, 2009, www.ligonier.org/learn/articles /essentials-unity-non-essentials-liberty-all-things/.

[16]Wendell Berry, *Jayber Crow* (Berkeley, CA: Counterpoint Press, 2000), 12.

[17]In N. T. Wright, *The New Testament and the People of God* (Minneapolis: Fortress Press, 1992), 1:121-44, Wright confronts the key makeup of a community's preunderstanding through the lens of worldview. Within a worldview, there are four major components: stories, answers to cardinal questions (such as, Who are we? Where are we? What is wrong in the world? and What is the solution?), symbols, and praxis or "a particular mode of being-in-the-world" (133). We cultivate stories in order to understand the world. And a key to storytelling is community, which is where stories are shared and shaped.

[18]Curt Thompson, *The Soul of Shame* (Downers Grove, IL: InterVarsity Press, 2015), 74.

[19]Regarding the body, see Romans 12:5; 1 Corinthians 12:12-14; Ephesians 4:16. Regarding the use of "one another," there are around one hundred uses than include commands such as "accept one another" (Rom 15:7 NIV); "forgive one another" (Col 3:13 NIV); "love one another" (Jn 13:34).

[20]Curt Thompson, *Anatomy of the Soul* (Wheaton, IL: Tyndale House Publishers, 2010), xiv.

[21]John Newton, "Amazing Grace," 1779.

[22]Lowney, *Heroic Leadership*, 7.

[23]James Davison Hunter, *To Change the World* (New York: Oxford University Press, 2010), 256.

[24]In addition to the four core values, the Jesuits embraced a fourfold value-laden prism through which they nourished a rich leadership culture and viewed their leadership enterprise. Lowney lists them, "1) We are all leaders, and we're leading all the time, well or poorly. 2) Leadership springs from within. It's about who I am as much as what I do. 3) Leadership is not an act. It is my life, a way of living. 4) I never complete the task of becoming a leader. It's an ongoing process." See Lowney, *Heroic Leadership*, 15.

[25]At Christ Community where I serve as senior pastor, we build around five values: cross, yoke, Bible, church, and city. See more at https://christcommunitykc.org/about/#values.

[26]Patrick Lencioni, *The Advantage* (San Francisco: Jossey Bass, 2012), 94.

[27]An excellent resource is Peter Greer and Chris Horst, *Mission Drift* (Minneapolis: Bethany House, 2014).

[28]Simon Sinek, *Start with Why* (New York: The Penguin Group, 2009), 39.

[29]Collins, *Good to Great*, 91

[30]Collins, *Good to Great*, 116.

9 CONNECTING SUNDAY TO MONDAY

[1]More of the author's story of pastoral malpractice can be found in Tom Nelson, "Who's Serving Whom?" *Leadership Journal* 35 (Spring 2014): 69-71, www .christianitytoday.com/pastors/2014/spring/power-to-people.html, where it was origi- nally published.

[2]John C. Knapp, *How the Church Fails Businesspeople* (Grand Rapids, MI: Eerdmans, 2012), xi-xii.

[3]See the great work of Elaine Howard Ecklund, Denise Daniels, and Rachel C. Schneider, "From Secular to Sacred: Bringing Work to Church," *Religions* 11, no. 9 (August 2020): 442. Read a part of their report:

> Hearing faith leaders talk directly about workplace issues is also relatively rare. Only 16% of practicing Christians said that their faith leader often/very often discusses how congregants should behave at work. This was more common among Evangelicals (28%) and less common among Mainline Christians (12%) or Catholics (7%; $p < 0.0001$). It was also more common among those who attend religious services multiple times a week (41%) compared to those who attend several times a year or less (5%; $p < 0.0001$). Finally, it was more common among younger respondents, with 18% those who are between ages 18-34 saying that their faith leader discusses how to behave at work often or very often, compared to 13% of those who are 65 or older ($p < 0.05$).

[4]For a more expansive exploration of a robust theology of work, see Tom Nelson, *Work Matters* (Wheaton, IL: Crossway, 2011).

[5]See Viktor Frankl, *Man's Search for Meaning* (Boston: Beacon Press, 2006).

[6]See James Davison Hunter, *To Change the World* (New York: Oxford University Press, 2010).

[7]Dorothy Sayers, "Why Work?" in *Leading Lives That Matter,* ed. Mark R. Schwehn and Dorothy C. Bass (Grand Rapids, MI: Eerdmans, 2006), 195.

[8]Bill Peel and Walt Larimore, *Workplace Grace* (Longview, TX: LeTourneau University Press, 2014), 19.

[9]Knapp, *How the Church Fails Businesspeople,* xiii.

[10]Amy Sherman, *Kingdom Calling* (Downers Grove, IL: InterVarsity Press, 2011), 151-68.

[11]For a more expansive discussion on regarding what is at stake in the Sunday-to-Monday gap, see Tom Nelson, "How Should the Church Engage?" in *The Gospel and Work,* The Gospel for Life Series, ed. Russell Moore and Andrew T. Walker (Nashville: B&H Publishing, 2017), 65-90.

[12]Denise Daniels and Shannon Vanderwarker, *Working in the Presence of God* (Peabody, MA: Hendrickson Publishers, 2019), 4-5.

[13]Sherman, *Kingdom Calling,* 141-222.

[14]Matthew Kaemingk and Cory B. Willson, *Work and Worship* (Grand Rapids, MI: Baker Academic, 2020), 2. This is an excellent resource to frame the conversation around the Sunday-to-Monday gap and equipping Christians for their Monday worlds.

[15]The teaching team at our church that I have the privilege of serving did a series on economics titled "Neighborly Love." The six-week sermon series is available on our

website (christcommunitykc.org/sermons). Also see Tom Nelson, *The Economics of Neighborly Love* (Downers Grove, IL: InterVarsity Press, 2017).

[16]See *Theology of Work Bible Commentary* (Peabody, MA: Hendrickson, 2014).

[17]Stephen Garber, "A Prayer for Labor Day," *Patheos,* September 9, 2015, www.patheos.com /blogs/visions-of-vocation/2015/09/476/ has a great example of a pastoral prayer from John Baillie for the labor force on Labor Day weekend. His prayer:

> O Lord and Maker of all things, from whose creative power the first light came forth, who looked upon the world's first morning and saw that it was good, I praise you now for this light that streams through my windows to rouse me to another day.
>
> I praise you for the life that stirs within me, I praise you for the bright and beautiful world into which I go, I praise you for the work you have given me to do . . .
>
> But you who are everlasting mercy, give me a tender heart towards all those to whom the morning light brings less joy than it brings to me.
>
> Those in whom the pulse of life grows weak, those who must lie abed through the all the sunny hours, The overworked, who have no joy of leisure, The unemployed, who have no joy of labor.

[18]Some of this section appeared previously in Tom Nelson, "Who's Serving Whom?" *Leadership Journal* 35 (Spring 2014): 69-71, www.christianitytoday.com/pastors /2014/spring/power-to-people.html.

[19]See Tom Nelson, *Work Matters*; Timothy Keller, *Every Good Endeavor* (New York: Penguin Random House, 2016).

10 A NEW SCORECARD

[1]Max DePree, *Leadership Is an Art* (Lansing: Michigan State University Press, 1987), 53.

[2]Dietrich Bonhoeffer, *Life Together* (New York: HarperCollins Publishers, 1954), 97.

[3]Lisa's comments come from a Zoom call with the author on March 8, 2021.

[4]"History," Chick-fil-A, Inc., accessed November 12, 2020, www.chick-fil-a.com/about /history.

[5]Dietrich Bonhoeffer, *Life Together*, 38.

[6]Personal email sent to Tom Nelson by Pastor Nathan.

[7]There are several great resources for equipping congregants. I would highly recommend David W. Gill, *Workplace Discipleship 101* (Peabody, MA: Hendrickson Publishers, 2020). In the area of discipleship regarding work and economic wisdom, see Tom Nelson, *Work Matters* (Wheaton, IL: Crossway, 2011) and *The Economics of Neighborly Love* (Downers Grove, IL: InterVarsity Press, 2017); Adam Joyce and Greg Forster, *Economic Wisdom for Churches* (Deerfield, IL: Trinity International University, 2017).

[8]The church where I currently reside as senior pastor, Christ Community Church Kansas City, has a pastoral residency program: a two-year mentoring program

designed to train and equip the church leaders of tomorrow. See fuller description here: https://christcommunitykc.org/pastoral-residency/.

If you are a pastor of a church and want help starting a program, see more at www.madetoflourish.org/.

[9]The leadership pathway has been called Razors Edge and is now called Church for Monday. Guiding this process has been and continues to be a curriculum-guided experience for our pastors to lead and deepen relationships with congregants.

[10]The apostle Paul reminds believers in Corinth of their accountability before Christ. See 2 Cor 5:10.

11 FINISHING WELL

[1]Stephen R. Covey, *Principle Centered Leadership* (New York: Summit Books, 1990), 42. Covey's second habit of highly effective people is "to begin with the end in mind." Covey makes the case that this habit is the endowment of human imagination and conscience.

[2]Throughout my ministry, I have asked myself these four questions to help me finish well:

1. What are my strengths and vulnerabilities?
2. Are weeds growing in my soul that need attention?
3. What mid-course corrections do I need to make now?
4. Who will I team up with to help me finish well?

[3]Covey, *Principle Centered Leadership*, 50.

[4]"The woman was very beautiful; she took care of the king and waited on him, but the king had no sexual relations with her" (1 Kings 1:4 NIV).

[5]This hopeful truth is transparently captured in David's own words. See Psalm 32 and 51.

[6]Claire Powless, "Was COVID-19 a 'Black Swan'?" *Continuity Central.com*, July 23, 2020, www.continuitycentral.com/index.php/news/business-continuity-news/5346 -was-covid-19-a-black-swan-and-why-this-is-an-important-question.

[7]Pastor Jim Baucom in Washington, DC, at Columbia Church shared this with a group of pastors as we debriefed navigating leadership during the pandemic.

[8]See James 1:5.

[9]C. S. Lewis, *The Screwtape Letters* (New York: HarperOne, 1996), 31. One of the leadership books I read almost every year is *The Screwtape Letters*. Few books have helped me better keep in mind the invisible war that is raging around me and in the world. This is particularly important for pastoral leaders as we now live in a culture where the imminent frame, which dismisses the spiritual realm, is the cultural mythos of our time.

[10]See Jesus' parable of the talents in Matthew 25.

[11]Martin Schleske, *The Sound of Life's Unspeakable Beauty* (Grand Rapids, MI: Eerdmans, 2020), 84.

[12]Gary Moon, *Becoming Dallas Willard* (Downers Grove, IL: InterVarsity Press, 2018), 240.

[13]Andraé Crouch, "My Tribute," *Keep on Singin'*, Light Records, 1972.

SCRIPTURE INDEX

MADE TO FLOURISH
A PASTORS' NETWORK FOR THE COMMON GOOD

The pastoral work you are called to do plays an important role in nurturing human flourishing and furthering the common good. We want to be a helpful resource as you faithfully equip your congregation to be followers of Jesus in all dimensions of life.

That's why we exist. Made to Flourish is a nationwide membership organization that equips pastors with a deeper understanding of the essential connection between Sunday faith and Monday work. Our goal is to help empower you to lead flourishing churches. As congregants begin to understand the intrinsic value of their daily work to God, it completely transforms their perspective on their work and how they do it.

Membership is free—we exist solely to provide you with relationships and resources to strengthen your ministry. We do this through a monthly newsletter, a resource-filled website, national events, online workshops and webinars, and city networks where you can meet with other local pastors.

By becoming a member, you will receive a welcome kit with several core faith-and-work resources, be connected to a city network, and receive special access to our events, seminars, and online learning opportunities.

WILL YOU JOIN WITH US TODAY?

Apply for the network at **madetoflourish.org/apply**.

For more written, video, and audio resources,
visit us at **madetoflourish.org**. You can also stay in touch by following us on Twitter (**@madetoflourish**) and liking us on Facebook (**facebook.com/MTFpastor**).

MADE TO FLOURISH

10901 Lowell Ave, Ste 130 | Overland Park, KS 66210
info@madetoflourish.org | www.madetoflourish.org

IVP PRAXIS

EQUIPPING LEADERS FOR MINISTRY

"...TO EQUIP HIS PEOPLE FOR WORKS OF SERVICE,
SO THAT THE BODY OF CHRIST MAY BE BUILT UP."

EPHESIANS 4:12

God has called us to ministry. But it's not enough to have a vision for ministry if you don't have the practical skills for it. Nor is it enough to do the work of ministry if what you do is headed in the wrong direction. We need both vision *and* expertise for effective ministry. We need *praxis*.

Praxis puts theory into practice. It brings cutting-edge ministry expertise from visionary practitioners. You'll find sound biblical and theological foundations for ministry in the real world, with concrete examples for effective action and pastoral ministry. Praxis books are more than the "how to" – they're also the "why to." And because *being* is every bit as important as *doing*, Praxis attends to the inner life of the leader as well as the outer work of ministry. Feed your soul, and feed your ministry.

If you are called to ministry, you know you can't do it on your own. Let Praxis provide the companions you need to equip God's people for life in the kingdom.

www.ivpress.com/praxis